ANGLO-AMERICAN
CRIMINAL JUSTICE

ANGLO–AMERICAN CRIMINAL JUSTICE

BY

DELMAR KARLEN

DIRECTOR OF THE INSTITUTE OF
JUDICIAL ADMINISTRATION
AND PROFESSOR OF LAW
NEW YORK UNIVERSITY

IN COLLABORATION WITH

GEOFFREY SAWER

PROFESSOR OF LAW
THE AUSTRALIAN NATIONAL UNIVERSITY

AND

EDWARD M. WISE

ASSOCIATE PROFESSOR OF LAW
WAYNE STATE UNIVERSITY

1967
OXFORD UNIVERSITY PRESS
NEW YORK AND OXFORD

© Oxford University Press 1967
Library of Congress Catalogue Card Number: 67-30319

Printed in the United States of America

Oh wad some power the giftee gie us
to see oursels as ithers see us!
It wad frae many a blunder free us,
An' foolish notion.

ROBERT BURNS

CONTENTS

CONTENTS

PREFACE

THIS book grew out of a recently completed interchange of experience in the area of criminal justice between judges and lawyers in the United States and England.

In July of 1963 a team of Americans paid a two-week visit to England to study criminal justice in that country in action, and to discuss their observations and reactions with English judges and lawyers. The American team consisted of the following:

Hon. William J. Brennan, Jr., Associate Justice, Supreme Court of the United States

Hon. Charles S. Desmond, Chief Judge, New York Court of Appeals

Hon. Roger J. Traynor, Then Justice, now Chief Justice of the Supreme Court of California

Hon. Emory H. Niles, Retired Chief Judge, Supreme Bench of Baltimore City

Hon. Bernard Botein, Presiding Justice, Appellate Division, New York Supreme Court, First Department

Major General Charles L. Decker, Then Judge Advocate General of the United States Army, now Director of the National Legal Aid and Defender Project

Hon. George Edwards, Then Commissioner of Police of Detroit, now Judge of the United States Court of Appeals for the Sixth Circuit

Hon. Frank S. Hogan, District Attorney, New York County

Edward Bennett Williams, Esq., Attorney, Washington, D.C.

Professor Delmar Karlen, Director, Institute of Judicial Administration.

The American team was received in London by an English team headed by the Rt. Hon. Lord Parker of Waddington, Lord Chief Justice of England, and comprising in addition other key judges, lawyers, and government officials.

Before the visit to London, each member of the American team prepared a paper on some aspect of criminal justice with which he was particularly familiar, describing American practice and comparing and contrasting it—so far as he was then able to do so—with what he knew about English practice. These papers were exchanged and discussed among members of the American team prior to their arrival in England, and helped to give focus to the observations and inquiries made there. After the visit, the team members revised their papers in the light of what they had learned. Each also answered a questionnaire designed to elicit his reactions to what he had seen and his views on what he considered good or bad in the practices of the two countries.

The revised papers and the answers to the questionnaires were transmitted to England for study by members of the English team in preparation for their forthcoming reciprocal trip to the United States. The visit occurred in September of 1964, at which time the composition of the English team was as follows:

Sir John Widgery, Judge of the Queen's Bench Division of the High Court

Sir Daniel Brabin, Judge of the Queen's Bench Division of the High Court

Hon. Graham Rogers, Judge of the Central Criminal Court (Old Bailey)

Mr. Mervyn Griffith-Jones, Then Senior Prosecuting Counsel, Central Criminal Court, but since elevated to the office of Common Serjeant, Central Criminal Court

Sir George Coldstream, Permanent Secretary to the Lord Chancellor

Sir Charles Cunningham, Permanent Secretary of the Home Office

Mr. Malcolm Morris, Q.C. and Recorder of Croydon

Mr. David Napley, London Solicitor and member of the Council of the Law Society

Mr. F. J. Odgers, Then of Emmanuel College, Cambridge, now Professor of Law, University of Liverpool

The English visit to the United States followed the same pattern as the earlier American visit to England. Again courts and other institutions concerned with the administration of justice were observed in action, and the reactions of the members of the English team were discussed with members of the American team. When the visit was concluded each member of the English team responded to a questionnaire designed to elicit his reflections upon what he had seen and heard in the United States. Contrasts and comparisons between the two systems were stressed, with the objective of discovering and revealing the strengths and weaknesses of each.

Then followed the preparation of this book. Both teams concluded that the best way to disseminate the results of the interchange to judges and lawyers generally was by means of a comprehensive description of the similarities and differences between the two systems of criminal justice as revealed in the reciprocal visits. Rather than rely upon isolated law review articles or speeches based upon the separate papers, each dealing with a fairly narrow topic, prepared by members of the American team, it was decided to entrust to the undersigned the preparation of a single, cohesive manuscript covering the entire subject of the interchange. It draws heavily upon the thoughts and reactions of all who participated.

In the preparation of the book, the labours of two men were indispensable. One was Professor Geoffrey Sawer of the Australian National University at Canberra, who spent his sabbatical leave during the year of 1964 at the Institute of Judicial Administration in New York; and the other was Edward M. Wise, now Associate Professor of Law at Wayne State University but in 1964–5 a Research Fellow at the Institute of Judicial Administration. When a manuscript had been completed in first draft form, it was submitted to various members of the British and American teams for criticisms and suggestions. These were freely given and have been taken account of in the final version.

On the English side, the interchange was sponsored by the British Council, which also supplied part of the necessary funds. On the American side, it was sponsored by the Institute of Judicial Administration, with funds supplied chiefly by the Walter E. Meyer Research Institute of Law.

This interchange was the second in what, it is hoped, will be a series. The first dealt with appellate procedure, resulting in a book by the undersigned entitled *Appellate Courts in the United States and England*, published by the New York University Press in 1963. Upon the conclusion of the current project, it is hoped that further interchanges of similar nature on other topics of interest to the legal professions of both countries will be developed.

It is expected that the current interchange, like the earlier one, will result in the judges and lawyers of each nation gaining a deeper understanding of the strengths and weaknesses of their own system and that they will be moved to work toward further improvements. In view of the fact that members of both the English and American teams occupy strategic positions and are deeply involved in major efforts in their respective countries to improve the administration of criminal justice, it seems likely that the insights they have derived from the interchange will quickly find their way into the main bloodstream of reform in both countries. As for commonwealth and other nations whose systems of criminal justice are based upon the English model, their judges and lawyers too may profit from seeing the original model placed alongside a newer version with the advantages and disadvantages of each pointed out.

The manuscript for this book was completed originally in December 1965 and accepted for publication in the spring of 1966. Subsequently several landmark decisions were rendered by the Supreme Court of the United States affecting and qualifying some of the discussion. The manuscript was revised to the limited extent necessary to take account of these major developments. Changes of a more minor nature also occurred in the interim, but no attempt was made to cover them through a complete revision of the manuscript.

DELMAR KARLEN

The Institute of Judicial Administration
New York
12 July 1966

FOREWORD

By the Right Honourable LORD PARKER OF WADDINGTON
Lord Chief Justice of England

THIS book records another important step in the interchange of ideas between lawyers on both sides of the Atlantic upon subjects which are of vital interest today.

The preservation of law and order and of a healthy relationship between police and public has always required the Courts to maintain a delicate balance between the powers of the police to detain and interrogate suspects, and the rights of the individual to protection against unreasonable interference with his liberty or property. As crime has increased in volume and sophistication the importance of this duty has become more and more apparent and the problems which it raises have multiplied.

Professor Karlen sets out to show how these and kindred problems in the administration of criminal justice are presently solved in the United States and in England respectively. His comparisons demonstrate how wide is the field of agreement, but it is in his elucidation of the differences that the real value of this book will be found to lie. Those of us who took part in the discussions to which the author refers are already considering how far we can improve our own procedures in the light of that experience and this book will make the lessons learnt in these discussions available to all. I commend it most heartily to all lawyers who are concerned to see efficient law enforcement and the protection of individual liberty advance together.

LIST OF ABBREVIATIONS

Abrahams

Abrahams, G., *Police Questioning and the Judges' Rules* (London, 1964).

Allen

Allen, Sir C. Kemp, *The Queen's Peace* (London, 1953).

Appellate Delay Report

A.B.A. Section of Criminal Law, *Committee on Appellate Delay in Criminal Cases: Report* (Chicago, 1964).

Barnes & Teeters

Barnes, H. E., & Teeters, N. K., *New Horizons in Criminology*, 3rd ed. (Englewood Cliffs, New Jersey, 1959).

Beaney

Beaney, W. M., *The Right to Counsel in American Courts* (Ann Arbor, Mich., 1955).

Black

Black, C. L., *Perspectives in Constitutional Law* (Englewood Cliffs, New Jersey, 1963).

Book of the States

The Council of State Governments, *Book of the States 1964/65*, vol. xv[1] (Chicago, 1964).

Brownell

Brownell, E. A., *Legal Aid in the United States* (Rochester, New York, 1951).

Chapman & St. Johnston

Chapman, S. G., & St. Johnston, T. E., *The Police Heritage in England and America: A Developmental Survey* (East Lansing, Mich., Michigan State University, 1962).

Cheatham

Cheatham, E. E., *A Lawyer when Needed* (New York, 1963).

Chute & Bell

Chute, C. L., & Bell, M., *Crime, Courts and Probation* (New York, 1956).

Cmnd. 2296

Home Office, *The War Against Crime in England and Wales, 1959–1964* (Cmnd. No. 2296, 1965).

Cmnd. 2742

Home Office, *The Child, The Family and the Young Offender* (Cmnd. No. 2742, 1965).

Cmnd. 2755

Interdepartmental Committee on the Court of Criminal Appeal: Report (Cmnd. No. 2755, 1965).

Devlin (1956)

Devlin, Lord P., *Trial by Jury* (London, 1956).

Devlin (1960)

Devlin, Lord P., *The Criminal Prosecution in England* (Oxford, 1960).

---

[1] *Book of the States* is a biennial: each is 1 v.+2 supplemental pamphlets every two years.

Elkin	Elkin, W. A., *The English Penal System* (Harmondsworth, 1957).
Fellman	Fellman, D., *The Defendant's Rights* (New York, 1958).
Fitzgerald	Fitzgerald, P. J., *Criminal Law and Punishment* (Oxford, 1962).
Fosdick	Fosdick, R. B., *American Police Systems* (London, 1920).
Freed & Wald	Freed, D. J., & Wald, P. M., *Bail in the United States: 1964* (Washington, D.C., 1964).
Freund	Freund, P. A., *The Supreme Court of the United States: Its Business, Purposes and Performances* (Cleveland, Ohio, 1961).
Giles	Giles, F. T., *The Magistrates' Courts* (London, 1963).
Glueck	Glueck, S., ed., *The Problem of Delinquency* (Boston, 1959).
Goodhart	Goodhart, A. L., *English Law and the Moral Law* (London, 1953).
Grossman	Grossman, J. B., *Lawyers and Judges (The ABA and the Politics of Judicial Selection)* (New York, 1965).
Halsbury	Simonds, G. T. Lord (ed.), *Halsbury's Laws of England*, 3rd ed. (London, 1959).
Howard	Howard, P., *Criminal Justice in England* (New York, 1931).
Jackson	Jackson, R. M., *The Machinery of Justice in England*, 4th ed. (Cambridge, 1964).
Karlen (1963)	Karlen, D., *Appellate Courts in the United States and England* (New York, 1963).
Karlen (1964)	Karlen, D., *The Citizen in Court* (New York, 1964).
Kennedy	Kennedy, Ludovic, *The Trial of Stephen Ward* (London, 1964).
Kenny & Turner	Kenny, C. S., & Turner, J. W. C. (ed.), *Outlines of Criminal Law*, 18th ed. (Cambridge, 1962).
Klare	Klare, H. J., *The Anatomy of Prison* (London, 1960).
LaFave	LaFave, W. R., *Arrest: The Decision to Take a Suspect into Custody* (Boston, 1965).
McCormick	McCormick, C. T., *Evidence*[1] (St. Paul, Minn., 1954).

[1] Handbook of the Law of Evidence.

Maitland	Maitland, F. W., *Justice and Police* (London, 1885).
Mayers	Mayers, L., *The American Legal System*, rev. ed. (New York and London, 1964).
Megarry	Megarry, R. E., *Lawyer and Litigant in England* (London, 1962).
Milton	Milton, F., *In Some Authority: The English Magistracy* (London, 1959).
Morris & Blom-Cooper	Morris, T., & Blom-Cooper, L., *A Calendar of Murder; Criminal Homicide in England since 1957* (London, 1964).
Orfield (1939)	Orfield, L. B., *Criminal Appeals in America* (Boston, 1939).
Orfield (1947)	Orfield, L. B., *Criminal Procedure from Arrest to Appeal* (New York, 1947).
Plucknett	Plucknett, T. F. T., *A Concise History of Common Law*, 5th ed. (Boston, 1956).
Polier	Polier, J. W., *A View from the Bench: The Juvenile Court* (New York, 1964).
Puttkammer	Puttkammer, E. W., *Administration of Criminal Law* (Chicago, 1953).
Rolph (1961)	Rolph, C. H., *Common Sense about Crime and Punishment* (New York, 1961).
Rolph (1962)	Rolph,* C. H., *The Police and the Public; an Inquiry* (London, 1962).
Rubin	Rubin, S., *Crime and Juvenile Delinquency*, rev. 2nd ed. (Dobbs Ferry, New York and London, 1961).
Rubin *et al.*	Rubin, S., *The Law of Criminal Correction* (St. Paul, 1963).
Salmond	Salmond, J. W. (ed. R. F. V. Heuston), *Salmond on The Law of Torts*, 12th ed. (London, 1957).
Sawer	Sawer, G., *Ombudsmen* (Melbourne, 1964).
Schwartz	Schwartz, M. L., *Cases and Materials on Professional Responsibility and the Administration of Criminal Justice* (Albany, New York, 1961).
Silverstein	Silverstein, Lee, *Defense of the Poor in Criminal Cases in American State Courts* (3 vols.) (Chicago, 1965).
Smith (1925)	Smith, Bruce, *The State Police; Organization and Administration* (New York, London, 1925).

Smith (1933)   Smith, Bruce, *Rural Crime Control* (New York, 1933).

Smith (1949)   Smith, Bruce, *Police Systems in the United States*, rev. ed. (New York, 1949).

Stephen   Stephen, Sir James FizJames, *History of the Criminal Law of England* (3 vols.) (London, 1883).

Street   Street, H., *Freedom: The Individual and the Law* (Harmondsworth, 1963).

Sussman   Sussman, F. B., *Law of Juvenile Delinquency*, rev. ed. (Dobbs Ferry, New York, 1959).

Tappan   Tappan, P. W., *Crime, Justice and Correction* (New York, 1960).

Tompkins   Tompkins, D. C., *Probation since World War II: A Bibliography* (Berkeley, Calif., 1964).

Trebach   Trebach, A. S., *The Rationing of Justice* (New Brunswick, New Jersey, 1964).

Vanderbilt   Vanderbilt, A. T., *Minimum Standards of Judicial Administration* (New York, 1949).

Wharton   Wharton, Francis, & Anderson, Ronald A., *Wharton's Criminal Law and Procedure*. Based on Wharton's *Criminal Law* (12th ed.) and Wharton's *Criminal Procedure* (10th ed.) (Rochester, New York, 1957).

Whitaker   Whitaker, B., *The Police* (Harmondsworth, 1964).

Wigmore   Wigmore, J. H., *Evidence* (10 vols.), 3rd ed. (Boston, 1940).

Williams (1958)   Williams, Glanville, *The Proof of Guilt: A Study of the English Criminal Trial*, 2nd ed. (London, 1958).

Williams (1962)   Williams, E. B., *One Man's Freedom* (New York, 1962).

Wootton   Wootton, B., *Crime and the Criminal Law; Reflections of a Magistrate and Social Scientist* (London, 1963).

ANGLO–AMERICAN
CRIMINAL JUSTICE

PART I

THE MACHINERY OF CRIMINAL JUSTICE

1

THE POLICE

IN the second part of this book we shall compare English and American law point by point at the successive stages through which a criminal prosecution passes. In this part we are concerned with the institutions by which criminal justice is administered: the police, the legal profession, the courts, and the penal institutions.

THE ROLE OF THE POLICE

The functions of the police in England and the United States are substantially the same, with only one important difference—their role in conducting criminal prosecutions in court. This difference will be considered at length in Chapter 2.

In both countries the primary purpose of the police is to maintain law and order, protecting life and property, and preventing crime. The constable walking his beat or the policeman cruising around in his squad car is a powerful deterrent to crime. Both English and American history record periods of almost incredible lawlessness before regular police forces were created. The difference between the conditions in Regency London or Frontier America and the comparatively Utopian conditions which now prevail marks a social revolution—strange as this might seem to the average citizen in either nation today who views with alarm the current state of criminal activity.

Instructions (which are still in use) to the first London policemen speak of 'the prevention of crime' as 'the principal object' and best means to 'all other objects of a police establishment'.[1] Most American policemen would agree. But, depending on the methods used, prevention is sometimes a debatable aim. Some preventive measures are generally acceptable to the public. Social case work with juveniles, practised by police forces both in England and the United States, and educating members of the public to better safeguard their houses and automobiles are familiar examples. Other preventive measures, however, can be oppressive. Searching on suspicion, for instance, is a preventive technique which many citizens resent. The limits on how far the police may go in preventing crime are partly a matter of law and partly a matter of public attitude, and are further discussed in Chapter 6.

A second purpose of the police is to detect crime, obtain proof of guilt, and prefer charges. This is a function which in the United States they share to some extent with the grand jury and the prosecutor's office. It is a function which in England is shared to a more limited extent with private prosecutors and other public bodies.[2] But by and large in both countries detective work is the job of the police. This is a unique feature of Anglo-American procedure. In continental Europe, proof of guilt is accumulated not only by the police but also by a judicial officer—for example, the *juge d'instruction* in France.

Setting the machinery of criminal justice in action is far from a mechanical operation.[3] The police exercise discretion as to whether or not they will prefer charges against an offender, considering the probable success and effect of prosecution, and weighing it against the social gain to be derived from merely letting the offender go with a warning.[4] Most Englishmen recognize and accept the exercise of such discretion, probably because they are accustomed to the idea of police control of prosecution. Americans tend to be concerned about police discretion, because they are not always confident that it will be exercised fairly, and because they are accustomed to leaving discretion whether to prosecute to the district attorney's office.

---

[1] Rolph (1962), pp. 7–8; Whitaker, pp. 18–19.

[2] Rarely do truly private prosecutions occur, except those which arise out of neighbourhood quarrels. There are, however, a fair number of prosecutions instituted by government departments and local authorities as distinct from the police.

[3] See Goldstein, 'Police Discretion not to Invoke the Criminal Process: Low-Visibility Decisions in the Administration of Justice', 69 *Yale L.J.* 543 (1960).

[4] However, in serious cases in England, ultimate control lies in the hands of the Director of Public Prosecution; and in serious cases in the United States, such control is in the hands of district attorneys.

A third and more doubtful police role is to administer public welfare regulations, some of which have little relevancy to regular police responsibilities. These regulatory duties, ranging from the licensing of fire-arms to the inspection of elevators and diseased animals, sometimes make the police disliked, and always draw off limited manpower to relatively minor work.[1] They are, nevertheless, a regular part of police activity both in England and the United States.[2] The most conspicuous examples of such work are the control of traffic and the enforcement of parking regulations. In both nations, progress is being made towards relieving the police of extraneous duties not directly related to the maintenance of law and order, as by the development of systems of traffic wardens or 'meter maids' to deal with parking offences.

ORGANIZATION OF POLICE FORCES

England

In England, police organization is more decentralized in theory than in fact.

There are 122 separate police forces in England and Wales, comprising over 80,000 policemen, or about 1 to every 600 people. The number of policemen has been increasing as the population has increased, but the number of separate forces has been continually decreasing as the result of amalgamations. In 1860 there were 226 forces; in 1939, 183; in 1949, 129. The forces in England range in size from the London Metropolitan Police, with over 20,000 men, to the police in Dewsbury, with just over 100. The one- or two-man police force, which is common in the United States, has not existed in England for over a century.[3]

Each of the English police forces is, with one striking exception, administered by a local police authority.[4] There are 37 county constabularies, each headed by a chief constable. In addition, 72 boroughs

---

[1] When police manpower is used to perform social welfare services, such as arresting drunks and vagrants for their own welfare or supervising juveniles, the effect may be detrimental to both the criminal justice system and the existing social service institutions. See Allen, 'The Borderland of the Criminal Law: Problems of "Socializing" Criminal Justice', 32 *Social Ser. Rev.* 107 (1958).

[2] Smith (1949), pp. 16–19; Whitaker, pp. 20–21.

[3] *Report of Her Majesty's Chief Inspector of Constabulary*, 1964, H.C. No. 251; see Chapman & St. Johnston, pp. 16–17.

[4] Allen (1953), pp. 116–17; Chapman & St. Johnston, pp. 15–18; Howard, 158–75.

have their own self-contained police forces, each headed by a chief constable. Finally, there are 11 combined forces resulting from the amalgamation of two or more formerly separate police forces.[1] All these are locally controlled, pursuant to Acts of Parliament.[2]

The one exception mentioned is the Metropolitan Police Force, which covers most of Greater London. This force is sometimes referred to by the name of its headquarters as 'Scotland Yard'. Since its establishment in 1829, it has been under the general control of the Home Secretary, a Cabinet Minister in the central government. The Home Secretary is the police authority for the London force. He recommends to the Crown the appointment of its Commissioner, and is answerable generally for its operations.

There is one autonomous enclave within the Metropolitan Police district. This is the old City of London—the one square mile in the business centre of the metropolis which has been traditionally jealous of its ancient privileges. In 1839 the City Corporation established its own police force wholly independent of the Metropolitan Police. Today it numbers 990 men.[3]

Growing Centralization

Although locally controlled, county and borough forces have since 1856 come more and more under the supervision of the Home Secretary. This has been accomplished through several devices:

1. The central government contributes money toward the cost of

---

[1] Chapman & St. Johnston, p. 16.

[2] The Municipal Corporations Act, 1835 (5 & 6 Will. IV c. 76) required each *borough* to provide a salaried and disciplined police force under the control of a watch committee of the borough council. In 1839 the County Police Act (2 & 3 Vict. c. 93) enabled Justices of the Peace in Quarter Sessions, at their option, to create a paid *county* constabulary. The County and Borough Police Act, 1856 (19 & 20 Vict. c. 69) made the creation of police forces in the counties mandatory, as in the boroughs, thus superseding everywhere in England such historical survivals as the parish constable and the night watch. Under the Local Government Act, 1888 (51 & 52 Vict. c. 41) control of the county police was transferred from the justices to a Joint Standing Committee, made up in part of representatives of the justices and in part of representatives of the newly formed county councils. Under the Police Act, 1964, the justices have been given a voice in the borough watch committees, although locally elected councillors are still in the majority. In both counties and boroughs, two-thirds of the members of the police authority must be members of the local councils, with the remaining one-third justices of the peace (Police Act, 1964, c. 48, §§ 2–3). The entire development of the professional English police force out of the old parish constabulary is traced in Allen, pp. 92–127; Maitland, ch. X.

[3] *Report of Her Majesty's Chief Inspector of Constabulary*, 1964, H.C. No. 251, pp. 80–81.

the local police. Since 1875 this Treasury subvention has amounted to about half the total cost. Grants-in-aid are conditional, not having to be paid if the Home Secretary is dissatisfied with the way a force is being run. It is rare that a grant is withheld, because ordinarily the mere possibility of that happening is sufficient to stimulate efficiency.[1] This device has been broadly employed by the British government to keep its hand on local activities and is not unlike that used by the federal government in the United States when making contributions towards state education and public welfare programmes.

2. Ten Inspectors of Constabulary, appointed by the Crown on the recommendation of the Home Secretary, visit the local forces to assess their efficiency and report to the Home Secretary as to whether they qualify for Treasury grants.[2] The Inspectors have no power to issue orders to the chief constables, but their advice in matters of organization and effective employment of police resources carries much force.

3. Since 1919,[3] the Home Secretary has possessed power to make regulations governing the pay, allowances, pensions, clothing, discipline, and conditions of service in all English police forces. His regulations have established uniform standards for the entire country.[4] Furthermore, the appointment of any chief constable, deputy chief constable, or assistant chief constable is subject to the approval of the Home Secretary, who also has power to compel a chief constable to retire on grounds of inefficiency.[5]

4. Joint or common services for all police forces have been established which are under the substantial control of the Home Office. It administers training programmes for police officers; maintains forensic science laboratories; and acquires and maintains radio equipment to be lent to the local forces.

Very few powers are left entirely in the hands of the local police authorities. While they are responsible for the organization of the force (subject to the Home Secretary's approval) and for providing it with accommodation and equipment, the day-to-day work of each

[1] Whitaker, p. 75.
[2] Police Act, 1964, c. 48, § 38; see Chapman & St. Johnston, p. 18.
[3] 9 & 10 Geo. V, c. 46. This Act, which grew out of unrest in the police service caused by the fact that the police were everywhere paid differently but everywhere underpaid, created the Police Federation, in effect a national trade union in which every policeman in the lower ranks (constable, sergeant, inspector) is automatically a member.
[4] Police Act, 1964, c. 48, § 33.   [5] Ibid., §§ 5, 29.

force is controlled by its chief constable who is entirely responsible for its discipline and, in matters of law enforcement, is accountable only to the courts.[1] The long-term trend is towards uniformity, enforced by the very wide powers which the Home Secretary possesses.

The 1962 Royal Commission on the Police was urged to abandon the surviving elements of local control in favour of a single national force such as exists in Northern Ireland, Holland, Denmark, Norway, and the states of Australia. One member of the Commission, Professor Arthur Goodhart, favoured this result, but the majority endorsed a continuation of local administration. This view was embodied in the Police Act 1964, which repealed or consolidated all the earlier statutes relating to the administration of the police outside the Metropolitan Police area. The Act retained the principle of local administration but strengthened the arrangements for central supervision over the police, and enlarged the powers of the Home Secretary to amalgamate police forces. Amalgamation has been proceeding, although against resistance, for some boroughs seem as anxious to have their own forces 'as independent nations are to possess their own airlines'.[2] Nevertheless, continued amalgamation appears to be the likely course of future development.

The United States

In the United States, police organization is highly decentralized both in theory and fact. American police systems began on the model of the English parish constable, sheriff, and night watch—relics which were superseded in England in 1856. They have continued to serve as models for many American forces, resulting in widespread inefficiency.

There are an estimated 40,000 separate police forces in the United States, comprising about 300,000 policemen.[3] As in England, there is roughly one policeman to every 600 people. The forces exhibit a very wide range of types, with police organization paralleling that of government generally at municipal, township, county, state, and federal levels. Each unit maintains its own police force, with considerable overlapping of jurisdiction.[4]

[1] Police Act, 1964, c. 48, §§ 4, 5.
[2] Whitaker, p. 87.
[3] Chapman & St. Johnston, p. 30.
[4] Chapman & St. Johnston, pp. 29–30; Puttkammer, pp. 38–41; Smith (1949), pp. 21–28 *passim*.

Federal

The federal government has a variety of police forces, with nearly every executive department and administrative board having an investigatory agency of its own.[1] A number of these agencies have grown into significant police forces, the most notable of which is the Federal Bureau of Investigation (FBI) in the Department of Justice, which investigates all federal crimes not immediately the concern of other agencies. Others include: (i) three units of the Treasury concerned with violations of federal laws relating to the collection of income taxes, alcohol taxes, and customs; (ii) the Bureau of Narcotics of the Treasury, concerned with violations of federal laws relating to narcotic drugs; (iii) the Secret Service Division of the Treasury, concerned with counterfeiting, forgery, and protection of the President; (iv) Post Office Department inspector, concerned with mail offences; and (v) the Immigration Border Patrol of the Department of Justice. The federal police agencies have authority to act anywhere in the United States, but they are not charged generally with keeping the peace. The authority of each is limited to a specific list of federal penal statutes.

Among these agencies there is a considerable fragmentation of jurisdiction, but along functional rather than geographical lines. Different aspects of the same criminal enterprise may be the concern of several agencies. For example, the engraver who counterfeits paper money is the concern of the Secret Service, but of the Post Office inspector when he counterfeits a postage stamp.

There is also an overlap between the federal agencies and state and local police. This is because the same act may be both a federal and a state offence. When investigating such an act, a federal agency will usually co-operate with the police of the locality where the offence took place. The FBI particularly comes into regular contact with police forces at every level of state government. Congress in recent years has been creating federal offences with a view towards allowing the highly professional and efficient FBI to enter the investigation of fact situations where local forces are apt to be inefficient. For example, under the National Stolen Property Act, the FBI is empowered to investigate thefts of over $5,000 when the stolen property is likely to have been taken across state lines. When the FBI enters a case it has authority to do so on its own initiative under federal law. Its position

---

[1] Chapman & St. Johnston, pp. 37–38; Smith (1949), pp. 190–203.

is quite different from that of Scotland Yard when assisting provincial forces in the investigation of serious crimes. Scotland Yard detectives can enter a case only at the invitation of the local chief constable.

State

Each state has its own police force.[1] The earliest state forces were established in the early part of the present century as an arm of the state executive to enforce locally unpopular laws. They were also used for strike-breaking. These origins for a long while gave the state police forces a bad name, but now they have outlived it. In nearly every state today the state-wide force is charged with policing traffic on the main highways; and some forces do no more than this. About two-thirds of the states have conferred full police authority on the state force; but in less than half of them is it actually exercised; and in probably only a dozen populous states is the force adequate to the task of general law enforcement outside the cities.[2] Where the state police are well developed, as in Pennsylvania, New York, New Jersey, Massachusetts, and Michigan, they tend to fill a void in rural law enforcement caused by the inadequacy or non-existence of local forces. Everywhere the performance of the state police tends to be substantially better than that of rural forces and often better than that of urban forces in the same states.

Nevertheless, state forces have not been allowed to supplant local ones. Even the most successful of them are careful not to encroach on the territory of rural sheriffs whose antipathy to the state police is known. They operate for the most part only in areas where there is no other form of organized police protection or where they are welcomed by local forces wishing to take advantage of their superior facilities. On the state level, as on the federal, there is some fragmentation and duplication of law enforcement activities among several agencies. In many states, for example, the state detective force or bureau of criminal identification is administratively separate from the highway patrol; in a few, the highway patrol is entirely independent of the regular state police establishment.

Local

In virtually every one of the more than 3,000 counties of the United

[1] See Chapman & St. Johnston, pp. 35–36; Puttkammer, pp. 43–50; Smith, pp. 164–90. See generally Smith (1925).   [2] Smith (1949), pp. 174–5.

States, there is a sheriff, usually with deputies.[1] In rural districts, his general peace powers have usually been retained, at least in theory, but in fact they are rarely exercised. Generally the sheriff is a political figure elected by popular vote for a short term, and generally he and his deputies are inexperienced and untrained in police work. Over the country as a whole, the sheriff system has broken down. The resulting vacuum has been filled partly by state police forces, and partly by special local police forces created to replace the sheriff and his ineffectual deputies, especially in the more populous suburban counties. These take several forms: (i) a uniformed highway patrol, placed administratively in the sheriff's office; (ii) an independent county police force; (iii) an independent parkway police force; (iv) a detective force operating out of the county prosecutor's office. Occasionally a county establishes two or more of these agencies, thus fragmenting police authority on the county level. Wherever they exist, county forces may overlap with the police of the small municipalities contained within the county. Efforts to consolidate police service within county lines usually have not been successful. Even if they were, the county in the United States is generally too small a unit to be the basis for satisfactory police organization. The English county constabulary has been effective because the greater population density of England has made a county a compact community. Only a few counties in the United States are of comparable population.

In over 20,000 townships and similar rural subdivisions into which the nation is divided for rudimentary local administration, the constable is retained as an elective officer, and vested by statute with general police jurisdiction.[2] However, the honour and compensation of the office are so small that in some instances it is never filled, being retained as hardly more than a symbol of local self-government. The typical rural constable is the true descendant of Shakespeare's Dogberry, with about the same degree of efficiency: he is almost always untrained and often incompetent; and his law enforcement activities are practically nil.

There are constables, marshals, or policemen in some 15,000 villages, boroughs, incorporated towns, other small municipalities, and quasi-public corporations such as special protection districts.[3]

[1] Smith (1949), p. 81. See generally ibid., pp. 81–89; Smith (1933), ch. II.
[2] Chapman & St. Johnston, pp. 32–33; Smith (1949), pp. 89–100. See generally Smith (1933), ch. 3.
[3] Chapman & St. Johnston, pp. 33–35; Smith (1949), pp. 100–1.

Even where a local force has been established to enforce only local regulations, it is usually vested by state law with general police authority. The larger the village, the more its force tends to acquire the characteristics of urban police. Some larger village forces are more efficient than the police of the smaller cities and manage to discharge their general authority quite adequately. However, at the lower end of the scale, the marshal of a very small village is likely to be not much more effective than the rural constable. The narrow municipal boundaries which he polices make his jurisdiction virtually meaningless and ineffective. His presence may even hamper an investigation in which federal, state, or county forces are involved. But his office is retained as a result of the stubborn home-rule sentiments which are sometimes harboured by even the smallest municipalities.

In well over 1,000 cities, there are urban police forces which exercise complete police authority.[1] Some of them are very large, the largest being the New York City force which numbers about 26,000 men. Many of them have achieved a high level of professionalization and offer the use of their facilities to smaller neighbouring forces. In terms of the strength of their manpower, these urban forces constitute the major part of the American police. In a handful of cities, including Boston, St. Louis, and Baltimore, the head of the police force is appointed by state authority, but in most cities, he is appointed by the mayor or equivalent municipal authority.[2] It is the city which ordinarily pays for the force, which is solely responsible to the city.

Fragmentation of Police Organization

The United States probably 'has the most decentralized police system in the world'.[3] It is characteristic that one cannot, even for a single state, give a list of statutes setting out the history or present state of police organization, such as can be done for England by reciting a half-dozen Acts of Parliament. Neither of the American legal encyclopedias—*Corpus Juris Secundum* or *American Jurisprudence*—attempts to gather the law of police organization under the one head 'Police', as Halsbury's *Laws of England*[4] does without trouble. The American law has to be sought in a *mélange* of federal, state, and local statutes and ordinances.

---

[1] Chapman & St. Johnston, pp. 33–35; Smith (1949), pp. 120–4.
[2] Smith (1949), pp. 208–9.
[3] Smith, 'A Preface to Law Enforcement', 291 *Annals*, Jan. 1954, p. 1.
[4] *Halsbury's Laws of England*, vol. 30, §§ 79–237.

Under the American federal system, it would not be constitution-ally possible for the national government to assert control over local police forces comparable to that which the Home Office has acquired in England. Control of police forces is a power reserved to the states, although the use of conditional grants-in-aid is a technique by which the federal government may seek to raise local standards. Legislation to this effect has recently been passed. It authorizes the Attorney-General of the United States to make federal grants to public or private agencies for the training of state and local law enforcement officers and correctional personnel.[1]

There was a movement towards state control over the police in the late nineteenth century, inspired by corruption in city governments and their police forces; but since this ran counter to the profound commitment of American politics to municipal home-rule, it has died out. There is presently no discernible tendency towards the central control of police standards which is characteristic of England, nor any towards the consolidation of forces. Amalgamation is not to be anticipated until the units of local governments themselves merge (as they ultimately may, although this movement has barely begun in the United States).

Fragmentation of the police has great practical disadvantages. The smaller forces are inadequate to deal with modern crime. Their stan-dards of competence are necessarily low and the geographic limits within which they have to operate are so small as to be crippling. In England a policeman has authority to act as such anywhere in the country;[2] in the United States, as a rule, he can act only within the boundaries of the governmental unit which hired him.[3] To some extent American forces have had to devise co-operative arrangements to cope with the resultant problems. Among the more successful modes of co-operation are joint communication networks, joint road-block systems; central identification and forensic laboratory services provided by the FBI, some state agencies, and larger city forces; and the use by smaller forces of FBI, state or city police training facilities.

Something of the degree of conflict and co-operation among the many autonomous American police forces is well illustrated in a recent episode. A group of two New York City detectives, an FBI

---

[1] Law Enforcement Assistance Act of 1965, 79 Stat. 828 (1965).
[2] Police Act, 1964, c. 48, § 19.
[3] Wharton, vol. 4, § 1614.

agent, and a New York State policeman went together into the State of New Jersey to keep watch for people attending the funeral of an underworld figure in Jersey City. The local police chief abruptly and abusively expelled them. In retaliation, the Jersey City police were denied facilities of the larger New York City force which they had been accustomed to use, such as the fingerprint registry, laboratories, and the Police Academy. The incident was reported in words more appropriate to transactions between sovereign nations as a rupture in 'diplomatic relations'; and a hastily concluded *rapprochement* was described as a *détente* inaugurating a new era of 'peaceful coexistence'.[1]

RECRUITMENT AND TRAINING OF POLICEMEN

In both England and the United States, there is a persistent struggle to get and keep competent policemen. In both countries the larger forces are generally below their authorized strength. One problem is police pay. The top salary for a London constable is £1,125 or about $3,150, although he is given tax-free accommodation, together with other allowances, worth about £350 or about $1,000 per annum, for a total annual pay of £1,475 or $4,150. American salaries vary considerably and it is difficult to equate them with English salaries. However, allowing for differences in the cost of living, and in the levels of pay for other employment, English salaries compare unfavourably with the best American salaries, which are about $8,000 in New York and Los Angeles.

A second problem is that of the inadequate number of men who want to become policemen, a significant proportion of whom are psychologically unsuited for the job. The leading American forces have been giving serious attention to this problem. In New York and Los Angeles, for example, the background and psychological fitness of each recruit is thoroughly explored. The same is true in England. Recruits are tested for their suitability for police work before they are accepted; and then are subject to close supervision and scrutiny during their probation period. Those who are psychologically unsuitable are not accepted for permanent employment.

A third problem is that of training. In England, eight regional training schools administered by the Home Office provide a uniform course of instruction for all recruits. A recruit attends an initial course of thirteen weeks' duration; then returns to his force to serve for about

[1] *N.Y. Times*, 20 Nov. 1964, p. 1, col. 4.

a year; then is brought back to a training centre for a two-week refresher course; then again returns to his force for about another year; and finally toward the end of his two-year probationary period returns for a final course of two weeks at the training school. In addition, the Home Office has established a National Police College at which courses are provided for the training of young policemen of outstanding merit, inspectors, and senior officers likely to reach the highest posts in the service.

The situation in the United States is uneven. The New York City recruit must pass a four-month course. Most other large cities have some sort of police school, but these often present no more than unrelieved lectures, to which there is no obligation to pay attention. In smaller forces, the newcomer may be handed a nightstick and a revolver and told to go to work. Some efforts have been made to improve this situation. A few states, notably New York, have established minimum standards of training for police recruits and have provided facilities at which basic and advanced training can be had. The FBI, in addition to conducting a national police academy for ranking police officers and police instructors, has provided teachers for schools run by state and local authorities. Such programmes have been particularly important in rural areas, but they have been directed mainly toward raising an average level of police competence which was, at the outset, exceedingly low.

In both England and the United States, the educational level of policemen is somewhat above the national average, although it falls short of what might reasonably be expected of a professional group. In the United States, while the FBI requires that its agents have university degrees in law or accountancy, even the best city forces require no more than a high school education. Only about half of English recruits have attended grammar school or its equivalent— which is, however, better than the national average of one in three. In both countries, attempts at creating a special 'officer class' by recruiting qualified outsiders to a high level in the force have been resisted by police associations and generally abandoned. It is now generally agreed that all must begin at the bottom and earn advancement, including the trickle of university graduates who enter police service. The need for increasing educational standards has stimulated experiments with systems in which men who are already in the police are offered higher education and the possibility of obtaining a university degree. The City University of New York, for example, provides several courses in police science which are conducted jointly with the City Police Academy; and part of the recruit training at the Academy can be credited towards a degree. In England, as already noted, the Police College is performing a similar service for outstanding young constables, some of whom are also given the opportunity of studying for a university degree at public expense.

A final problem affecting recruitment is the matter of tenure. Until recently in England, police officers were subject to summary removal by the local authority, without a hearing and without the necessity of good cause being shown. That is no longer true as a result of the decision in *Ridge* v. *Baldwin*,[1] the principles of which have now been embodied in the Police Act of 1964. In the United States, the situation varies widely from community to community. In some places, police officers enjoy the same sort of tenure as is enjoyed by their English counterparts: in others, they are subject to summary removal.

PUBLIC ATTITUDES TOWARDS THE POLICE

The English tradition, which is cherished, is that the police should not be a quasi-military organization but rather a group of citizens performing on a regular basis the duty of every citizen to enforce the criminal law. Originally, however, the establishment of a police force was seen as the beginning of a new military tyranny.[2] The example of the French police-spy system was a terrifying bogey. Throughout the Victorian era, the police were regarded by some persons as strike-breakers and enemies of the working class; but at the same time they were beginning to attract strong support from other large segments of the public. Now and for some time past it has been the boast of Englishmen that their police are not only respected but liked by the average citizen. Although sporadic scandals have occurred, relations between the police and the public are on the whole very good, with the police receiving a strong vote of public confidence. However, as the English police—now faced by organized criminal gangs accustomed to using modern tools and methods—adopt appropriate counter-organization, the traditional view of the police as a somewhat specialized collection of ordinary citizens becomes anachronistic. The image of the 'Bobby' as a kindly father figure and friend to all is beginning to be obsolete and be replaced by a complex range of popular attitudes more appropriate to the altered nature and functions of the police.

[1] (1964) A.C. 40.   [2] Rolph (1962), pp. 8–10.

Americans have often contrasted British attitudes enviously with the poor relations between public and police which have characterized many parts of the United States. Despite early opposition to a uniformed police force as being 'militaristic' and 'undemocratic',[1] the American police have developed on the pattern of semi-military organizations, in which there are 'troops', 'corporals', 'sergeants', 'lieutenants', and 'captains'. The American police habitually carry fire-arms, which the English police do not. This seems an unavoidable difference since the criminal population of the United States is largely armed, while that in England is generally not. To some extent (as the English have feared) the armed policeman intimidates the citizen instead of attracting his sympathy and support. But the military aspects of the American police are not primarily responsible for their adverse public relations. Rather, the persistent criticisms have been that the police are ignorant, corrupt, and brutal.[2] Sensational exposés of the links between policemen, politicians, and criminals have occurred often in the past and are still occurring.

In the United States, as might be expected from what has just been said, there is a greater sensitivity to the need of cultivating better relations with the public and of replacing the 'tough cop' with an officer who is not only better trained but also better mannered, and less likely to indulge in abusive and profane language. The more advanced forces have gone further than the English in creating public relations programmes and specialists to supervise them, as they have also probably gone further in using psychological testing on recruits to weed out those likely to abuse power or crack under strain.

A point on which the experience of the two countries agrees is that popular respect for the police has no relation to the issue of centralization of control. In the United States, the FBI enjoys the highest reputation, and state forces are generally better regarded than local ones. In England, it was Home Office control of standards which established the police as an efficient organization worthy of popular respect and affection.

COMPLAINTS AGAINST POLICEMEN

Police conduct giving rise to disputes with the public lies in an area where there are differing views on the proper scope of police activity

[1] Fosdick, pp. 216–25 (1920).
[2] See, e.g., Barnes & Teeters, pp. 216–25; Gourley, 'Police Public Relations', 291 *Annals*, Jan. 1954, pp. 135–6.

and evolving doctrines as to the scope of police power. Many of the disputes have arisen in connexion with political and civil rights demonstrations where a normally law-abiding section of the population is involved with the police in ways which are not subject to wholly clear rules. These factors cause difficulties both for internal administrators and for judges and juries. Unless convinced that the officer is acting within his powers, many citizens are prone to accuse him of misconduct. Unless convinced that he is acting outside his powers, the average policeman retorts that to restrict him is to coddle criminals. Both sides are, to some extent, in a false position. The citizen, without admitting it, may think he should be able to get away with a certain amount of illegality. The policeman, without admitting it, may think he should have a certain amount of discretion to exceed his strict powers when convinced he is dealing with a law-breaker.

In both England and the United States there is a difference of opinion as to the proper procedure for hearing and remedying citizen complaints that the police have exceeded their powers.[1] In all forces in England and in all sizeable American forces there is some system within the force itself for considering such complaints. These systems do not, however, satisfy a very vocal part of the public. The feeling is expressed increasingly in both countries that the police ought to be subject to review by an independent agency. Internal disciplinary measures, so the argument runs, work only in cases of clear and obvious illegality such as brutal assaults and bribery; they are not effective in close cases where the police are loath to admit a mistake; the result is a lack of public confidence; and only external review will restore the public's faith.

External review in the form of a number of judicial remedies has always existed in both countries. The argument for a separate reviewing authority presupposes that these have been insufficient to deter police illegalities.

One indirect form of judicial control over the police is the power of the courts to reject evidence obtained by illegal means. We shall discuss exclusionary rules of evidence at length in the second part of this book, and there see that the American rules are considerably more stringent than the English. Nevertheless, their influence on the police is uncertain. Clearly the police are careful not to go into court with a case which exposes their worst abuses, for the American judiciary has

---

[1] See Trebach, pp. 218–30; Whitaker, p. 134; Note, 'The Administration of Complaints by Civilians Against Police', 77 *Harv. L. Rev.* 499 (1964).

slowly educated the police not to use the 'third degree'. It is debatable, however, whether it has done more than substitute subtler techniques of interrogation and stimulate police perjury.

A similar form of control is judicial criticism of police activities. In England the judges seem able to make their views on what is fair procedure felt by the police,[1] and the police generally conform. American judges are not so influential. The American police show little enough regard for judicial holdings, much less for judicial dicta. The judges are reluctant to label any wrongful police practice as harmless error lest the police take it for permission to continue the condemned activity.

In both countries civil actions for damages lie against individual police officers on the grounds of assault and false arrest.[2] Such actions have succeeded on occasion, but there are formidable obstacles. First, the complainant is not the most persuasive witness as to an incident in which there are, as a rule, only two parties: himself and the policeman. Furthermore, he may have a criminal record, which, despite the worth of his claim, can be used to impeach his testimony. Second, the complainant will probably be unable to bear the expense of litigation unless he is eligible for and able to secure legal aid.[3] This is not a serious problem in England, but it is in the United States, where civil legal aid is less well developed. Finally, the assets of the individual policeman are likely to be very small, so that even if the complainant recovers damages, he may be unable to collect unless payment is made out of public funds. Again, this is a more serious problem in the United States than in England, where the practice of public payment of damages awarded against a policeman is well established. The practice was formalized by the Police Act, 1964,[4] which provides for civil actions to be brought directly against the chief constable as a representative public defendant. A few American states likewise permit civil suits against municipal bodies.[5] This improves the position of the complainant, but it reduces the impact of

[1] Devlin (1960), pp. 22–23.

[2] For a discussion of whether civil remedies are designed to indemnify innocent persons injured by unlawful police activities or to serve as a deterrent to unlawful police practices, see LaFave, pp. 412–20.

[3] Foote, 'Tort Remedies for Police Violations of Individual Rights', 39 *Minn. L. Rev.* 493 (1955).   [4] Police Act, 1964, c. 48, § 48.

[5] e.g. *Mich. Stat. Ann.* § 5.3376(1) (Supp. 1963). In addition to those states permitting payment from public funds, most states require that peace officers post bond. However, these requirements are generally applied to traditional categories of officers—sheriffs and constables—but not to policemen in large metropolitan forces. LaFave, p. 421 and nn. 45–50.

the suit on the individual policeman.[1] He does not stand to suffer direct financial loss, although his career may be adversely affected and he may be subjected to disciplinary proceedings.

In both countries there is the possibility of criminal prosecution against erring officers. But this has most of the disadvantages of a civil action. In England, the complainant would have to bear the expense of prosecution himself, although if successful he might be awarded costs. In the United States, he would have to convince a district attorney that prosecution was feasible. The district attorney might be reluctant to act against police on whose co-operation his office relied.

The police in both countries have generally claimed that internal and judicial review are sufficient checks on police misconduct and that any attempt to create a special inquiry system external to the force and outside the ordinary course of law would be prejudicial to police morale, discipline, and control. Nevertheless, there has been increasing pressure for the introduction of such a system either in the form of a special tribunal or an 'ombudsman'[2]—a commissioner of investigations charged with hearing complaints against all government departments including the police. This pressure has had some effect. Some American cities have established disciplinary review boards in which both the police and the general citizenry are represented; some have attempted to make their internal complaint procedures more judicial in nature; and a few, beginning with Philadelphia in 1958, have established citizen review boards entirely independent of the police. In England, Home Secretaries have occasionally set up *ad hoc* independent inquiries into a police matter. In addition, under the Police Act, 1964,[3] a chief officer may call in, or may be required to call in, an officer of another force to investigate a complaint, and if there is any suspicion that a criminal offence may have been committed, he must submit the report of the investigation to the Director of Public Prosecutions. Finally, the Home Secretary is accountable to Parliament for the actions of the police.

[1] This is also the case if the police carry false arrest insurance. Two related practices that may remove this defect of the civil action as a sanction, are the assessment against the entire force of a *pro rata* share of money damages recovered against an officer in a false arrest action, and the requirement that the entire force contribute to a pool to be held to pay such recoveries. LaFave, p. 423 and nn. 57–58

[2] See, e.g., Sawer; Hurwitz, 'Denmark's Ombudsman: The Parliamentary Commissioner for Civil and Military Government Administration', 1961 *Wis. L. Rev.* 169.   [3] Police Act, 1964, c. 48, § 49.

2

THE PROSECUTION

DIFFERENT APPROACHES TO THE SAME PROBLEM

THE essential functions of the prosecution are the same in England and the United States. In both countries prosecutors have three major tasks to perform: first, they must make a decision on whether or not to bring criminal charges against an alleged offender, second, they must put the accusation into proper form and place it before the proper judicial authorities; and third, they must present to the court evidence tending to establish the guilt of the accused. In both countries the prosecution is, theoretically, on an equal footing with the defence, with each side presenting its evidence to the court, and the court acting as an impartial umpire in reaching a decision based solely on the evidence presented to it by the parties.[1] This system is markedly different from that in Continental Europe, where the judges are expected to investigate a complaint and find the facts for themselves. The Anglo-American system places the entire burden of proving a criminal charge on the prosecution.

Despite these similarities, American and English methods of prosecution are profoundly different. The key to the difference lies in the American district attorney, a public legal officer whose job it is to institute and conduct all criminal proceedings.[2] England has no comparable figure.

In England, any person can bring a prosecution.[3] Even when the prosecutor is a policeman, as he is in most cases, he prosecutes by virtue of his right as a private citizen and not by virtue of his office. This is seen in the way cases tried summarily in the lower courts are named. The title of a case reads as if it were a private suit between two parties: the complainant (who is probably a police officer) and the defendant. In more serious cases in the higher courts, the prosecution

---

[1] For a discussion of the relative advantages of the prosecution and the defence, see Chapter 6 below.

[2] In this respect, the United States resembles Scotland and the continental countries, which also have public prosecutors.

[3] However, the magistrate may refuse to issue a summons, which will usually stop the proceedings.

is in the name of the Crown, but it is usually initiated by some named individual, who in legal theory is acting in a private capacity. In practice, most prosecutions are instituted by police officers as part of their normal duties. In the United States, on the other hand, all prosecutions are brought in the name of the state, and are conducted by the district attorney acting as the state's agent or representative.

PROSECUTION IN ENGLAND

The work of prosecution in England is widely diffused.[1] If a private citizen wishes to prosecute one of his neighbours, he can, if he chooses, handle the whole case by himself. He may, however, want a lawyer's assistance, in which case he retains a solicitor. The solicitor will prepare the necessary papers, interview witnesses, call them to testify, and conduct the prosecution's case at the preliminary hearing or summary trial. He may retain a barrister to present the case in court if it is unusual or complex. But if the case is serious enough to require indictment and jury trial in a higher court (Assizes or Quarter Sessions), the complainant's solicitor will have to retain a barrister or allow the complainant to conduct the case himself. Only a barrister— an entirely distinct species of lawyer—is allowed to represent a party at Assizes and at most Quarter Sessions.

The Police

English police are theoretically in the same position as private complainants. If they decide that an offender shall be prosecuted, they prefer charges against him in the name of one of their officers. That officer (who may or may not be a senior man on the force) then goes into court to conduct the case for the prosecution. The alternative is for the police, like the private complainant, to retain a solicitor or barrister to present the case in court. This is becoming more and more common. With the extension of free legal aid, the defendant is likely to have a lawyer on his side, and the police like to be equally well represented. Also significant is the fact that there has been some criticism of police presentation on the theory that it is hard for a police officer to have the degree of detachment from the case at hand which a lawyer is supposed to have. Nevertheless, most prosecutions are handled by police officers alone without the help of lawyers.

In London, the Metropolitan Police force has a Solicitor's Department, staffed by over thirty solicitors. They are not consulted in the

[1] Devlin (1960), pp. 16–22; Fitzgerald, pp. 157–8; Jackson, pp. 119–30.

majority of police prosecutions, which are still handled by police officers themselves, but only in difficult or serious cases, or in those where the defendant is legally represented. In such cases, a member of the Solicitor's Department may appear for the police in the lower court, or as happens in about half the cases referred to the Department, a barrister may be retained to appear. If the case is one which must be tried in a higher court, the Solicitor's Department, like a private solicitor, has no choice but to retain a barrister to present the case.

Outside of London, the great majority of minor prosecutions are also handled entirely by the police. With regard to serious cases, practice varies widely from one community to another. The chief constable may give the work of prosecution to one or more local firms of solicitors in private practice. There is a tendency to give cases to a single solicitor who is either on the staff of the town or county, or paid a salary for handling prosecutions. Sometimes it is necessary to employ not one but several police solicitors because of the size of the area to be covered.

Private Prosecution

Most citizens are satisfied to let the police or police solicitors initiate criminal proceedings. Private prosecution is negligible in volume. There are no figures on the proportion of all prosecutions started by the police, but there can be no doubt that they are far more numerous than any other kind.[1] For serious cases, the statistics available show that the police account for 88 per cent. of the prosecutions and that the remaining 12 per cent. are initiated largely by other public bodies.[2] The few strictly private prosecutions are likely to be undertaken by large commercial firms—banks, insurance companies, and the like— for offences that interfere with their business, or by societies such as the N.S.P.C.C. and the R.S.P.C.A. which prosecute offences involving cruelty to children and animals. There is also a small class of minor offences which are normally privately prosecuted, the most notable example being simple assault. Since in English law a criminal conviction or acquittal for assault bars a subsequent civil proceeding against the offender, the victim is given the choice of prosecuting or suing for damages.[3]

[1] Jackson, pp. 120–2.   [2] Devlin (1960), pp. 20–21.
[3] Offences Against the Person Act, 1861, 24 & 25 Vict., c. 100, § 45; see Salmond, *Torts*, § 90, p. 296 (12th ed. 1957).

Less than 4 per cent. of serious ('indictable') offences are prosecuted by government departments specially concerned with the particular offences. For example, the Board of Inland Revenue prosecutes income tax violations, the Board of Trade, commercial frauds, and the Post Office, mail offences. Such departments have staffs of solicitors, but if the case is one which must be tried by a jury in a higher court, again a barrister must be retained to conduct the prosecution's case at trial.

The Director of Public Prosecutions

The remaining 8 per cent. of serious crimes (and under 1 per cent. of minor crimes) are prosecuted by another public official—the Director of Public Prosecutions.[1] He is appointed by the Home Secretary, after consultation with the Attorney-General, from among barristers or solicitors of ten years' standing. His staff includes thirty-five qualified lawyers,[2] who may be either barristers or solicitors, although when working in the Director's office, they perform only the functions of solicitors. When one of the Director's cases goes to trial in a higher court, he must go outside his own staff for a barrister to conduct it. Furthermore, he does not have any investigative facilities of his own, as do the larger American prosecuting offices, but must rely entirely on the police.

Within the limits indicated, the Director occupies an important role in the system of English prosecutions. He is required to prosecute any case punishable by death, and any case where his participation is ordered by the Home Secretary. He may prosecute, if he sees fit to do so, any case referred to him by any other government department. He may also prosecute any case that appears to him to be of such importance or difficulty that his intervention seems necessary, having the power to step in and take a case over from any private or police prosecutor who started it. There is a substantial list of offences which the police are required to report to the Director, so that he can decide whether or not to undertake prosecution from the outset, including all offences that immediately affect the public interest, such as sedition, espionage, misconduct by public officials, counterfeiting, and most offences of an especially serious nature such as manslaughter, rape, and sexual offences against children. Finally, the Director may, on

[1] Devlin (1960). See generally Mathew, 'The Role of the Director of Public Prosecutions in the Administration of Justice', 1957 *Proceedings, ABA Section of Criminal Law* 54–63.   [2] Jackson, pp. 126–7.

request, give advice on the conduct of a case to any private or official prosecutor, and he may authorize any of them to incur special costs—as for scientific evidence—to be paid out of public funds.

The Attorney-General and the Solicitor-General

Though appointed by the Home Secretary, the Director is responsible to the Attorney-General, who, like his American counterpart, is a member of the government and conducts its legal business. Most of the litigation with which he is concerned is civil, but both through the Director of Public Prosecutions and in his own right, the Attorney-General has potentially a considerable amount of control over criminal cases. There are a number of offences which cannot be prosecuted without his permission, including cases in which the government itself is concerned—for example, violations of the Official Secrets Act—and also non-governmental offences, such as incest, where the right of private prosecution might be misused. The Attorney-General also has the power to stop any criminal action tried 'on indictment' (i.e. in one of the higher courts), by the entry of a *nolle prosequi*—an order directing that the case be terminated. This power is in practice rarely used, being employed for the most part only when some technical reason makes it impossible to dispose of a case in any other way. Finally, the Attorney-General or his nominee acts as counsel in all cases undertaken by the Director of Public Prosecutions in which a barrister's appearance is required. The Attorney-General himself appears only in two or three such cases a year, usually Official Secrets Act cases or appeals to the House of Lords. In the other cases, he nominates barristers in private practice to handle the trial or appeal. Outside London, nomination is on a case by case basis, but for cases tried at the Old Bailey in London, he selects in advance, on the basis of merit, a panel of eight barristers who are then known as standing 'Treasury Counsel'. They continue in private practice, and in the course of it may appear for the defence as well as for the prosecution.

For the purposes just mentioned, the Solicitor-General is the *alter ego* of the Attorney-General. He often conducts litigation, both criminal and civil, for the Crown.[1]

Some of the government bodies which prosecute in their own right also have standing counsel. These are not employees of the government, but practising barristers who have been retained to represent the government whenever a prosecution occurs.

[1] See Law Officers Act, 1944, 7 & 8 Geo. VI, c. 25.

Private Barristers

There are about 2,000 practising barristers in England,[1] almost all of whom are available for criminal work on either the prosecution or defence side. To a limited extent, Treasury Counsel tend to stick to prosecuting and a few other barristers to the defence, but the great majority of barristers are likely to appear for either side indifferently. This distribution of work avoids the occupational bias which afflicts many American lawyers making repeated appearances for one side only.

PROSECUTION IN THE UNITED STATES

In describing prosecution in the United States, it is necessary to deal separately with the three levels of government: federal, state, and local.

Federal Prosecution

The American federal government has its own system of courts and prosecutors, entirely distinct from the courts and prosecutors in each of the fifty states. The federal judicial system is divided into ninety-two districts, each having its own trial court and its own United States Attorney. His job is to represent the federal government in both criminal and civil litigation, so that he prosecutes in federal court all federal crimes committed within his district. The United States Attorney is always a lawyer appointed by the President, with the approval of the Senate, and he in turn appoints a staff of lawyers to assist him. His selection and the selection of his assistants is largely a matter of political patronage. The jobs usually change hands with each change in administration, although in the larger offices there is some tendency for an incoming United States Attorney to keep on experienced members of his predecessor's staff.

The United States Attorney is not entirely autonomous, his office being part of the federal Department of Justice. While he has wide discretion in running his office, he is ultimately under the supervision of the Attorney-General of the United States, who is both the head of the Department of Justice and a member of the President's cabinet.

The United States Attorneys are not concerned with the great bulk of crimes committed in the United States. They handle only the prosecution of federal crimes, which are relatively few in number, since the

[1] Devlin (1960), p. 22; Megarry, pp. 6–7.

federal government is one of limited, enumerated powers, and has no jurisdiction to define crimes for the nation as a whole.[1] Ordinary crimes are a matter of state law, prosecuted in the state courts by state officials of two kinds: attorneys-general and district attorneys. The attorney-general works on a state-wide basis; the district attorney on a local—usually a county—basis.

State Attorneys-General

Each of the fifty states has an attorney-general. He is directly elected in forty-one states, appointed by the governor in seven, by the legislature in one, and by the state supreme court in another. In two small states, Delaware and Rhode Island, the attorney-general's office is in charge of all criminal prosecutions, there being no district attorneys in those states. In the remaining forty-eight states, the attorney-general has few duties in connexion with prosecution of criminal cases, his main task being to represent the state government in civil litigation. His responsibilities in the criminal field are limited to a few crimes likely to have state-wide ramifications (like violations of certain taxing and regulatory statutes) and situations where local law enforcement and prosecution have broken down because of corruption or incompetency.[2] The great bulk of offences are left to be prosecuted on a local basis by the district attorneys.

Local District Attorneys

The key figure in American prosecutions is, therefore, the officer whom we have been calling the district attorney. This is his most popular designation, although in some states he is called the 'commonwealth attorney', 'circuit attorney', 'state's attorney', 'county prosecutor', 'county attorney', 'solicitor', or 'prosecuting attorney'. As a rule, he is virtually autonomous, his office not being administratively subordinate to the state's attorney-general or any other official. He is usually locally elected for a term of two or four years, although in one state (Connecticut) he is appointed by the court, and in another (New Jersey) by the governor. Normally, the only formal prerequisites for election or appointment are that the candidate be of voting age and a lawyer. The office is a salaried post. Depending upon the volume of work, the district attorney may appoint one or more assistants.

[1] Karlen (1964), pp. 14–19.
[2] See Sunderland, 'Circumventing the Corrupt Prosecutor', 48 *J. Crim. L., C. & P.S.* 531 (1958).

He may also, in many states, allow the lawyer for a complaining witness to participate in a particular prosecution. This resembles the English private prosecution, but differs in one essential: while the district attorney can accept private help, he can also refuse it. It is in fact rarely offered, for the pattern of public prosecution is dominant.[1]

In most rural counties, a single district attorney is enough, but in larger communities, large staffs are needed. The district attorney's office in New York County (that part of New York City known as Manhattan) has an annual budget of nearly $2 million and includes on its staff 260 employees, including ninety-two lawyers, and seventy detectives, as well as investigators, accountants, clerks, secretaries, stenographers, process servers, and technical specialists. In most places, appointment to the district attorney's office is a matter of political patronage, but there are a few exceptions. Assistants in the Los Angeles office are civil servants, and the New York County office —whose chief has, for over twenty years, himself been elected on nomination by all parties—has also developed a career service, uninfluenced by political connexions.

In many places, the district attorney's is not a full-time job, he and his assistants being free to engage in private practice. Even in some large offices where the district attorney and his chief assistants do not engage in private practice, junior men may be allowed to do so. The only restriction on them, as a rule, is that they limit themselves to civil litigation and not appear for the defence in criminal cases. This restriction is designed to avoid undue influence on their associates in the office, but it incidentally serves to keep them prosecution-minded. The New York County office is again almost unique in requiring the members of its staff to devote full time to their work.

The district attorney enters a criminal case at the point where police investigation stops. The only cases he does not handle, as a rule, are those tried in traffic and juvenile courts. These are, in a sense, prosecuted by the police, somewhat as in England, except that the arresting officer, who is usually the only policeman in court, functions more like a witness than a prosecutor. All felony and most misdemeanour prosecutions are controlled from an early stage by the district attor-

[1] Some states allow a person interested in getting a conviction to hire a private lawyer to assist the public prosecutor. For example, in *Neill* v. *State*, 89 Okla. Crim. 272, 207 P. 2d 344 (1949), the widow of the deceased employed an attorney to assist in a murder prosecution. See also Note, Private Prosecution: 'A Remedy for District Attorneys' Unwarranted Inaction', 65 *Yale L.J.* 209 (1955).

ney's office, which carries them through sentence or acquittal and, if necessary, through appeal.

The district attorney has concentrated within his own office powers and functions which in England are distributed among a number of institutions:

1. He or his assistants do much of the preliminary work which in England is done by the police. This is especially true in large offices which have investigating forces of their own. In particularly difficult cases, such as those involving commercial frauds, or official corruption, the district attorney's office frequently initiates and carries through the whole of the investigation. In especially serious cases, such as homicides, an assistant district attorney may accompany police investigators to the scene of the crime.

2. The district attorney has a degree of control over the activities of the grand jury, which possesses broad investigatory powers, including the power to compel possible prosecution witnesses to testify before it. The district attorney or an assistant invariably attends the sessions of the grand jury, and so shares in all the advantages of its power. This gives him a great investigative instrument which the police in England do not possess.

3. It is the district attorney who, in the United States, sifts through cases to determine which shall be prosecuted and which shall not.[1] Such discretion is usually vested in the police in England, subject to ultimate control by the Director of Public Prosecutions.

4. The district attorney's staff does all of the work which in England is done by the police or their solicitors in preparing cases for trial, and by solicitors or barristers in trying them before the courts. Since the legal profession in America is not divided, there is nothing to prevent the same practitioner from acting both as a solicitor and as a trial advocate. It is more usual than not for the same lawyer to handle the whole of a case from beginning to end, for specialized trial lawyers are still somewhat of a luxury. Only the larger cities can support them. But, on the other hand, within a large district attorney's office there may be more specialization than is imposed on English prosecutors by their divided legal profession. In such an office a separate group of assistants will be assigned to try cases in the higher courts; another group will be assigned to argue appeals; another to handle 'racket' cases (arising out of systematic criminal activities by groups of professional criminals).

[1] See Karlen (1964), pp. 40–41.

5. Finally, the district attorney has power effectively to compromise or to terminate a prosecution. There is no exact equivalent in England, where no prosecutor can on his own motion drop the proceedings once he has started them. He can, if he wishes, offer no evidence and ask the court for permission to withdraw the charges. The decision is the court's, but the court as a matter of practice refers it to the Director of Public Prosecutions. Conversely, the Director may advise the police against a prosecution and may enforce his advice either by taking over the proceedings or by asking the Attorney-General to stop them through entry of a *nolle prosequi*. Nevertheless, these are extraordinary powers which are not often used. They involve the sort of decisions about which questions are asked in Parliament. The American district attorney, on the other hand, is virtually a free agent when it comes to dropping or compromising charges. Even in those states where withdrawal of charges is a judicial question, the judges tend to accede to the district attorney's requests as a matter of routine.[1]

Politics

In practice, the district attorney has powers of control over the course of a prosecution which are at least as great as those of the judges. There is some advantage to having a single individual with responsibility for the whole process of prosecution, but the political milieu in which a district attorney works creates a danger that his great powers will at times be used unwisely.

The effect of politics, however, differs at different times and places. As a result of the local political situation, the district attorney's office may be filled with inexperienced party hacks or with a competent staff; it may serve as a sinecure for an incompetent lawyer, or as a stepping stone to higher political office; it may be inefficiently inert or it may be infused with the ambition to make a good record for a coming election. In short, politics tends both to distort and correct the conduct of elected prosecutors. It undoubtedly leads to abuses, but also curbs some of the worst excesses. The positive value of politics needs to be emphasized. It makes the system work better than might be expected, and makes more formal controls relatively ineffective if not illusory. Public opinion, reinforced by the sanction of defeat at the polls, is the most effective control over an elected district attorney.

Formal controls are of three types. The first is direct or indirect

[1] Note, 'Prosecutor's Discretion', 103 *U. Pa. L. Rev.* 1057, 1064–72 (1955).

removal of the district attorney from office. Directly, the state legislature can impeach him in nearly all states; in others, the governor can remove him. Indirectly, he can be effectively removed by conviction for malfeasance in office, or by disbarment. Second, the district attorney may be subject by statute to the general surveillance of the state attorney-general, as he is in over thirty states. Third, the district attorney's deliberate inaction in a case may be circumvented by appointment of a special prosecutor in matters of great public concern. In about twenty states the attorney-general has power to make such an appointment; and in seven others, the courts possess that power. However, nearly all of these controls involve a clash of one set of elected officials with another; and there is for this reason a general disinclination to use them. It is easier, safer, and often quicker to leave questions of the prosecutor's misconduct to the electorate.

Thus, elective politics is both a grave weakness of American prosecution and its main corrective influence. The English avoid both the disease and the cure by a nearly complete divorce of criminal law administration from political considerations.

3

THE DEFENCE

THE defence of a criminal case may be conducted by the accused himself or by a lawyer. It was not always so. At common law, the second alternative was not permitted except in minor cases—where it was least needed. Counsel were not permitted for persons accused of treason or felony. In England, legal representation for the defence was not allowed in treason trials until 1696, and was not fully allowed in felony cases until 1837.[1] Early American law was more generous, so that by 1800 the federal constitution and the law of every state then in existence guaranteed the accused the right to have the assistance of counsel for his defence—if he could afford to pay for it.[2]

The right to counsel having been established, a major difficulty remaining was to provide representation for indigents. This is now recognized as one of the most significant problems of criminal justice in both nations. In the United States as a whole, about 60 per cent. of all criminal defendants are too poor to retain lawyers, and in the large cities the figure is 75 per cent.[3] In England the situation is much the same. Hence, in the vast majority of criminal cases in both countries, provision of some form of free legal aid is the only alternative to requiring the accused to represent himself. In England legal aid has been established within the traditional structure of the legal profession. In the United States there has been a tendency to establish separate legal aid societies and public defender offices to supplement the services traditionally provided by lawyers in private practice.

THE LEGAL PROFESSION IN ENGLAND

There are about 22,000 solicitors and about 2,000 barristers practising in England,[4] or roughly one solicitor for every 2,000 persons and one barrister for every 23,000. The difference between these two kinds of lawyers is often loosely expressed by saying that the barrister tries cases in court while the solicitor is an office lawyer whose job is to

---

[1] Plucknett, p. 435.   [2] Beaney, pp. 18–26.
[3] Lumbard, 'The Adequacy of Lawyers now in Criminal Practice', 47 *J. Am. Jud. Soc.* 176–7 (1964).   [4] Megarry, pp. 6–7.

advise clients and prepare cases for trial. This is not strictly accurate. On the one hand, the barrister does more than advocacy, for he is often a specialist in some field of law, and as such may be consulted solely for his opinion on a particularly difficult problem. On the other hand, the solicitor handles a great number of cases in court. While barristers have an exclusive right of audience in the higher courts, both criminal (i.e. Assizes and most Quarter Sessions) and civil, solicitors have an equal right to appear in the lower courts, both criminal and civil. The lower courts, where barristers appear relatively infrequently, account for the vast bulk of all litigation. As we shall see in the next chapter, the proportion of all criminal cases finally disposed of in the Magistrates' Courts—where solicitors have the right of audience—is about 97 per cent. of the total. Considering the volume of cases handled by them, solicitors on the whole do far more courtroom work than barristers.

The solicitor works directly for a lay client while the barrister does not.[1] A barrister may not accept employment from a member of the public, but only from a solicitor who, understandably, consults him only on matters of special difficulty or where trial in a higher court is involved. This leads to different modes of practice as between the two branches of the profession. Solicitors tend to work in firms, at locations accessible to clients, conducting a large amount of routine business from their offices. While they may specialize in a broad division of the law such as real estate or commercial transactions, they must be prepared to deal with any subject of concern to their clients. They tend to become consultants and confidants with regard to all of their clients' affairs. Barristers, on the other hand, practice alone, partnerships being prohibited. Their chambers are concentrated near the law courts in London, and in a few of the large cities like Birmingham, Liverpool, Manchester, and Leeds. Apart from counselling on points of law (they tend to specialize in narrower divisions of the law than solicitors) most of their work is in court. They are seldom in on a case from the beginning to the end, but only on those phases of it which require their special talents. Occasionally, however, in the case of a very serious offence like murder, a barrister may be consulted almost immediately upon arrest, and he may subsequently conduct the trial and appeal, if any.

Solicitors used to have a lower social status than barristers. The

[1] See pp. 39–40 below for exceptions arising out of the use of the 'dock brief' and the courtroom assignment of counsel.

tendency to regard them as an 'inferior' branch of the profession has almost, but not entirely, died out. It is kept alive by the barristers' exclusive privilege of appearing in the higher courts; by the fact that solicitors are still expected to go to barristers' chambers to tender briefs, participate in conferences, etc.; and by the tradition that most judges are to be drawn only from the Bar (as barristers are collectively called). By recent legislation solicitors as well as barristers may be appointed stipendiary magistrates or chairmen or deputy chairmen of Quarter Sessions, but only a few solicitors have been so appointed to date.

THE LEGAL PROFESSION IN THE UNITED STATES

In the United States, where there are almost 300,000 lawyers, or about one to every 666 people,[1] the English division of the legal profession has never existed. Admission to practice entitles a lawyer to perform every function associated with legal representation, from initially interviewing and advising a client through appearance at trial and upon appeal. The most widely used terms to describe a legal representative are 'lawyer' and 'attorney' which are normally interchangeable, while 'the bar' is used in the United States to describe the entire legal profession.

Within the American bar there is some informal specialization in the sense that an attorney may avoid appearing in court or he may spend most of his time there. There is also the same sort of specialization by legal subjects that is found among solicitors and barristers in England. Both kinds of specialization are common in large legal partnerships. These firms, however, do not ordinarily take criminal work, so that most of the attorneys who work in criminal law practice singly or in small firms, where they are accustomed to perform all the work associated with the defence of a criminal case. On the whole, such practitioners would dislike having to present a case in court unless they themselves had prepared it for trial. While it is not unknown for one attorney to engage another to handle a trial or appeal, this happens rarely, and it requires the consent of the client, who ordinarily expects that the attorney he has engaged will conduct the whole case personally at all stages. Most American lawyers practise in a manner which is more closely comparable to that of an English solicitor than to that of an English barrister.

[1] Griswold, 'Law and Lawyers in the United States', p. 5 (1964).

LEGAL EDUCATION

As to the training of lawyers, the two nations have developed along different paths. In the United States, law schools have virtually sup-planted apprenticeship. The general pattern for admission to the bar is for a student to take a college course for three or four years; then to take a law school course for three years; and then to pass a bar examination administered by the state in which he intends to practise. In England, the aspiring solicitor must undergo a combination of schooling, apprenticeship, and examination. Admission to practise without a formal law course after five years' apprenticeship is possible, but the usual course for an able aspirant is to take an undergraduate university course for three or four years; then to take a six months' law course; then to pass an examination given by the Law Society; and then to serve as an apprentice for two years.

The training requirements for barristers are substantially more relaxed than for solicitors. The aspiring barrister in England still is not required to undertake a formal law course, though most do. A call to the bar requires only eating a prescribed number of dinners for three years at one of the four Inns of Court in London (upon which occasions the neophyte meets senior members of his intended profession and absorbs from them some of the traditions of that profession; he is also afforded the opportunity of witnessing and participating in moot court arguments); and then passing an examination given by the Council of Legal Education, a body controlled by the Inns. Between 1959 and 1965, newly admitted barristers were required to undertake a year's pupilage in the chambers of a senior barrister, which was, in effect, an apprenticeship, but one coming after admission. This formalized what had long been the practice of the vast majority of junior barristers. Since October 1965, the new barrister is required to undergo six months of such pupilage before he is allowed to practise.

DISCIPLINE AND BAR ORGANIZATION

In formal organization of the profession, the American and English patterns are widely different. For English barristers, the scheme of organization is rigid, with education, admission, and discipline firmly in the hands of four Inns of Court—Lincoln's Inn, the Middle Temple, the Inner Temple, and Gray's Inn. English solicitors are less closely organized. The Law Society, to which most of them belong, is a voluntary association which, by statute, establishes and administers the requirements for admission to practise. A Disciplinary Committee—a separate statutory entity, not part of the Law Society, but composed of past and present members of the Council of the Society—has the power, subject to appeal to the courts, to strike a solicitor from the rolls.

American lawyers, on the whole, are less organized than either branch of the English profession. Legal education is largely left to the law schools. Admission to the bar is controlled by the courts on a state by state basis. Discipline is likewise a judicial function, which in some places is only sporadically exercised. There are bar associations on all levels: national, state, and local. Membership in the state bar associations of about half the states is compulsory. The remaining state bar associations and all national and local bar associations are voluntary organizations with no official power.

QUALITY OF REPRESENTATION

It is often observed that English lawyers, on the whole, entertain a higher sense of ethics and professional responsibility than those in the United States. This may be partly attributable to the fact that disciplinary action against unethical practices is fairly certain in England. It may also be due in part to the attitude which pervades all of English life that any game—including the practice of law—must be played strictly according to the rules.

In a growing number of communities in the United States, the defence of criminal cases is largely in the hands of legal aid lawyers and public defenders, who are generally upright, capable men. However, to the extent that private practitioners occupy the field or operate alongside of legal aid lawyers and public defenders, the quality of representation ranges from excellent through mediocre to poor.[1] At its worst, it involves seeking official favours for clients or persuading the clients that they are being given special treatment.

Negotiation of a sort with public officials is perfectly proper, for American criminal law leaves much room for discretionary action by prosecutors and judges; and part of the defence lawyer's legitimate

---

[1] See Wood, 'Informal Relations in the Practice of Criminal Law', 62 *Am. J. Sociology* 48 (1956). This comparative study of criminal and civil lawyers suggests that the former tend to dissociate themselves from the business community, are much more active in political party work, have a more 'liberal' voting preference, and generally have a lower status among members of the bar and the community at large. Ibid., pp. 49–53.

work consists of seeking discretionary decisions favourable to his client—whether to dispense with bail, to reduce a charge, or to impose a light sentence. But because the prosecutor and the judge are usually elected, they are thought to be sensitive to political influence and disposed to grant improper favours to lawyers they know. The aura of evil is vastly greater than the reality, for defence lawyers of the worst sort are disposed to overreach their poor and gullible clients and demand high fees for securing imagined official favours, when their real corruption consists of doing nothing and giving the client a false impression of legal legerdemain.

The economics of criminal law practice has an important effect. While there are in every American city a few able and honourable private lawyers who specialize in criminal cases, they attract only about 5 per cent. of all criminal cases,[1] usually those involving clients who can afford to pay substantial fees. Other defendants cannot afford a lawyer at all or can pay very little. This means that the bulk of criminal cases must be handled by legal aid lawyers or public defenders, or by private practitioners who depend for their living on volume and a quick turnover of clients. It is uneconomical for such men to do much in the way of preparation on the law or the facts. The result is that the private criminal bar in America has a bad reputation, which tends to be self-perpetuating, and to repel able lawyers. Despite the growing academic respectability of criminal law as a subject in the law schools, top students are still attracted mostly to corporate tax and commercial practice. Mounting concern with providing adequate counsel to indigent defendants is tending to change this situation, but much remains to be done.

Another factor affecting the performance of defence counsel is the lack of appellate supervision over them. Because no appeal can be taken from an acquittal, there is seldom any appellate scrutiny of the way in which defence counsel conduct themselves in court at the trial level. They are not subject to reprimand in the same sense that prosecutors are. This is also true in England, but there adequate substitute controls are found in the discipline exercised by the Inns of Court.

One reason the English have avoided the stigma which attaches to criminal practice in the United States is that English prosecutors and courts are, and are known to be, almost entirely free from influence, proper or improper. The essential skills of a criminal lawyer are those of an able advocate. These are the same skills required in civil cases,

[1] Lumbard, op. cit., p. 177.

with a result that there are, among both barristers and solicitors, few specialists in criminal matters but many specialists in litigation.

Another reason is that the legal aid system, which we shall describe presently, leaves the defence of indigents to lawyers in private practice, but assures them of reasonable fees. Especially among barristers, many a bright beginner makes his way by handling legal aid cases. But it is not the young men alone who are involved. Legal aid cases constitute an important part of the practice of almost all barristers who handle criminal law cases, including the most distinguished 'silks' or Queen's Counsel. For many of these men, legal aid cases account for about half of their total practice. Thus the defence as well as the prosecution of criminal cases is distributed widely among the members of the bar.

UNPOPULAR CAUSES AND CLIENTS

The English are also untroubled by the close identification of lawyer with client which characterizes criminal practice in the United States. Like the English solicitor the American lawyer is retained by and deals directly with his client, but, unlike the solicitor, he also acts as trial advocate for the client when public attention is most sharply focused on him. Furthermore, loose standards of professional probity have sometimes allowed attorneys to maintain close associations with the underworld in fact as well as appearance. The net result is a tendency on the part of the public to regard lawbreakers and the attorneys who represent them as fellow criminals.[1] Distrust of defence lawyers affects many aspects of criminal procedure in the United States, including the matter of discovery, where it supports the stock argument that it would be unsafe to disclose the prosecution's evidence in advance of trial.[2]

The identification of lawyer and client is particularly troublesome when defendants are politically or socially unpopular[3]—for example,

---

[1] Steinberg, 'A Comparative Examination of the Role of the Criminal Lawyer in Our Present-Day Society', 15 *W. Res. L. Rev.* 479, 482 (1964).

[2] A 1963 District of Columbia Survey shows that the two most important factors—in the opinion of both prosecutors and defence counsel—which favour discovery are: (1) the prosecutor's personal acquaintance with defence counsel and (2) the likelihood of a guilty plea. 'Discovery in Federal Criminal Cases: A Symposium', 33 *F.R.D.* 47, 116 (1963). For arguments favouring a more liberal discovery procedure in the federal courts see 33 *F.R.D.* pp. 61–63, 84–86, 91 (1963). And see generally Chapter 7 below.

[3] See Cheatham, pp. 13–38; Schwartz, pp. 74–87 (1961); Williams (1962);

persons charged with subversion or espionage, or civil rights demon-strators. Lawyers who represent such persons are often subjected to personal vilification, social reprisal, and loss of practice. As a result, most lawyers will not accept unpopular causes or clients. England avoids this difficulty.[1] In part this is due to widespread public under-standing of the duties of an advocate, but in part it is due to the structure of the profession, providing lawyers with insulation from public rancour. The solicitor is spared the publicity which comes of conducting a prolonged major trial, and the presence of a barrister diffuses attention between the two. The barrister is separated from the client not only in the courtroom, where the defendant is ordinarily in the dock rather than at counsel's table, but in other ways as well. He is engaged by the solicitor, not the client. Fees are negotiated not by the barrister but by his clerk with the solicitor, and are required to be fixed in advance in the case of any paying accused. A barrister's economic prospects depend on the impression which other lawyers have of the quality of his craft rather than upon public opinion con-cerning the cases he handles. The barrister is further insulated by the so-called 'cab rank' principle to the effect that he is obliged to accept any case offered to him if it is within his competence, if the fee ten-dered is suitable, and if he has no prior conflicting commitment. This means that most barristers may not and do not refuse to undertake the defence of criminal cases.

THE VIGOUR OF DEFENCE

There are, however, some respects in which the defence of criminal cases in England seems to Americans to be less vigorous than is desirable.

Members of the bar, including those who have become judges, constitute a close-knit homogeneous fraternity.[2] This has important advantages, leading to a corporate spirit among barristers which assures that high professional standards will be met. On the other hand, it makes for fairly narrow social horizons. There is nothing in the training or practice of English barristers which necessarily en-larges their view of life beyond the confines of the law courts and the Inns. The tendency of counsel to feel closer to the judge than to the

Downs & Goldman, 'The Obligation of Lawyers to Represent Unpopular Defendants', 9 *How. L.J.* 49 (1963).
[1] See Steinberg, op. cit., pp. 485–6 for a general comparison of the criminal bar and practice in America and England. [2] Wootton, pp. 32–33.

accused appears (at least to some American observers) likely to inhibit the presentation of a strong defence.

There is a general readiness in England to assume that the only skill a barrister needs is the ability to present a good argument in the courtroom—as if advocacy involved little more than the drawing of inferences from evidence. This leads to the assumption that any barrister can be brought into a case at the last minute. Adjournments of trial because counsel is engaged elsewhere are uniformly denied on the theory that another barrister can always be briefed overnight. Experienced barristers do, indeed, develop a fine capacity for picking up a case as it goes along, sometimes on very slight previous instruction, and for hammering home the essential points. By American standards, however, this capacity is an inadequate substitute for proper preparation on the facts.

The English system does little to encourage the kind of careful preparation for trial which characterizes the work of the best American practitioners. In England, a solicitor rarely thinks of using a private investigator, and tends to rely heavily on the client to find and produce witnesses. The barrister is limited in his contact with the client, and is prohibited from contact with ordinary witnesses.

Except in very special circumstances, the barrister is not allowed to interview witnesses—other than experts—before trial.[1] His conferences with the accused himself, if any, tend to be few and formal in the simple case. (In more difficult cases, however, the barrister almost always goes through the client's story with the client himself and the interviews between them may be many and lengthy.) The heavy burden of case preparation is on the solicitor, not on the man who must present the case in court. The barrister gets his case as interpreted and distilled in the brief of the solicitor. This avoids the imputation that counsel has manufactured evidence and it has the advantage of allowing the barrister to form an objective assessment of the client's chances in court, uncoloured by the sort of emotional bond which may develop when client and lawyer are too closely identified. But it also involves the risk of inadequate communication and co-ordination of the defence. A saving feature of the English system is the fact that relatively little defence preparation is needed in the ordinary case in view of the full disclosure of the prosecution's case on the preliminary hearing.[2]

---

[1] Megarry, p. 46.
[2] See Chapter 7 below.

THE DEFENCE OF INDIGENTS

Both in England and the United States a large majority of defendants cannot afford a lawyer. In both countries for at least two centuries the judges have assigned counsel to poor persons accused of crime, and in both countries the legal profession has undertaken this work as a matter of charity. In neither country, however, has the assigned counsel system ever been entirely adequate to furnishing representation for all defendants who have needed it. Furthermore, the system puts an unfair burden on the lawyers who accept its obligations, requiring them to assume the cost of what ought to be a public service. In the twentieth century, these drawbacks have become especially noticeable, with the result that in both countries alternative and more adequate systems of legal aid have been developed.

The English System

While legal aid in England is today largely a matter of statute, two traditional devices for furnishing an indigent with counsel survive. One is the 'dock brief', by which a prisoner whose case is brought on for trial in the higher courts (Assizes and Quarter Sessions) may choose any barrister then present in the courtroom to undertake his defence. That barrister must take the case if the defendant can produce the nominal fee of £2. 4s. 6d. or about $6.25. Any defendant, regardless of his financial means, is entitled to counsel on these terms, but his defence is not likely to be a good one, for the 'dock brief' permits no time for preparation, and it does not allow for the important preliminary services of a solicitor.[1]

The second common law form of legal aid in the higher courts is for the court itself to ask a barrister to undertake a defence, as when the defendant has failed to apply for statutory legal aid or has applied too late. Like the 'dock brief', this does not provide for the services of a solicitor. Barristers assigned under it may be compensated if the court orders the prosecution to pay the costs of the defence, including counsel's fee, but this is not as satisfactory as the scheme of statutory legal aid about to be described. Nevertheless, the power of the courts to appoint counsel is still sometimes used in lieu of the statutory scheme. The Lord Chief Justice has stated that it is wrong for

[1] Cheatham, pp. 45–49; Jackson, pp. 138–47; Parker, L.C.J., 'The Development of Legal Aid in England since 1949', 48 *A.B.A.J.* 1029 (1962); *Working Party on Legal Aid in Criminal Proceedings, Final Report* (H.M.S.O. 1963).

committing magistrates to rely upon the exercise of the power by the trial court when they themselves are confronted with the decision of whether to grant statutory legal aid. In 1961 roughly 30,000 defendants were tried at Assizes and Quarter Sessions. Statutory legal aid was employed in 11,471 of these cases, but another 1,368 cases were undertaken by counsel at the request of the court.[1] In other words, about 4 per cent. of all cases in the higher courts and about 10 per cent. of all those involving free legal assistance were defended by court-appointed counsel outside the statutory legal aid system.

Statutory legal aid in criminal cases in England began in 1903. It was originally limited to trials in the higher courts, and included a requirement that the accused had to disclose the nature of his defence before aid could be granted. The system was revamped and extended to all courts by the Poor Prisoners' Defence Act, 1930.[2] This Act is still in force, although considerably amended by the Legal Aid and Advice Act, 1949[3] (which also established a comprehensive system of legal aid in civil matters).

The statutory scheme makes a distinction between legal aid in the magistrates' courts and legal aid in the higher trial courts. A person charged with a criminal offence will appear before a magistrates' court either for preliminary hearing on the charge for which he will later be tried in a higher court, or for summary trial of the charge against him. In either event, if he needs legal aid, he must obtain a 'legal aid certificate' from the magistrates, entitling him to the services of a solicitor. Only in the case of a preliminary hearing on a murder charge does the certificate entitle him to the services of a barrister as well. The defendant is assigned his solicitor by the court clerk from a list of those who have volunteered to undertake legal aid work, although the clerk usually respects any preference that the defendant may have for a particular solicitor. For work done under a 'legal aid certificate', payment is made out of a Legal Aid Fund which is provided by Parliament, and administered by the Law Society (the solicitors' association). Fees are determined according to a scale set out in Home Office regulations made under the 1949 Act.

For trial in a higher court—Assize or Quarter Sessions—a defendant must obtain a 'defence certificate'. This may be granted either by the committing magistrates at the preliminary hearing or by the court of trial at the commencement of proceedings there. It allows the defendant the services of both a solicitor and a barrister. As with a 'legal

---

[1] Jackson, p. 146.   [2] 20 & 21 Geo. V, c. 32.   [3] 12, 13, & 14 Geo. VI, c. 51

aid certificate', the solicitor is selected from a panel of volunteers. He then selects a barrister who likewise must have indicated interest in taking legal aid cases. For work done under a 'defence certificate', payment is made from local government funds, reimbursed by the national government. Fees are determined by the clerk of the court of trial, again using a basic scale of payments set out in administrative regulations.

In general, fees for legal aid work are assessed on the principle of allowing 'fair remuneration according to the work actually and reasonably done'. This is an easier determination to make in England than it would be in the United States, first, because the English legal profession, apart from legal aid, has developed fairly clear-cut customary standards of remuneration; and second, because court officials have had long experience in valuing legal services in civil cases, where they are included in the costs assessed against the losing side. Solicitors sometimes feel that legal aid fees fall short of what a paying client would be charged, but, on the whole, the system has proven satisfactory. There has been no shortage of practitioners ready to put their names on the list of those willing to undertake legal aid cases.

In the United States, the English practice of allowing indigents to choose their own lawyers from a list might result in an overloading of particularly skilled or famous lawyers. That danger is avoided in England because trial advocates are not chosen directly by the accused, but by solicitors who know better than to choose famous counsel for minor cases, particularly in view of the fact that English courts are unwilling to adjourn proceedings to suit the convenience of counsel. Barristers adjust the work they accept to the likelihood of their actually being in court on the day set for trial. In practice, solicitors, who are unlikely to develop the type of reputation gained by barristers or American criminal trial lawyers, are chosen by the court clerk and not by the accused. This permits the clerk to rotate legal aid work evenly among registered practitioners. One by-product of the spreading of work broadly throughout the legal profession is the general feeling that criminal practice is as respectable as any other type of practice.

American Systems

There is no uniform system of providing for the defence of indigents in the United States,[1] nor is it likely that there will be one in the

---

[1] Att.-General's Comm. Rep., *Poverty and the Administration of Federal*

foreseeable future. The tendency is to leave each community to determine its own solution to the problem of providing representation for poor defendants.

The traditional method is the assigned counsel system, whereby a defendant who cannot afford a lawyer has one appointed for him by the court. This is still the only system of legal aid in thirty-one states, and more specifically in 2,900 out of 3,100 counties in the country. About a dozen states either make no provision for compensating assigned counsel or provide compensation only in capital cases.[1] The remainder provide compensation out of either state or county funds, but it is generally felt among lawyers that the amounts allowed are inadequate. The system generally has other drawbacks, including uneven distribution of assigned cases among the bar, a tendency not to appoint counsel early enough in the proceedings, and lack of facilities or lack of reimbursement for investigation by the defence. None of these defects is inherent in the system for there are communities which avoid some or all of them. The problem is largely financial. In populous communities, a wholly adequate assigned counsel system would doubtless cost more than a salaried defender system either on a public or private basis.[2]

As of 30 April 1964 there were 136 defender offices in the United States.[3] Of these, 111 were public defender offices, established by local or state governments and supported by public funds; 13 were privately supported, charitable organizations; and twelve were offices partly supported by private effort and partly by appropriations from public funds. These defender organizations were found in nineteen states and the District of Columbia, but only four states (Massachusetts, Rhode Island, Connecticut, and Florida) had a public

Criminal Justice, pp. 12–57 (1963); Brownell, *Legal Aid in the United States* (1951); Cheatham, pp. 39–58; Silverstein, vol. i (1965); Special Comm. to Study Defender Systems, *Equal Justice for the Accused* (1959); Trebach, pp. 95–130, 205–12.

[1] In a recent case, a federal trial court awarded appointed counsel over $3,800 as just compensation for services rendered under the theory of governmental taking of an attorney's services for public use. *Dillon* v. *United States* 230 F. Supp. 487 (D. Ore., 1964). The Ninth Circuit, in an unreported case decided 16 June 1965, reversed. The court observed that compensation was a matter for legislative action and that 'the obligation of the legal profession to serve indigents on court order is an ancient and established tradition'.

[2] Institute of Judicial Administration, *Report to the Mayor of the City of New York on the Cost of Providing Defense for Indigents in Criminal Cases* (1965).

[3] National Legal Aid and Defender Ass'n., *Statistics of Legal Aid and Defender Work in the United States and Canada*, p. 2 (1963).

defender system which covered every county. Elsewhere offices were usually confined to metropolitan areas.

Private defender offices are an offshoot of the charitable organizations which still account for the bulk of legal aid in civil matters in the United States. There are several hundred legal aid societies of this type, but few of them have extended their service to criminal cases, and of those which have, half rely in part upon public subsidy in the form of free office space, or assigned counsel fees, or an annual cash grant. The Legal Aid Society of New York City is an example of a service which, though originally private and still controlled solely by its own governing board, is today substantially subsidized in its criminal work by city funds.

Public defender offices, as their name implies, are supported entirely by governmental grants and under public control. The method of selecting a public defender varies greatly. He may be chosen by popular election, by the courts, by a committee of citizens appointed by the courts, by civil service examination, or by local governing officials.

Considerable variation exists in the range of work which defender offices, public or private, can or do undertake. In Los Angeles, the public defender is charged by law with the defence of all indigents who request his services, and he has a large staff of lawyers and investigators who are able to interview any defendant shortly after his arrest. Elsewhere, the public defender office may consist of a single lawyer serving part-time, or may be limited by law or by lack of funds to providing representation only at trial and only in certain classes of cases. A similar disparity exists among private defender offices. For cases which a defender office cannot handle, the courts must fall back on the assigned counsel system.

There has been some opposition in the United States to public defender systems. One objection is that it is improper for the same government to control both the prosecution and the defence, this amounting to an intolerable degree of state control over individual liberty. The English Rushcliffe Committee,[1] whose report resulted in the Legal Aid Act of 1949,[2] rejected the use of a public defender system for this reason (even though England is generally a more highly socialized society than the United States). A second objection is that an organized defender system cannot provide the same whole-hearted service as is provided by lawyers in private practice. Fears have often

[1] Committee on Legal Aid and Advice (Rushcliffe Comm.), *Report*, Cmnd. 6641 (1945).   [2] 12, 13, & 14 Geo. VI, c. 51.

been expressed that a defender office will tend to make deals too easily with the prosecution. However, several inquiries which have been made into the workings of defender systems suggest that these fears are largely unfounded. They also suggest that a cordial but proper relationship between professional defenders and professional prosecutors has advantages, permitting, for example, informal discovery of the government's case. This is something that prosecutors are reluctant to allow to private defence attorneys, for whom they generally have less respect.

Legislation on defence of indigents has tended to adopt the principle of local option, allowing each community to establish the type of system it prefers. The Criminal Justice Act of 1964,[1] which establishes a system of compensated legal aid for the federal courts, allows the judges of each United States District Court to choose a plan that will provide for representation: (1) by private attorneys; (2) by a bar association or private legal aid agency; or (3) by some combination of the first two. A proposal for a public defender office as a fourth choice was deleted from the federal statute because of opposition in Congress. Increasingly, however, the public defender system is provided as one of the alternatives in state legislation on the subject. The Criminal Justice Act and similar state legislation may ultimately lead to the development of an *élite* and officially recognized criminal bar with special requirements for training, apprenticeship, and the like. Recently the Federal government announced a large-scale programme of financial aid to local communities in their efforts to provide legal defence for indigents.[2]

The Scope of Legal Aid

In the United States, legal aid to indigents is thought of largely as a consequence of the constitutional right to counsel. If the right is denied, then the defendant's conviction must be reversed. The Sixth Amendment to the Constitution has long been interpreted to require that an indigent defendant has a right to be assigned an attorney in a federal court, but until recently it was held that state courts were constitutionally required to assign counsel only in capital cases, and in other cases where, under the circumstances, absence of counsel would be a denial of fundamental fairness. In 1963 this position was

---

[1] 78 Stat. 552 (1964), 18 U.S.C. § 3006A.
[2] *N.Y. Times*, 30 Nov. 1965, p. 31, col. 3.

overturned. In *Gideon* v. *Wainwright*,[1] the Supreme Court held that a state court must provide trial counsel for an indigent—at least in every felony case, and possibly in every case of a serious nature; and in *Douglas* v. *California*,[2] the Court held that a state must provide counsel for an indigent appealing as of right from his conviction. These decisions have given tremendous stimulus to the development of legal aid systems in the United States. Their effect is to require all communities to do what some communities have been doing as a matter of grace. As the constitutional right to counsel is further extended,[3] legal aid systems will be compelled to follow suit.

Legal aid in England, by contrast, has not traditionally been regarded in terms of a right to counsel, but rather in terms of judicial discretion. The statutory test is whether the defendant's means will allow him to provide for his own defence and whether it is desirable in the interests of justice that he should have free legal aid. This allows the courts a wide discretion, the exercise of which may even be influenced by considerations such as the number of legally aided cases, the state of the calendars, and the prospective cost to taxpayers. Nevertheless, recently there has been a substantial rise in the number of grants made. In magistrates' courts, the 'interests of justice' clause used to be further qualified by the requirement that legal aid had to be justified 'by reason of the gravity of the charge or of exceptional circumstances'. This restriction was removed in 1963. Lord Chief Justice Parker, who took office in 1958, has strongly encouraged a more generous approach to granting legal aid than his predecessor, Lord Goddard, to the point of saying that it should be given even on a plea of guilty in a superior court. Even more significant is the fact

---

[1] 372 U.S. 335 (1963). See also Note, 'Effective Assistance of Counsel for the Indigent Defendant', 78 *Harv. L. Rev.* 1434 (1965).

[2] 372 U.S. 353 (1963).

[3] Recent Supreme Court decisions involving capital cases have given the accused the right to counsel at the preliminary hearing and the arraignment. *White* v. *Maryland*, 373 U.S. 59 (1963); *Hamilton* v. *Alabama*, 368 U.S. 52 (1961). Under the reasoning of the *Gideon* case, op. cit., this right to counsel might be held also to apply in non-capital cases at any critical stage (although problems would arise as to the time when the proceedings against the accused become 'critical'. Compare *Alden* v. *State*, 234 F. Supp. 661 (D. Mont. 1964) with *United States ex rel. Cooper* v. *Reinke*, 333 F. 2d. 608 (2nd Cir. 1964).). In some states, at the preliminary hearing the judge decides only whether the accused is to be bound over to the grand jury and if so whether he should be admitted to bail; the defendant is not required to plead to the charge. Where this is so, the Supreme Court has indicated that *White* v. *Maryland* above, is not necessarily controlling. See *Pointer* v. *Texas*, 380 U.S. 400 (1965).

that the Court of Criminal Appeal has quashed several convictions where it considered legal aid to have been improperly refused.[1] In effect, the English courts seem to be approaching the point where free aid will be available for every indigent tried or sentenced in the higher courts, and perhaps to every indigent tried in a magistrate's court—at least if the prosecution is legally represented. A Departmental Committee headed by Mr. Justice Widgery of the High Court is presently reconsidering on a broad and fundamental basis the whole question of legal aid in criminal cases.

There are a number of problems regarding the scope of legal aid which are common to both countries. One is eligibility for legal aid services. The English statute requires that a defendant be without the means to provide his defence, but there is no prescribed test of sufficiency of means, and doubts are resolved in favour of the defendant. He can, however, be required to make a written statement in prescribed form as to his means. In the United States, there is usually a similar flexibility, but there is also a tendency to put eligibility in terms of whether the defendant can afford 'counsel' in the narrow sense. This fails to account for other expenses of defence such as bail, investigation, and witness fees.[2] Neither country has given adequate attention to the problem of the accused who can pay part but not all of the expenses of his defence.[3]

Another problem concerns the many defendants in both countries who, although eligible for free aid, waive it and plead guilty.[4] To some

[1] e.g. *Regina* v. *Phillippe*, reported in *The Times* (London), 15 Dec. 1964, p. 19. The Lord Chief Justice stated: 'If legal aid had been granted, it was more probable than not that the result would not have been the same. It would therefore be unsafe to allow the verdict to stand.'

[2] See Att.-Gen.'s Comm. Rep., *Poverty and the Administration of Federal Criminal Justice*, pp. 39–40 (1963). Compare the practice in Scandinavian countries, where appointed counsel may consult with experts and use government laboratories at the expense of the state. Ibid., p. 34.

[3] Ibid., pp. 7–8, 40–41; Silverstein, pp. 110–12.

[4] Although it appears that a significant number of defendants intelligently waive counsel and plead guilty, it is difficult to isolate the reasons for waiver. A defendant may want immediate adjudication so that he may begin serving his sentence without delay. Or he may want to expedite the proceedings in the hope of gaining freedom through probation. See Note, 'The Right of an Accused to Proceed Without Counsel', 49 *Minn. L. Rev.* 1133, 1134, and n. 9 (1965).

For the recidivist, pleading guilty without counsel may be explained by the defendant's knowledge of his own susceptibility to conviction. He may feel that the bargaining rapport which he believes to exist between himself and the prosecution will be lost if an attorney is involved. Or he may fear that if he demanded trial and lost, his past record would incline the judge to be severe in sentencing.

extent, the problem can be solved by properly explaining his rights to the defendant, but the decision as to whether he needs counsel really requires a professional assessment of his case, which he cannot get under the English legal aid scheme or the American assigned counsel system until he makes his decision.[1] The American defender system can avoid this dilemma, at least if the defender office is in a position to interview all defendants before or upon their first arrival in court.

A related problem is to provide legal advice as soon as needed after arrest. A person of means sometimes asks to speak to his lawyer in person or by telephone at this point in the criminal process. An indigent cannot. In theory, the English system allows a person immediately after arrest to apply by letter to the magistrate's court for a legal aid certificate entitling him to the services of a solicitor, but in practice the certificate is usually not granted until the defendant appears in court for a preliminary hearing or for summary trial, if it is granted at all. In fact, legal aid is allowed in no more than 10 per cent. of committal proceedings before magistrates. In the United States, the general practice has been to offer legal aid either at or shortly before the arraignment at which the defendant must plead to the charge. Only a few states have assigned counsel at the first appearance or preliminary hearing before a magistrate.[2] Today, as a result of a recent Supreme Court decision,[3] an indigent person in custody is entitled to insist upon being represented by assigned counsel before he can be interrogated.

Finally, there is the question of legal aid on appeal. The English problem has been to provide prompt and adequate legal aid during the crucial ten-day period within which an application for leave to

He may expect that if he puts the state to less trouble and expense, he will receive a more favourable sentence. See Newman, 'Pleading Guilty for Considerations: A Study of Bargain Justice', 46 *J. Crim. L., C. & P.S.*, pp. 780, 783–6 (1956).

[1] For a discussion of the problem of whether an accused waiving counsel fully understands what an attorney could do for him, see Note, op. cit., pp. 1139–44.

[2] Note, 'The Preliminary Hearing—An Interest Analysis', 51 *Iowa L. Rev.* 164, 169 n. 34 (1965). For a collection of recent state cases, see National Legal Aid and Defender Ass'n., *Newsletter*, 'The Right to Counsel at the Preliminary Hearing', vol. ii, No. 4 (6 July 1965).

If the defendant does not have counsel at his initial appearance before the magistrate, it is likely that he will waive the preliminary hearing. However, some states have developed a procedure whereby an unrepresented defendant who has waived his preliminary may, when counsel is later appointed for him, have the preliminary examination rescheduled. Miller & Dawson, 'Non-Use of the Preliminary Examination: A Study of Current Practices', 1964, *Wis. L. Rev.* 252, 271–4.

[3] *Miranda* v. *Arizona*, 34 U.S.L. Week 4521 (U.S. 14 June 1966).

appeal to the Court of Criminal Appeal must be filed. It has not fully succeeded in this regard, although proposals for improving the system are under consideration.[1] In the United States, it is now required that a state provide free counsel and a free transcript of the record for a prisoner appealing as of right.[2] Whether counsel must also be provided in appeals and other post-conviction proceedings which are not a matter of right is an open question so far as the federal constitution is concerned. Some but not all states provide counsel in such situations.[3]

[1] See Chapter 10, below.

[2] *Douglas* v. *California*, 372 U.S. 353 (1963); *Griffin* v. *Illinois*, 351 U.S. 12 (1956).

[3] See Silverstein, i, pp. 137–44. According to a 1963 survey, 38 states provided some type of representation by counsel in post-conviction proceeding, ibid., p. 141.

4

THE CRIMINAL COURTS

THERE are two fundamental contrasts between the criminal courts in England and the United States. One is that in England the vast bulk of the work is done by unpaid, lay Justices of the Peace, whereas in the United States it is done by paid professional judges. The other is that politics plays a minor role in England and a central role in the United States in the selection of members of the judiciary at all levels. In order to understand these differences, it is necessary first to compare the court structure of the two nations.

THE ORGANIZATION OF COURTS IN ENGLAND

Trial Courts

England has basically two levels of criminal trial courts.[1] On the lower level are the Magistrates' Courts which sit without a jury; on the higher level are Quarter Sessions and Assize Courts which sit with a jury. Virtually every criminal case in England initially comes before a magistrates' court. The magistrates either try it themselves or hold a preliminary inquiry into whether the evidence is sufficient to warrant trial by jury in a higher court. The basis for determining when a case must be referred to a higher court is the nature of the offence. For this purpose, offences fall into five categories:

(*a*) Those triable only in the magistrates' courts.

(*b*) Those normally triable in the magistrates' courts, but which must be tried in the higher courts if the accused demands trial by jury—as he has a right to do in most cases punishable with more than three months' imprisonment.

(*c*) Those triable either in the magistrates' courts or in the higher courts at the election of the prosecution and the magistrates, subject, however, to the defendant's right to insist upon trial by jury in a higher court.

(*d*) Those normally triable in higher courts but which may be tried in a magistrates' court if the magistrates think that desirable and if the accused consents.

(*e*) Those triable only in the higher courts.

[1] Jackson, pp. 92–119; Kenny, pp. 537–59.

In practice, the great bulk of cases—about 97 per cent. of the total—are tried by the lower courts. Almost all of the remaining 3 per cent. begin in the magistrates' courts and, after preliminary hearing, are committed to a higher court for trial. As a rule, only the gravest offences go to the higher courts. Where the defendant has a choice between trial before a jury or trial before magistrates, he is likely to choose the latter. The only notable exception is when he is being tried for a motoring offence punishable by imprisonment or loss of licence, in which case he is likely to choose trial by jury in the not unreasonable hope that he may be acquitted. In the ordinary case, trial before the magistrates is quicker and the sentence is likely to be less, the maximum punishment that they are empowered to impose being six months' imprisonment for one offence or twelve months for two or more offences, together with a fine of £100. There is a procedure whereby the magistrates, after trying and convicting the accused, may refer his case to a higher court (Quarter Sessions) for sentencing if they discover that he has a particularly bad record or if for some other reason they consider their own sentencing powers inadequate. The higher court may then impose any penalty up to the maximum provided for the offence. Despite this procedure, most cases remain in magistrates' court from beginning to end. About 80 per cent. of all 'indictable offences'—meaning those which could go before the higher courts—are in fact tried in the lower courts.

There are about 1,000 magistrates' courts in England, staffed by about 16,000 magistrates. Throughout most of the country these are unpaid, part-time justices of the peace who more often than not are untrained in the law. Justices are required in nearly every case to sit in groups of two or more—up to seven.

London is an exception. Although it also has lay magistrates, the bulk of criminal cases there are handled by a group of paid, professional, full-time 'metropolitan stipendiary magistrates'. Arrangements have recently been made, however, for the lay justices in London to deal with a much larger part of the work than they have in the past. A few cities outside London also maintain professional 'stipendiary magistrates'. There are forty-nine such magistrates in all of England, of whom thirty-six are in London. A stipendiary magistrate can sit alone for the trial of a case.

The higher level of criminal courts consists of (1) Assizes, (2) Quarter Sessions, and (3) certain special courts in London and in the cities of Liverpool and Manchester.

For the purpose of Assizes, England and Wales are divided into seven circuits. Three times a year for most circuits, four times a year for others, one or two judges of the Queen's Bench Division of the High Court of Justice (consisting of the Lord Chief Justice and thirty-seven other judges) go out from London on a pre-arranged itinerary to handle the cases which the local magistrates have committed for trial at Assizes. There are certain kinds of cases which must be committed to Assizes—notably homicide; but in other cases, the magistrates have a choice as to whether they will send a case for trial at Assizes or at Quarter Sessions. Generally they choose Quarter Sessions unless there are special reasons, such as unusual difficulty or gravity of a case, which make it desirable that it should be heard by a High Court judge.

Courts of Quarter Sessions, which have concurrent jurisdiction with Assize courts except for a few of the most serious crimes, are of two kinds: county and borough. Every county, of which there are fifty-nine in England, has a County Quarter Sessions Court, consisting of justices of the peace for the county, sitting in benches of up to nine. In small rural counties the sessions are held four times a year for relatively short periods of time, but in large and thickly populated counties, the courts are in almost continuous session. One of the justices—who must be a lawyer of standing, or a judge serving part time in the capacity of a justice of the peace—acts as chairman of each court. Most counties also have similarly qualified deputy chairmen, thus making it possible for more than one court to sit for the county at a time. In ninety-three cities there are Borough Quarter Sessions, independent of the counties in which they are located, in which justices have no part. Instead there is a single judge known as a 'Recorder', who is a barrister of at least five years' standing, and who is paid for his services on a part-time basis. In most boroughs the courts of Quarter Sessions sit four times a year for varying periods of time, but in the larger cities where deputy and assistant recorders have been appointed to help dispose of the work, they may sit almost continuously.

The sittings of Assizes and County and Borough Quarter Sessions throughout the nation are co-ordinated in such a way that an accused person will be tried either in the county or borough in which he is committed, or in a neighbouring county or borough within eight weeks of his committal.

In the London area, Quarter Sessions and Assize courts are

established on a permanent basis. The Central Criminal Court, commonly known as 'the Old Bailey', acts as Assize Court for the Greater London area, holding sessions continuously throughout the year. The court has eight permanent judges—the Recorder of the City of London, the Common Serjeant, and six additional judges; and in addition, a judge from the Queen's Bench Division is always present on a rotating basis to try the most serious cases. The Central Criminal Court also serves as the court of Quarter Sessions for the City of London proper—the autonomous mile-square area in the heart of the metropolis. The rest of Greater London is divided into five areas, in each of which Courts of Quarter Sessions sit almost continuously throughout the year. Lay justices participate in these courts, but always with a salaried chairman or deputy chairman of considerable legal experience who has been appointed on a full-time basis. If an occasion arises when there are no lay justices available to participate, the legal chairman may sit alone.

Another exception to the usual pattern of courts is found in the industrial cities of Liverpool and Manchester, located in south Lancashire. Since 1956, both cities have had Crown courts, each with a fulltime judge called 'Recorder'. These courts sit continuously and do the work of Quarter Sessions for the two cities, as well as most of the Assize work for the whole of south Lancashire.

Appellate Courts

Courts of Quarter Sessions also have appellate jurisdiction. A defendant can appeal from a magistrates' court against his conviction if he did not plead guilty; and, regardless of his plea, he can appeal against his sentence. Appeals to County Sessions are heard by a court of up to nine justices of the peace, including the legally qualified chairman; in a borough, appeals are heard by the recorder sitting alone, except in the case of an appeal from a juvenile court, where he sits with two juvenile court justices who act as 'assessors' (non-voting advisers). In an appeal against conviction on an issue of fact, there is a full rehearing of the case, in which the witnesses are called again, so that the 'appeal' really is a trial *de novo*. Appeal work is done without a jury.

Either the prosecution or defence can appeal a point of law directly from the magistrates' court to a tribunal consisting of three Queen's Bench judges, known as a Divisional Court of the Queen's Bench Division of the High Court. Appeals to the Divisional Court also lie on a point of law which has been initially appealed from the magistrates to Quarter Sessions.

A defendant who has been convicted after trial in Quarter Sessions or Assizes may seek review in the Court of Criminal Appeal. This is not a court having permanent personnel of its own, but rather a tribunal consisting of the Lord Chief Justice and two, or occasionally four, other Queen's Bench judges, sitting temporarily to hear appeals.[1] A defendant must obtain leave from either the trial judge or the Court of Criminal Appeal to appeal against his conviction on a question of fact; and to appeal against sentence, he must obtain leave from the Court of Criminal Appeal; but he may appeal as of right on a question of law. Where a defendant has been convicted in a magistrates' court but sentenced by Quarter Sessions he may also, by leave, appeal against sentence to the Court of Criminal Appeal.

From the Court of Criminal Appeal or from a Divisional Court, a further appeal may lie to the House of Lords. First, however, the court from which the appeal is taken must certify that a point of law of general public importance is involved; and then that court or the House of Lords must grant permission for the appeal.

THE ORGANIZATION OF COURTS IN THE UNITED STATES

Federal Courts

In the United States, the federal government and each of the fifty states has its own separate system of courts.[2] The federal system consists of (1) 'District' (trial) Courts, (2) intermediate 'Courts of Appeal', and (3) the Supreme Court of the United States. The ninety-two district courts have jurisdiction over all criminal matters arising under federal law. There is at least one such court in each of the states, territories, and the District of Columbia, but some of the larger states are divided into two, three, or four districts. The total number of district judges is over 300, and, in addition, each district court has one or more part-time United States Commissioners, whose job is to hold preliminary hearings in criminal cases. In rural districts, these commissioners are sometimes laymen; in urban districts, they are usually lawyers. Each district court also empanels one or more grand juries, which, independent of any preliminary hearing, must indict a

---

[1] See Chapter 10 below for recent proposals to reorganize the court.

[2] For general descriptions of American court systems, see Institute of Judicial Administration, *A Guide to Court Systems* (3rd ed. 1962); Mayers, pp. 367–403; 10 *New York Judicial Conference Report* 175 (1965); Karlen (1964), ch. 1.

defendant before he can be tried on a serious charge. Trial in the district court is before a single judge and a jury unless trial by jury is waived.

From conviction in a district court, the defendant may appeal as of right to a federal court of appeals. There are eleven such courts in the United States, established on a regional basis, each with from three to nine judges, who sit in panels of three.

After a decision in one of the courts of appeal, further review is possible in the Supreme Court of the United States, consisting of nine justices, all of whom sit together in every case. The Supreme Court also has ultimate appellate jurisdiction over all matters arising in the state courts where a controlling issue of federal or constitutional law is involved. For the most part, the jurisdiction of the Supreme Court is discretionary with the court, not subject to being invoked as a matter of right.

Federal courts try only the relatively few offences which are made punishable by act of Congress.[1] For the most part, these are offences which impinge on some particular interest of the federal government like regulating interstate commerce or providing postal service. The federal government, possessing only such powers as are vested in it by the Constitution, cannot define or punish crime in general throughout the nation, for that is one of the many powers reserved to the states.

State Courts

The overwhelming bulk of criminal cases in the United States are tried in state courts. Each of the fifty states has its own system of courts to try crimes committed within its borders and made punishable by its laws. The court systems of the various states differ one from another, but have many elements in common.

In every state there are at least two levels of trial courts for criminal matters. On the lower level are those empowered to handle (in addition to minor civil cases) petty offences or minor misdemeanours, and to conduct preliminary hearings in more serious cases. In rural areas, these courts usually consist of a single lay justice of the peace; in more heavily populated urban centres—even in the same states— they are likely to be manned by professional judges, sitting full-time or part-time. Relatively few states have replaced their diverse local

---

[1] Some exceptions exist. e.g., removal to the federal courts in civil rights cases, such as criminal trespass prosecutions; removal to the federal courts by a federal officer in a state criminal prosecution.

courts by a uniform system of district courts, all manned by full-time professional judges. On the upper trial level, every state has a court of broad jurisdiction, usually comprehending the more serious criminal cases as well as the larger civil cases, sitting in county or other regional divisions. Such courts frequently have jurisdiction to hear 'appeals' from courts on the lower level, but these are not genuine appeals but rather trials *de novo* similar to those conducted in the English Courts of Quarter Sessions. Some large cities also have specialized systems of criminal courts, distinct from the civil courts and differing from the courts in the rest of the state.

On the appellate level, two-thirds of the states have a single court of appeals which hears both civil and criminal matters, and the remaining one-third have in addition a system of intermediate appellate courts established on a regional basis, thus allowing the possibility of two stages of appellate review.[1] Only Oklahoma and Texas have courts of criminal appeal distinct from their courts for hearing civil appeals.

SIMILARITIES AND DIFFERENCES

There are significant parallels between court organization in England and the United States. Both systems have distinct sets of courts for rural and for heavily populated areas; both have inferior and superior trial courts with intricately defined jurisdictional differences between them; both impose appellate duties on their superior trial courts; and both have a fairly complex pattern of appellate jurisdiction depending on such questions as to whether an appeal is taken on an issue of law or of fact.

Differences between the courts in the two nations, however, are more striking than the similarities. England relies heavily on the services of unpaid justices of the peace. This entails a somewhat cumbersome court structure because provision must be made for a very large number of lay judges and for different combinations of lay and professional judges in different localities, but it provides a system which is relatively inexpensive, and which has the further advantage of introducing a substantial lay participation into the work of criminal justice. In the United States, very much less reliance is placed upon lay justices, and citizen participation in the administration of criminal justice is sought primarily through grand and petit juries.

England sends a far greater share of serious criminal cases to its

[1] 15 *Book of the States* 125.

inferior courts than does the United States. The trial jurisdiction of English magistrates' courts has been progressively widened during the past century so that it now includes not only most misdemeanours but also many felonies. In the United States, the jurisdiction of inferior courts is more limited. This is partly because of the low quality of lay justices in the United States, but not entirely. The tendency is to limit even a fully professional inferior court like the Criminal Court of New York City to misdemeanours only.

English criminal tribunals are generally kept distinct from civil tribunals. The County Courts and two divisions of the High Court handle only civil cases, whereas the Quarter Sessions courts handle only criminal cases. Magistrates' courts are concerned mostly with criminal cases, civil jurisdiction being limited to matrimonial matters. Only the Queen's Bench Division of the High Court is committed to double duty in both civil and criminal matters. The United States, on the other hand, has tended to develop general purpose tribunals, exercising both civil and criminal jurisdiction, with specialized courts being the exception rather than the rule. This must not be taken to mean that England has chosen to develop a corps of specialized criminal judges; quite the contrary. The Crown Court system of Lancashire and the Central Criminal Court system in London have not been followed elsewhere because the English are reluctant to turn anyone into a full-time criminal judge. In law, as in most other walks of life, there is a preference for the amateur.[1] In order to keep men fresh for criminal work, the tendency is to continue criminal judging as a part-time job instead of merging the civil and criminal courts. A recent manifestation of this attitude is found in an arrangement which was introduced in London in April 1965, whereby County Court judges serve as deputy chairmen of Quarter Sessions on a rotating basis, each judge sitting at Sessions for one month in every twelve. At present only County Court judges who have had extensive criminal experience are being used for this purpose, but it is expected that ultimately all the London judges will so serve. Similarly, other judges holding high judicial office and doing primarily civil work, as on the Court of Appeal, often serve part-time as justices of the peace, participating in the work of the Quarter Sessions courts.

A further difference between court organization in the two countries is the character of their respective systems for appeal. England

[1] See Evershed, 'The Judicial Process in Twentieth Century England', 61 *Columbia L. Rev.* 761, 762 (1961).

was slow in developing appellate review for criminal cases, the Court
of Criminal Appeal having been established only in 1907. Until then,
there was no regular system of appeal from Quarter Sessions or Assize
courts. Even now, the Court of Criminal Appeal is an *ad hoc* tribunal
with fairly restricted jurisdiction. Recently, however, changes in its
organization, jurisdiction, and procedure have been recommended by
a high level Interdepartmental Committee.[1] The jurisdiction of the
House of Lords is even more restricted, so that criminal appeals are
seldom heard before it, although they are becoming less rare than in
earlier years. In the United States, on the other hand, appellate tribunals are easily accessible and, in the larger states, numerous, with
intermediate tribunals as well as courts of last resort providing for
two or more stages of review. The existence of the federal system provides further opportunities for review. Not only do federal tribunals
exist side by side with state courts, sometimes with overlapping jurisdiction, but as we shall see more fully in Chapter 10, they are, in
effect, a second hierarchy of courts, to which a convicted defendant
can turn, either on appeal or collaterally, once he has exhausted the
opportunities for review in the courts of his own state.

JUSTICES OF THE PEACE

The justice of the peace system has existed in England for about six
centuries.[2] During that period, it has fluctuated widely in prestige and
authority. At the height of their power, the justices were among the
most influential men in England, conducting almost the whole of local
government. They have since lost most, but not all, of their general
governmental powers; and there have been times in the past hundred
years when it seemed likely that they would lose their judicial powers
as well and be displaced by professional magistrates. In the past
twenty years, however, largely through reform of the process of
selecting justices, the prestige of the system in England has been
greatly augmented. It now seems likely to last for a long while.

The United States copied the English system of lay justices of the
peace, but unfortunately this happened at a time when the English

---

[1] Cmnd. 2755.

[2] For an excellent historical study see Allen, pp. 131–83. See also Giles;
Jackson, pp. 92–104, 157–77; Milton; Williams (1958), pp. 305–26. A comprehensive study is Royal Commission on Justices of the Peace, 1946–8, *Report*, Cmnd.
7463 (1948). See also Royal Commission on the Selection of Justices of the Peace,
Report, Cmnd. 5250 (1911).

system was at its lowest ebb.[1] American justices have never enjoyed the wide authority or prestige of their English prototypes, and now they are widely regarded as being ignorant, corrupt, or both. There is mounting pressure in the United States to abolish the justice of the peace system altogether, and this has been done in a few states. Where the political influence of the justices is sufficient to prevent their outright abolition, reform of the system has been undertaken—not so much by changing the method of selection, which remains essentially political, as by introducing measures for training the justices or for closer state supervision over them.[2]

The Scope of Their Jurisdiction

The criminal jurisdiction of English justices is much greater than that of justices in the United States. In both countries, justices are empowered (a) to conduct preliminary inquiries into cases triable in the higher courts, and (b) to 'hear and determine' other cases. It is the wider range of such cases in England which primarily accounts for the greater jurisdiction of the English justices. Their power is augmented by the fact that they also serve on one of the higher trial courts—county Quarter Sessions—attending by rotation in panels of two to eight, and sitting with a legally qualified chairman. The chairman presides at the trial, but lay justices have an equal voice with him on sentence and on the decision of appeals.[3]

Finally, lay justices in England compose the juvenile courts for the special handling of young offenders in accordance with modern concepts of criminology.[4] In this capacity, they perform the same services which in the United States are commonly performed by full-time professional judges sitting in specially created tribunals. Juvenile courts in England are established within the justice of the peace system, and are, in form, nothing more than special sittings of the magistrates' courts. The justices for an area make up from among their ranks a panel of members under 65 years of age who are thought to be especially suited for work with children. A juvenile court consists of three justices drawn from this panel and must include at least one woman and one man. In London, which differs from the rest of the

---

[1] For a general discussion of the American justice of the peace system, see Institute of Judicial Administration, *The Justice of the Peace Today* (1965); Mayers, pp. 140–5.

[2] The Institute of Judicial Administration, *The Justice of the Peace Today* (1965).   [3] Jackson, pp. 101–6, 165–6.   [4] Ibid., pp. 184–96.

country, justices are appointed to the Juvenile Court Panel by the Lord Chancellor who chooses them for this purpose after an interview by a selection board. They sit with the stipendiaries.

There is currently under consideration in England a proposal for the Home Office to revise the method of handling juvenile cases. Under this proposal, special magistrates' courts would be established to sit as 'family courts' in dealing with children under the age of 16 whose cases cannot be handled administratively; and to sit as 'young offenders' courts' in dealing with criminal offences of persons aged 16 to 21. Even with this change, juvenile work would still be primarily the responsibility of part-time lay magistrates rather than that of full-time professional judges.[1]

American justices of the peace are ordinarily limited to trying offences which carry no more than three or six months' imprisonment; and there are many states which limit them to offences punishable by no more than one month's imprisonment or a fine of not more than $100. Such limitations restrict them to hearing and determining little more than traffic infractions, and to preliminary hearings in other cases.[2] As for juvenile matters, justices of the peace in many parts of the nation are completely excluded from dealing with them.

The Volume of Their Work

Although there are professional paid judges who sit as magistrates in London and a few other cities, by far the greater number of all criminal trials throughout the nation as a whole are handled by lay justices. Theirs is a far larger share of the total criminal work than falls to justices of the peace in any state of the United States.

Not surprisingly, therefore, England has a proportionately greater number of lay magistrates than does the United States—some 16,000 (excluding several hundred honorary and *ex-officio* justices, as well as about 2,000 on the 'Supplemental List', who have retired from active judicial work) for a population of 46,000,000. American states differ widely in the number of justices they have *per capita*, but all have proportionately fewer than in England. This can be seen by comparing the English figure with those of the two largest American states, California and New York, each of which has a population of

[1] Cmnd. 2742. [2] For instance, in New York State in 1963 about 90 per cent. of all cases handled by justices of the peace involved violations of traffic laws or town ordinances. Another 6 per cent. were private civil actions and only 4 per cent. concerned penal and indictable offences. 10 *New York Judicial Conference Report* 206–7 (1965).

over 16,000,000. California has 288 justices of the peace,[1] and New York about 2,500.[2]

It is not only the amount of work that justices do which requires England to maintain so large a number of them. It is also their manner of operation. In magistrates' courts and Quarter Sessions they do not sit singly, but in panels. These panels are rotated often, sometimes with each sitting of the court, so that a particular justice may not sit more than once a month. Throughout the country the average is about one day in every two weeks for each justice. For preliminary hearings, for the trial of certain petty infractions, and for such work as the issuing of summonses and warrants, only one justice is required, although in practice two or more are usually available. For most trials in magistrates' courts, the number of justices varies from two to seven, three or five being the most common. For trials in County Quarter Sessions, five or seven justices usually sit, taking turns. The county justices are grouped, for convenience, into 'petty sessional divisions'. The number of divisions per county varies from one to twenty-four according to the size of the county, and there are roughly 1,000 divisions in England. Usually there is one court in each division but in some of the larger ones there may be two or more courts sitting in different towns. Each justice normally sits in a court for the division in which he lives, but in an emergency he may sit in another division within the same county. In the boroughs, there is always only one petty sessional division covering the whole borough area, but courts may sit in more than one place within this area. Each petty sessional division has its own court-room provided by the local authorities or, in London, by the Home Office. The frequency with which a magistrates' court sits varies with the locality. In some rural divisions, it may be no more than once a month, but in urban divisions, it may be every day, with six courts going at once.

In the United States, the practice of pooling and rotating justices of the peace is virtually unknown. Each justice constitutes a separate court. A few localities make an effort to provide him with proper court-room facilities but, on the whole, he sits either at his home or place of business, and then only when a case is brought to him. One of the reforms currently being considered in some states where it has proved impolitic to abolish the system entirely is to require the justices for an area to take turns sitting in a fixed court having proper facilities.

[1] 20 *California Judicial Council Report* 127 (1965).
[2] 10 *New York Judicial Conference Report* 175 (1965).

Their Selection, Tenure, and Training

The American system of selecting judges is at its worst in the selection of justices of the peace. While a candidate for higher judicial office has to be politically acceptable, he is also expected to be qualified for the post. A candidate for justice of the peace needs only to be a local resident and of voting age. The term of office is short: six years in a few states, but four or two years in most. Furthermore, the American justice, unlike his counterpart in England, is paid for his services. Sometimes he receives a small salary from the local government; sometimes he is paid out of litigants' fees in a manner inviting unfair decisions, where, for example, the justice does not promptly get compensated unless there has been a conviction. Unlike England, America has not developed the tradition that the office of justice of the peace is an opportunity to render important public service. It is regarded rather as an opportunity to make a trifling amount of money.

In most American states the popular election of justices has proved too firmly entrenched to be changed. Where this is so, one of the significant compromise reforms is to require the justices to undertake a course of training. New York provides that a justice who is not a lawyer may not assume office until he has completed a special training course administered by the state's Judicial Conference;[1] and California requires that all candidates for justice of the peace, unless they are lawyers, must pass an examination administered by the Judicial Council before they can qualify for selection.[2]

In England, justices of the peace are appointed by the Crown to serve until retirement at age 75 or earlier removal. In practice, appointments are made by the Lord Chancellor[3] who is both the highest judicial officer in England and a member of the Cabinet. His own position is political, but by strong tradition he keeps politics out of judicial appointments. This tradition works remarkably well in the selection of the higher judiciary—and it has worked reasonably well in the selection of justices of the peace. A problem, however, arises because of the fact that justices are so numerous that about 1,000 vacancies have to be filled each year. To aid him in the process of selection, the Lord Chancellor appoints an advisory committee for each borough and county, whose members are drawn from all sections and groups in the community, including each of the three leading

---

[1] *N.Y. Sess. Laws* 1962, ch. 705, § 3.
[2] *Cal. Govt. Code*, § 71601.
[3] Jackson, pp. 160–5.

political parties. Members are appointed on the understanding that it is their job to find candidates best suited for the office of magistrate, and that they must not regard themselves as representatives of their parties; but some of them tend to forget these instructions. Their nominations, while based largely on merit, also try to balance the political complexion of the courts so that members of one party will not dominate. This is tame compared to the uses of politics in selecting judges in the United States, but it has given rise to controversy in England. Another criticism is that the advisory committees are generally composed of people active in public affairs who in turn tend to nominate others active in public affairs. Since the English have come to regard lay justices much as the Americans regard the jury— as broadly representative of community values—the argument is that justices ought to be drawn from as wide a base as possible, not from the small group actively engaged in public affairs.

As in the United States, English justices are not chosen for their knowledge of law, but this has not proved to be a serious drawback. Whereas American justices are entirely on their own, having to do their own paper work and find the law for themselves, English justices have available the service of a paid clerk,[1] who is appointed, subject to Home Office approval, from among solicitors and barristers of five years' standing. There is a clerk for each petty sessional division. In some, it is a full-time post, but in most it is a part-time job, held by a solicitor who is also engaged in private practice. He not only keeps court records, performs administrative tasks, and helps poor and ignorant complainants and defendants, but also acts as legal adviser to the justices. Sometimes he retires with the justices into chambers. It has been held that he should not do so unless the justices expressly ask him to advise them on a point of law, but there is a feeling among some members of the profession that this is an unfortunate ruling, curtailing the possible usefulness of the clerk. Often he examines witnesses for the court in the course of the hearing, in which case there is a possibility that he will come to dominate the proceedings. This need not happen, however, and does not happen in well-regulated courts.

Despite the way in which English justices have been able to handle the vast judicial burden placed upon them, some persons in England believe that lay justices ought not to sit until they have received some training in their duties, particularly sentencing. For some time there

[1] Jackson, pp. 166–72; see also Departmental Committee on Justices' Clerks, *Report*, Cmnd. 6507 (1944).

has been statutory provision for locally administered instruction of justices, but the results have been uneven. In the spring of 1964, the Lord Chancellor proposed that instruction should become compulsory for all newly appointed justices, as in New York. A national advisory board has been established to map out the form which such training should take.

PART-TIME PROFESSIONAL JUDGES

In both the United States and England, lawyers may serve as justices of the peace. In New York, for example, 20 per cent. of the justices are legally qualified; and lawyers also serve as part-time judges in many of the smaller city and municipal courts. There is nothing in the United States, however, that compares to the highly-developed use in England of lawyers of standing as part-time judges in the superior trial courts, i.e., as Recorders in Borough Quarter Sessions, as 'legally qualified' chairmen of County Quarter Sessions, and as Commissioners of Assize.

There are ninety-two part-time recorderships in England, as well as a fluctuating number of deputy and assistant recorderships for places where Borough Quarter Sessions sit in two or three divisions. Recorders are nominated by the Lord Chancellor and appointed by the Crown from among barristers of over five years' standing. All are in active practice at the time of their appointment. Recorders are obliged to attend at least four of their borough sessions each year. If sessions have to be held more frequently a Deputy Recorder may be appointed; and in addition Assistant Recorders may sit when the work is so heavy that two or more courts have to be held in the borough at the same time. Recorders are paid fixed annual salaries ranging from £100 to £1,000 according to the size of the borough. In addition, they receive a daily fee (£20 in the small boroughs and £30 in the larger ones) for each day on which they sit. This remuneration usually does not compensate the Recorders for the loss which they sustain in their practice as a result of their undertaking Quarter Sessions work; but such service provides the Recorders with judicial experience and a possible path to full-time judicial office as well as an opportunity for important public service.

In County Quarter Sessions, the part-time offices of Chairman and Deputy Chairman are required to be held by 'legally qualified' persons. This does not mean simply that they must be lawyers, but that either they are appointed by the Crown (on advice of the Lord Chancellor), upon application of the Court of Quarter Sessions, from among barristers and solicitors of ten years' standing, or they are elected by the justices of the county from among the holders of high, full-time judicial office. There are 62 chairmen and about 200 deputy chairmen in England. Of these, 27 chairmen and 113 deputy chairmen receive remuneration. The chairmen receive annual salaries varying from £100 to £1,000 a year, plus daily fees of £30 for each day on which they sit. The deputy chairmen receive no annual salaries but are paid £30 per day. As in the case of Recorders this remuneration does not ordinarily compensate a practising barrister for the resulting loss to his practice. In a number of counties, the chairmanship is held by a High Court or County Court judge who has volunteered for part-time criminal work. Currently, 2 Lords of Appeal, 1 Lord Justice, 19 High Court, and 41 County Court judges serve in this capacity. A judge who volunteers to sit at Quarter Sessions does so without additional remuneration and is expected to fit his Quarter Sessions work in with his normal judicial duties, i.e. normally during vacations or on days on which he is not required to sit in his regular court.

There is a practice in England by which a Queen's Counsel of high standing can be used to fill in for an incapacitated Queen's Bench judge on his circuit of the Assize Courts or to help handle especially heavy case loads on Assize. This is done only when the necessity arises, but for a barrister to be sent in this way as a 'Commissioner of Assize' is often the final step between a Recordership and a High Court bench.

These three types of part-time professionals participate in virtually every Quarter Sessions case and a few Assize cases tried in England. Even so, they handle under 2 per cent. of the total of criminal cases.[1] Over 97 per cent. are tried, as we have said, by justices of the peace in the lower courts. The remaining serious cases, considerably less than 1 per cent. of the total, are tried at Assizes by full-time judges of the Queen's Bench Division.

FULL-TIME PROFESSIONAL JUDGES

Since England relies so heavily on part-time justices and judges, the relative number of full-time judges doing criminal work is considerably less than that in the United States. In all of England there are less

[1] Interdepartmental Committee on the Business of the Criminal Courts, *Report* Cmnd. 1289 (1962).

than seventy-eight professional judges who devote substantially the whole of their time to criminal cases. These include:

(a) Up to forty Metropolitan Stipendiary Magistrates in London;
(b) Thirteen Stipendiary Magistrates in cities outside of London;
(c) Five chairmen and eight deputy chairmen of the five Quarter Sessions courts of Greater London;
(d) Two full-time chairmen for the County Sessions of Kent and Lancashire;
(e) Two Recorders for the Crown Courts of Manchester and Liverpool;
(f) Eight judges sitting permanently at the Central Criminal Court in London.

Of these, fifty-nine sit in Metropolitan London. In New York City, which has a population almost as large, there are 108 professional judges devoting the whole of their time to criminal work: 78 on the Criminal Court and 30 in criminal parts of the Supreme Court within the city.

Besides these full-time judges in courts which are exclusively criminal, and those who serve part time as justices of the peace in County Quarter Sessions, the only other full-time professionals in England who try criminal cases are the 35 judges of the Queen's Bench Division. They divide their time between civil and criminal work. By contrast, in New York State—which has one-third the population of England—there are 288 professional judges who divide their time between civil and criminal work: 85 on the Supreme Court outside the city, 81 in the County Courts, 45 in the Family Court (which hears juvenile cases),[1] 16 in the Nassau County District Court, about 26 judges of small city courts serving full time, and 35 judges in Federal District Courts sitting within the state. These are in addition to the 108 judges in New York City whose full time is spent on criminal cases.

These figures, of course, change yearly. In New York, as in every state, there is a tendency to add to the number of professional judges. A similar tendency is at work in England: the Crown Courts were established in 1956; the authorized number of Metropolitan Stipendiaries was raised from 27 to 35 in 1959, and to 40 in 1964; and the number of judges sitting in the Central Criminal Court was raised from 5 to 8 in 1963. The chairmanships of several busy County

---

[1] For a description of the work of the Family Court, see Chapter 5.

Quarter Sessions are now on a full-time basis, as those of London and Middlesex have long been. But even these increases are unlikely to change the fact that England manages its judicial business with a far smaller proportion of full-time judges than any American state.

SELECTION AND TENURE OF PROFESSIONAL JUDGES

In both England and the United States full-time judges are lawyers either by virtue of statutory requirement or tradition. However, their backgrounds and manner of selection are very different.[1]

In general, American judges at all levels are chosen for short terms; by local election; and largely on the basis of political considerations. In general, English judges are chosen for indefinite terms; by central appointment; and almost wholly on the basis of fitness and ability.

The English Pattern

In England stipendiary magistrates may be appointed from among barristers or solicitors of seven years' standing, although most stipendiaries have been chosen from the former group. High Court judges must be barristers of ten years' standing, but it is rare for anyone to be appointed who has not been at the bar for at least twice that time. Since barristers are almost always specialists in litigation, a new judge usually brings to the bench an extensive experience of practice in the courtroom.

In the United States it is not unusual for an office lawyer or an academic lawyer without substantial experience in litigation to become a judge. This is one consequence of the undivided legal profession. On the other hand, there is a tendency to draw a disproportionate number of judges from the ranks of former district attorneys, for the progression from politically selected prosecutor to politically selected judge is a natural one. It is sometimes thought that this entails a danger that the new criminal judge will bring with him to the bench an occupational bias; but sometimes it develops that former district attorneys are extremely zealous in their protection of the rights of accused persons. The English avoid the problem by not having professional prosecutors.

Judicial selection in England is essentially non-political. This has

---

[1] Jackson, pp. 256–71; Mayers, pp. 16–24; Erskine, 'The Selection of Judges in England: A Standard for Comparison', 39 *A.B.A.J.* 279 (1953). See also Grossman, *Lawyers and Judges* [*The ABA & the Politics of Judicial Selection*] (1965).

not always been so and it is not necessarily inherent in the English system of appointment. Appointments are made in the name of the Crown, but are effectively in the hands of political figures. The Prime Minister, guided by the Lord Chancellor, nominates judicial members of the House of Lords, the Court of Appeal, and the heads of the divisions of the High Court; the Lord Chancellor himself nominates the other judges of the High Court as well as the lesser judiciary, including justices of the peace. It is only by a fairly recently developed tradition that party politics plays no part in this process, but this tradition is very strong today.

The Lord Chancellor's selection of a judge is usually based upon informed knowledge of his fitness and probity, supplemented in some cases by knowledge of the man's performance as a judge if he has served as a Recorder, Chairman or Deputy Chairman of County Quarter Sessions, or Commissioner of Assize. With only about 2,000 barristers to choose from, it is likely that the Lord Chancellor and his close advisers personally know any candidate under consideration. The Lord Chancellor, as a distinguished member of the bar, is also in touch with the Inns of Court and can take account of their views; and, in addition, he consults with the head of the court to which an appointment is being made.

Stipendiary magistrates hold office until the age of 72, but their tenure may be extended to age 75 if the Lord Chancellor considers this to be in the public interest. Provincial stipendiaries are subject to removal by the Lord Chancellor 'for good cause' and metropolitan stipendiaries may be removed by him 'for inability or misbehaviour'. Recorders may also hold office until they reach 72 (which may be extended by the Lord Chancellor to 75) and may be removed for inability or misbehaviour. Chairmen of County Sessions are appointed for fixed periods, usually for three or five years, but may be re-appointed, as they usually are, until they reach 72. Superior judges hold office 'during good behaviour'. In theory they can be removed by Parliament, but this procedure has never been used. There are dangers in lifetime tenure, the worst of them being senility. This has been met in large part by providing for the retirement of superior judges at age 75. There is also the danger that a judge will be out of step with modern times—a danger aggravated by the fact that appointments are made only from among the successful senior members of a bar which tends to be conservative in outlook. On the other hand, the judges in England are all Benchers of their respective Inns of

Court, where they regularly come in contact with other Benchers, including barristers in active practice. Among the Benchers all are equal, and informal criticism is freely made. This tends to keep the English judges abreast of the times and prevents their undue isolation. On the whole the English system has produced judges of outstanding ability who enjoy a very high degree of public confidence and international esteem.

The American Pattern

In the United States federal judges, like English judges, are appointed to serve 'during good behaviour' until retirement. The quality of federal judges is generally agreed as being higher than that of state judges—a fact which is sometimes attributed to the appointive system and to life tenure. The federal system of selection, however, is not free from politics. While appointments are not made exclusively on a party basis, political pressures have a powerful impact. Appointments to the federal bench are made by the President, acting on the advice of the Attorney General, and are subject to confirmation by the Senate. By convention, the Senate gives a veto power to a senator from the candidate's home state. As a result, candidates are nominated only after consultation with the senators or other leaders of the President's party in the state concerned. The American Bar Association has a committee which investigates and reports to the Attorney General on a candidate's qualifications, but its recommendations are not binding, and men found by this committee to be unqualified have sometimes been appointed.

The great majority of states provide for the popular election of judges and for short-term tenure.[1] A handful of states allow the Governor to appoint the judges, and a few others give that power to their legislature. In three of the states judges hold office during good behaviour, but in most states their terms vary from two to twenty-one years for appellate judges, and from two to fifteen years for trial court judges. The median term is about six years.

There are three types of elective systems. In one, candidates for judicial office, like other candidates, run on tickets in which their party affiliations are stressed. In another, they run on non-partisan ballots without party affiliations disclosed (despite the fact that loyal

---

[1] 15 *Book of the States* 123–5. For example, courts of last resort in 36 states have judicial terms of ten years or less. See, generally, American Judicature Society Information Sheet No. 19, 15 Jan. 1965.

service in partisan politics tends to be a prerequisite for nomination). In the third, the so-called 'Missouri Plan', judges are initially chosen by the Governor or other appointing authority from names submitted to him by an impartial nominating committee, and, after having served on the bench for a short probationary period, they are required to run for popular election, not against other candidates but 'against their own records'. The question put to voters is simply whether Judge X shall be retained in office. This system is gaining favour throughout the country as the most satisfactory balance of two views widely held in the United States: (1) that the influence of politics on judicial selection is an evil to be avoided; and (2) that a judge should be responsible to the people for the conduct of his office. The first view is supported not so much on the ground that political selection results in corruption or party bias as upon the ground that a judge may spend too much time in seeking re-election and may be induced to hesitate over an unpopular decision, and upon the further ground that the judiciary may be deprived of the services of able lawyers who are unwilling to curry the political favour required for nomination or expose themselves to the expense and humiliation of a political campaign. The second view stems historically from the extreme notions of democracy entertained in American political thought during the Jacksonian era of the nineteenth century, but it has been reinforced by modern emphasis upon the lawmaking function that the courts perform. Whatever the merits or faults of the elective system of choosing judges, they are somewhat ameliorated by the fact that many, if not most, American judges originally come to office by reason of their being appointed to fill vacancies caused by death, resignation, or retirement. Once in office, they are likely to be re-elected, sometimes in pursuance of a local professional tradition that sitting judges ought to be retained.

5

PENAL INSTITUTIONS

In the last four chapters we have been discussing the institutions which administer criminal justice up to the point where a decision is made regarding disposition of an offender. Beyond that point, the agencies of special importance are the services concerned with probation, prisons, and parole or after-care. It is to these that we now turn our attention. Because institutions for juveniles and adolescents have become so specialized a part of the penal system in both England and the United States, we shall also devote a separate section of this chapter to facilities for the treatment of young offenders.

PROBATION

Probation is the practice by which a court, rather than imprisoning an offender, permits him to remain at liberty, subject for a period of time to certain stated conditions and to the supervision and guidance of a probation officer. If, during that period, the offender stays out of trouble and observes the conditions of his probation, nothing further will be done in his case. But if he does not comply with these restrictions, he becomes liable to be imprisoned for the offence of which he was originally found guilty.[1]

Probation developed during the nineteenth century when several English and American courts independently hit upon the idea as a method of dealing with first offenders, particularly juveniles, for whom a prison sentence seemed likely to have harmful consequences without compensating advantages. These courts relied mainly on police officers or on religious and philanthropic volunteers to act as probation supervisors. In 1878 the American state of Massachusetts enacted the first law providing for regular supervision of conditionally released offenders and for a salaried probation service. Since then in both countries official probation services have gradually superseded private volunteers. Government-controlled and financed services now

---

[1] See generally Chute & Bell (1956); Elkin, pp. 41–57; Home Office, *The Probation Service in England and Wales* (1964); Jackson, pp. 196–204; Tappan, pp. 539–84; Tompkins (1964).

exist throughout England, in the American federal court system and in all of the American states.

In neither nation is probation regarded primarily as a matter of leniency or grace on the part of the court. Rather it is regarded as a means of rehabilitating an offender if he is willing to co-operate. England stresses co-operation by requiring the offender, if over 14, to consent to probation and to express his willingness to comply with the terms of the probation order. No such requirement is imposed in the United States. England also, again unlike most American states, imposes a minimum limit of one year for any term of probation in order to prevent it being ordered for a period too short to permit an effective attempt at rehabilitation.

When specialized services are needed by a probationer, probation officers, both in England and in the better American systems, are authorized to obtain them from whatever resources are available in the community, sometimes paying for them out of probation service funds. A probationer may, for instance, require medical or psychiatric aid, in which case the probation officer uses his knowledge of local facilities to put the probationer in touch with an appropriate clinic or hospital. In both countries an offender may be required to seek such specialized aid as a condition of his probation. This sort of condition is commonly used in New York City as a method of dealing with the growing number of young narcotics addicts.

England has developed a system of probation homes and hostels[1] to provide for the group residence of probationers, which so far has been little copied in the United States. These homes and hostels, which are usually small establishments accommodating from fifteen to twenty-five residents, are run by voluntary bodies, but must be approved and are largely financed by the Home Office. They are used for probationers over the compulsory school age but under 21 who are required by the terms of their probation orders to live in them. Those who live in probation hostels work at ordinary jobs during the day but are obliged to return to the hostels at night and to contribute to the cost of their maintenance. These ordinarily are young people whose home environments are thought likely to impede their rehabilitation but who are not considered bad enough to require fully institutionalized training. Those who live in probation homes (as distinguished from hostels) work mainly on the premises. There seems to be a certain inconsistency in combining probation with residential

[1] Elkin, pp. 76–81.

treatment, but the combination has been found helpful for a few persons who require close supervision, for a relatively short time and without the strict discipline found in a correctional institution. In neither hostels nor homes are the residents, strictly speaking, in legal custody, and in this sense also the system differs from custodial forms of treatment.

In view of its origins, administration of the probation system by the courts was natural in its early stages. Even today the varied duties of probation officers bring them into close and continuous contact with the courts, and make it desirable that some judicial oversight of their work be maintained.

The tasks of the probation officer are to supervise the offender and to see that he is dealt with if he breaks his promise to behave. In line with the modern conception of his role, the probation supervisor devotes his main effort to helping the probationer to a better life, but if he is able to do nothing else, he must at least see that the conditions of the court's probation order are observed. Probation officers differ in their view as to what justifies them in bringing a violation to the attention of the court, but their decisions in particular cases are bound to depend largely on their estimate of what action the court will take. In most of the United States, courts have complete discretion as to whether or not they will revoke probation. English courts have a like discretion, and also the option of imposing a small fine while continuing the offender on probation or, in the case of a young offender, of requiring him to spend some of his time during his probationary period in attending one of the new 'Attendance Centres' (which we shall describe in the section on juvenile delinquency).

In both England and the United States, the few studies which have been made conclude that probation is generally successful.[1] The feeling among most experts is that it can be extended with advantage to many cases where it is not now used. This can be done, however, only if there are probation officers available in sufficient numbers and with sufficient training to handle the work. In this respect England appears to be in a better position than the United States, although the situation is not entirely satisfactory in either nation.

[1] A 1933 Home Office investigation supports the following conclusions: (a) the probability of success of probation increases with the age of the offender while its use decreases; (b) the percentage of success is higher at all ages with girls and women than with boys and men. Elkin, pp. 54–56. Comparative international data indicate that in most countries probation achieves a 70 to 80 per cent. 'success rate'. Tappan, pp. 576–84, 581.

Pre-sentence Investigations

Once probation officers evolved, it was soon recognized that they could perform a useful service by investigating an offender's background, character, outlook, problems, and failings before he was sentenced, in order to guide the court in deciding upon an appropriate penalty. With the development of large probation staffs, this has become a regular and major feature of the work of probation officers in both England and the United States. In England the officer preparing the pre-sentence report is normally appointed to supervise the offender if probation is ordered. This principle is not always followed in the United States, especially in the larger services like that attached to the Supreme Court in New York City, where investigatory and supervisory officers are organized into separate divisions. Some observers believe that the two functions should be kept separate because of different qualities of mind and personality required for the different jobs. In New York and a few other American states, a court may defer sentencing for several months while releasing the offender on probation for a short period to see if he can benefit by it. This allows for more thorough observation by the probation service than would otherwise be possible. Under the youthful offender law in New York, by which offenders between 16 and 19 can, if the court chooses, be treated substantially as older juvenile delinquents, probation officers are also used to investigate an offender's eligibility for this special kind of treatment. A further use of the investigatory resources of the probation service which has developed in New York City is the practice of having probation officers furnish the criminal courts with factual information pertinent to decisions regarding pre-trial release on bail—information not available to most magistrates.

Miscellaneous Tasks

In England and some places in the United States, probation officers have been given tasks which have nothing to do with the treatment or supervision of convicted offenders. For example, they may be made responsible for the supervision of children who have not committed specific offences but who are adjudged to be in need of care or protection outside their homes. Probation officers may also undertake adoption inquiries, ascertain amounts required for the maintenance of minor children under support orders, and act as conciliators in matrimonial disputes. In American juvenile courts they sometimes provide what is called an 'intake service', in which an informal adjustment of a complaint against a child is made before the case reaches the judge.[1] In a majority of cases the probation officers are able to compose differences with the complainant without bothering the court, and to refer the child or his family to an appropriate social agency for whatever help may be required.[2] In England the Home Office has recently recommended the institution of a similar programme which is designed, so far as possible, to take children 'outside the ambit of the criminal law and of the courts, to make, if possible with the agreement of their parents or guardians, such arrangements for their welfare as are appropriate'.[3]

Administration of Probation Services

In light of the many tasks which make probation officers function as an arm of the court, it is not surprising that they should normally be assigned to particular courts for considerable periods of time and develop close relations with the judges. As against this court orientation, however, there is some pull towards a different principle of organization by which the probation service is made part of an agency having responsibility for parole as well. This is primarily a matter of economical public administration, but has the disadvantage of splitting the allegiance of probation officers between the courts in which they serve and a state administrative agency.[4]

As a result of pressures alternately pulling the probation service towards and away from the courts, there is considerable variation in the organization of probation services in the United States.[5] In ten states, including California, the service is under the control of the courts and is locally financed. Appointment to the service is in some of these states subject to civil service, but elsewhere, especially when the courts themselves are under a régime of political influence, it tends to be governed by partisan political considerations. In four states, including New York, court administration and local financing is supplemented by state subsidy. Within New York City, the Supreme Court has its own probation service, while the City Office of Probation provides officers in the Criminal and Family Courts. Six states have both local, judicially administered systems and a state

---

[1] See Note, 'Informal Disposition of Delinquency Cases: Survey and Comparison of Court Delegation of Decision-Making', 1965 *Wash. U.L.Q.*, p. 258; Tappan, pp. 393–4.

[2] Polier, p. 44.   [3] Cmnd. 2742, p. 12.   [4] Tappan, p. 575.

[5] Chute & Bell, pp. 175–213; Tappan, pp. 574–5.

service which fills rural gaps. Nine states have a centralized state-wide service, and also some local services in the larger cities. Twenty-one states, all relatively small in area or population density, have only a centrally administered service.

In only thirteen states does the central service extend to juveniles, this aspect of probation being administered in the other thirty-seven on a local basis.

The state services are under executive departments, not under judicial control. In twenty-seven states they are combined with the parole service. Federal probation officers are appointed by the district courts and controlled by them, but there is a probation branch in the Administrative Office of the United States Courts. In 1964 a special committee of federal judges was appointed to study probation, looking towards greater uniformity of standards throughout the federal court system. Similarly, many of the states with local services have a central commission or authority to recommend standards and policies, and sometimes also to supervise performance and receive reports on the conduct of the probation service. In the larger probation systems, consistency in standards and performance is promoted by the fact that their staffs are wholly professional, have been trained in the same social work schools, and keep up an exchange of information and ideas with their colleagues throughout the country. But among the smaller services there are great differences in quality, depending largely upon how willing the local government is to provide the funds for probation work. In many areas staff members have had no special training for their jobs. There are still many local areas of the United States where the courts are without any probation services.

In England probation is locally administered but centrally supervised—a pattern which we saw in Chapter 1 is also characteristic of the organization of the English police, and one which has resulted in a high degree of uniformity throughout the country. Every magistrates' court in England is required by law to have at its disposal the services of at least two probation officers, one man and one woman. For purposes of administering the probation service, the country is divided into eighty-nine probation areas, in each of which there is a probation committee, a majority of whose members are chosen by the magistrates from among their own ranks, and the remainder of whose members may be chosen from Recorders or Chairmen of Quarter Sessions and outside persons whose experience will be helpful. The probation committee appoints probation officers and is responsible for making them available to the superior trial courts (Quarter Sessions and Assizes). For each magistrates' court there is also a case committee, similarly selected, which exercises general supervision over the work of probation officers in the area. Detailed supervision, however, is carried out by chief probation officers within the service (as it is in the United States, where there is generally no equivalent to the English case committee).

Probation committees have a budget provided in equal parts from local government funds and from a central grant administered by the Home Office. Until April 1965 probation in London was administered by the Home Office, but that responsibility has now been transferred to a committee of judges and magistrates representative of courts in the Metropolitan London area.

As with the police, the power of the purse held by the central government has led to a situation in which the Home Office exercises very close supervision over probation throughout England. The entire service is subject to inspection by the Home Office, which also lays down rules regarding the powers and conduct of probation committees and the duties and conditions of service of probation officers, including a national salary scale. The education of probation officers is in the hands of the Home Office assisted by the Training Committee of the Advisory Council for Probation and After-care, which selects and plans the training of candidates for the service, and provides a pool from which local committees must make their appointments; and the final appointment of a probation officer must be confirmed by the Home Office. Finally, the Office has power to combine probation areas. This power has been frequently exercised in recent years and is considered a major factor in ensuring efficient administration of the service.

Caseloads and Workers

The English probation service now numbers nearly 2,400 and was expected to go up to 2,750 during 1966[1]—a number recommended as adequate by a committee which reviewed the workings of the probation service in 1962. The proper caseload for a male probation officer in England is considered to be from fifty to sixty cases. The actual average caseload today is under sixty, although there are areas where it has been as high as 100 cases. Reasonably satisfactory caseloads

[1] Cmnd. 2296, p. 10.

have been achieved in part through the emergency appointment of many probation officers who lack prior training.

In the United States, the number of probation officers is considered by American experts to be totally inadequate. It has been estimated that there are only 7,000 probation officers in the entire country, while the number needed for children's courts alone is about 15,000.[1] The generally accepted proper caseload for a probation officer in the United States is fifty cases for supervision; but where the officer also has the duty of investigation, the ideal is thirty-five cases for supervision and six for investigation. In fact, the average caseload is three times greater and in some places considerably higher.[2] Even in New York City, where there are about 600 probation workers (as compared to 200 in London), the service is considered overburdened with excessive caseloads, especially in the juvenile courts.[3] Under these conditions it is often believed impossible to give a probationer anything but perfunctory supervision.

In the United States new probation workers are generally required to have a much higher degree of formal education than applicants in England. Although American standards vary, the larger services require at least a four-year college degree; New York City and Los Angeles now also require either a Master's degree or two years' experience in social work (although the latter may sometimes be acquired in a probation trainee programme). In England, on the other hand, the normal training for persons entering under the age of 27 is a two-year university social science course, followed by up to twelve months' specialized training after appointment. For older persons the normal training is a twelve months' specialized course. Government grants are available during such training. Some American observers wonder whether standards in the United States are not unnecessarily high, making recruitment more difficult than it need be and producing too precious a type of probation worker.

AMERICAN PRISONS

In the United States there are three levels of prison systems:[4] local, state, and federal.

[1] Tappan, p. 582.

[2] Chute & Bell, pp. 189–90. The figures are based on a 1948 study of 172 departments in 45 states. The average caseload ran to 123·9 cases for supervision; most workers also made investigations.   [3] Polier, pp. 44–45.

[4] See generally American Academy of Political and Social Science, 293 *Annals*, 'Prisons in Transformation' (1954); Tappan, pp. 584–708.

Local governments provide 'county jails' in most of the country's 3,000 counties and an estimated 10,000 cities and towns. These serve several purposes: (1) the temporary holding of persons awaiting trial, (2) the detention of persons who have been convicted and who are awaiting transfer to other institutions, and (3) the imprisonment of convicted misdemeanants and minor offenders. They range in size from village lock-ups with a few beds to city prisons designed for several thousand inmates. Their standards vary enormously but in general their condition is very bad. The various kinds of prisoners are often housed together in crowded, run-down quarters, and in unsegregated proximity. In many instances, the jail, lacking any constructive programme of work, training, treatment, or recreation, provides a school for beginners in crime. The population of such jails at any given moment probably approaches 90,000, and the number of prisoners who pass through each year is nearly two million. In view of these swollen figures, there would probably be little opportunity for rehabilitation even if the necessary funds and facilities were available, which they are not in most cases. State inspection and supervision has sometimes resulted in improvement, as has inspection by the federal government which temporarily detains its own prisoners in local jails. However, more than three-quarters of these institutions are considered unfit for federal prisoners.

Each state government operates its own system of prisons for the incarceration of persons convicted of the more serious state crimes. In many states liability to imprisonment in a state prison for a year or more is the principal way of defining a 'felony'. Treatment in these institutions ranges from the latest methods of rehabilitation to enforced idleness. State prisons generally offer more favourable opportunities for treatment and training than local jails, but many states have too small a prison population to make diversified facilities feasible. In only about a dozen states is the number of state prisoners over 5,000 and in only four does it exceed 10,000. As a result, there are some states in which a single prison is used for all convicted felons. Only in the most exceptional cases have state governments pooled their resources, e.g. sharing facilities for women prisoners. Even in states where several prisons are operated, there has been little versatility in the types and programmes of these institutions. The California system, with over seventeen establishments, is a notable exception; and a few other states have been moving ahead in this regard in recent years.

Finally, the federal government operates a separate system of prisons with a total population of over 20,000. This is the most diversified prison system in the United States and it is commonly regarded as the most effective. In 1964 it contained thirty-six institutions of different types and sizes, including maximum security penitentiaries for the close custody of serious offenders, medium security penitentiaries for more tractable prisoners, reformatories for inexperienced offenders, 'correctional institutions' for short-term prisoners, open camps for those requiring little custodial control, and special institutions for juveniles and youths, as well as pre-release guidance centres, a detention headquarters, and a medical centre for the more difficult mental and medical cases.[1]

ENGLISH PRISONS

In England the prison population, including persons in temporary detention, is about 30,000.[2] There are over 100 institutions administered by a central prison service, and a massive building programme is at present under way, twenty-seven new establishments having been opened between 1959 and 1964.[3] Apart from special institutions for young offenders, which we shall discuss in the next section, English prisons can be classified in three groups,[4] not entirely dissimilar to the three types of American prisons just described.

First, there are local prisons. It is to one of about twenty-five local prisons that every offender is first sent upon conviction. Persons awaiting trial are also held there, but separately from those who have been convicted. These local prisons resemble American county jails, most of them being old, overcrowded buildings, unsuited to modern methods of treatment and training. Some are very large by English standards, a few housing over 1,000 prisoners. All are closed, maximum security establishments. There are a few special local prisons with open (minimum security) conditions to which prisoners serving short sentences may be transferred, but the mass of short-term prisoners are kept in the closed local prisons.

[1] Federal Bureau of Prisons, *Annual Report*, p. 14 (1964).

[2] This figure is kept down because imprisonment is not the most common method of treatment adopted by the English courts. In 1958, of all adult persons found guilty of indictable offences only 29 per cent. were imprisoned, the remainder being dealt with in some other way. Home Office, *Prisons and Borstals*, p. 4 (4th ed. 1960).   [3] Cmnd. 2296, p. 11.

[4] Elkin, pp. 110–236; Home Office, *Prisons and Borstals* (4th ed. 1960); Home Office, *The Sentence of the Court*, pp. 24–32 (1964).

Second, there are regional prisons which offer constructive training to prisoners who are serving sentences of more than one year. Selection for a regional prison is made by the authorities at the local prison to which an offender is first sent by the court. Some of these training prisons are open, some closed. Some regional prisons were set aside in whole or part for certain young recidivists who had been sentenced to a special régime of corrective training; however, with the improvement of training in the regional prisons generally, corrective training now differs little from an ordinary medium-term sentence of imprisonment, and in fact no prison is now devoted wholly to corrective training.

Third, there are a number of central prisons which receive from all over England prisoners whose sentences are for more than three years. One is an open establishment; the rest are closed. In practice, allocation to one or the other of them is made centrally by the Home Office. All long-term prisoners ultimately get into a central prison, but because of overcrowding they may have to wait some months in a local prison before they can be transferred to it.

The three types of English prisons just described correspond to the length of sentences of the prisoners assigned to them. Within each type there is also sub-classification according to the degree of custody: maximum, medium, or minimum. English prisons are further broken down according to a third principle: the class of offender. Convicted prisoners are divided into three classes: (1) young prisoners under 21; (2) the 'star' class, embracing most of those in prison for the first time; and (3) the ordinary class, embracing most of those who have been to prison before. First-timers may, however, be put in the ordinary class if their records are particularly bad and repeaters may be put in the star class if their records are especially good. So far as possible the English prison system aims at keeping these classes of prisoners in separate institutions. If this is not possible, as is the case in most local prisons, at least the classes are segregated within the same institution.

As a result of this elaborate system of classification, prisoners in a particular institution tend to have similar records, substantially the same amount of time to serve, and roughly the same prospects of rehabilitation. In consequence no single English prison is exactly comparable to those American state penitentiaries in which all types of convicted felons are lumped together under one roof.

PENAL REFORM

The American prisons, when constructively managed, try to make up for their lack of diversity by giving each prisoner a programme of treatment and training best suited to his needs within the limits of the facilities available. There is an approximation to the English system only in the small number of jurisdictions which have sufficiently varied facilities to allocate prisoners to the institutions from whose programmes they will most benefit. Some of these jurisdictions have gone further and established reception centres in which a new prisoner can be observed, studied and then assigned to an appropriate institution in the prison system. This is generally recognized by prison administrators to be a good practice. The construction of similar observation centres is projected in England, and one has already been opened at Risley in Lancashire. At present, however, allocations of prisoners to institutions are made in local prisons which lack the resources for the sort of intensive study of an offender's personality that is commonly deemed to be desirable in planning his course of treatment.

Among prison officials in both England and the United States, there is broad agreement on the essentials of an effective penal system. More perhaps than in any other area of criminal justice, these officials have exchanged information, visited each other, and studied each other's voluminous specialized literature. They agree that over-crowded prison buildings in which inmates are kept idle under high-security conditions are ineffective. In both countries prison administrators have been among the first to favour the development of a wide range of correctional institutions in which the restrictions imposed are no greater than necessary to maintain order; in which the inmates may be influenced to lead useful and law-abiding lives; and in which individual prisoners can be provided with programmes appropriate to their special needs. However, the translation of these ideals into practice has been obstructed by financial considerations. The provision and staffing of an appropriate range of institutions is extremely expensive, so that performance constantly lags behind promise. In the interim, both countries have no choice but to continue to use large numbers of prison buildings built to nineteenth-century plans, in which rehabilitative efforts are almost impossible. The older English local prisons often house 900 to 1,000 men, whereas the English prison authorities have concluded that the optimum number of inmates for a single institution is about 300.[1] American opinion likewise favours smaller institutions, although in the case of state prisons the commonly approved standard allows a population of 1,200.[2] Today there are over fifty American prisons in twenty-nine different states which exceed this figure, nearly all of them walled fortresses, some housing between 4,000 and 5,000 inmates.

In England penal reform is easier than in the United States because of the fact that prisons are centrally administered. All prisons have Boards of Visitors or Visiting Committees, the latter being a survival from the days before 1877 when the county jails were run wholly by the justices in Quarter Sessions. In 1877 they were brought within the control of a National Prison Commission, whose Commissioners were responsible to the Home Secretary; and in 1963 the Commission was converted into a Prison Department within the Home Office, which now directs the operations of all penal establishments in England. The Home Office is also the central authority in England for the police, the probation service, criminal statistics, and child welfare, and generally the prevention of crime and the treatment of offenders. Thus the Home Office is in a position to formulate a complete penal policy for the entire country. It has recently laid the foundations for such a policy in a series of departmental committee reports and in two remarkable White Papers containing many highly important proposals which promise to profoundly affect the character of the English prison system.[3] Already the prison authorities have gone forward with a programme which emphasizes the establishment of open institutions, the building of new types of institution such as a special psychiatric prison, the provision of half-way houses for long-term prisoners approaching release, expanded education and vocational training, and advanced therapeutic techniques such as group counselling (which was pioneered in California). Such developments are expected to receive still further impetus from the work of a Royal Commission on Penal Reform which is currently sitting to examine the 'concepts and purpose that should underlie the punishment and treatment of offenders'.

In the United States there have also been developments. As new prisons are built, the old fortress concept is being discarded, with the trend strongly towards open or medium security prisons for 400, 500,

---

[1] Klare, pp. 20–21.   [2] Tappan, pp. 645–6.
[3] Home Office, *Penal Practice in a Changing Society*, Cmnd. 645 (1959); Cmnd. 2296; see also Cmnd. 2742.

or 600 inmates. Clinics, half-way houses, forestry camps, farms, and domiciliary facilities have been opened. The more populous states have set up diagnostic centres. California and the federal government operate what are sometimes claimed to be the best prison systems in the world. Both are staffed by qualified and adequately paid personnel; both operate a full range of diversified institutions; and both maintain sophisticated classification services and provide a balanced programme of employment, education, vocational training, and recreation. Thirteen states, including the larger ones, have separate departments of correction responsible to the Governor; fourteen others have made the prison authority a division within some broader department, e.g. public welfare; and in a few states there is a full-time and salaried board of prisons or a board of control in charge of all state institutions.

In most states, however, innovations have been on a very limited scale, partly because the administrative structure of the prison system is an impediment to reform.[1] In nearly half the states there is no full-time body in charge of the penal system. Most of the systems are administered by part-time and unsalaried boards. There are some states in which there is no central prison authority at all but only local trustees for each institution. Finally, throughout the United States local jails are not administered by the state governments, and in less than one-third of the states is there any state control or inspection of them.[2]

In the federal government the Bureau of Prisons is within the Department of Justice. Thus its Director is responsible to the Attorney-General, a member of the President's Cabinet, and the head of the major law enforcement agencies of the federal government. In this respect the Attorney-General, somewhat like the Home Secretary in England, is in a position to co-ordinate national policy on crime prevention and control. There are, indeed, indications that his office will assume an increasingly active role along these lines. There is now developing in the United States a trend towards attacking problems of crime and punishment through greater federal aid to the state governments. In 1961, for instance, Congress authorized $30 million to be spent over a three-year period to test new approaches to the control of juvenile delinquency. In a message of 8 March 1965 President Johnson proposed major legislation authorizing assistance by the Attorney-General to local authorities in improving crime

[1] Tappan, pp. 614–21.   [2] Ibid., p. 663.

control programmes and announced the appointment of a Presidential Commission on Law Enforcement and Administration which is drawing up a comprehensive programme for federal action.[1] The legislation was enacted.[2]

YOUNG OFFENDERS

In both England and the United States, young offenders are dealt with differently from adult offenders. During the nineteenth century one of the goals of penal reform in both countries was to prevent the detention of such children in ordinary prisons where they might come under bad influences. The development of probation was one aspect of this movement. Beginning with the state of Illinois in 1899, the notion that children ought to be handled on different principles from adult offenders led ultimately to the establishment in both countries of special juvenile courts in which the welfare of the child became the controlling consideration.

Adolescents over the juvenile court age (usually 16) are generally tried in the regular criminal courts. However, it has long been recognized that they present different problems of treatment from those of adult offenders.[3] This recognition was reflected in the reformatory movement of the late nineteenth century in the United States, which insisted on special facilities for the training and discipline of adolescent offenders, and in the development, beginning in 1902, of the Borstal system in England. The English Borstal system flourished, but the American movement stagnated after a few years and has only recently been revived.

Juvenile Courts in England

In England, as we observed in Chapter 4, a juvenile court is a specially constituted sitting of justices of the peace.[4] The justices for each magistrates' court area choose from among themselves a panel of those thought most suitable for work in the juvenile courts. The court is drawn from this panel and usually consists of a chairman and two other members, and must include at least one man and one woman. A juvenile court holds separate sessions from the ordinary

---

[1] *N.Y. Times*, 9 Mar. 1965, pp. 1, 20.

[2] Law Enforcement Assistance Act of 1965, 79 Stat. 828 (1965).

[3] Home Office studies emphasize that youthful offenders present a unique problem, statistics showing that the probability of their success on probation is less and the rate of their re-conviction greater than for adult offenders. Elkin, pp. 54–55; Home Office, *The Sentence of the Court*, pp. 42–44 (1964).

[4] Jackson, pp. 184–96.

magistrates' court, preferably on different days and in a different room. The general public is not admitted and the Press is not allowed, unless the court specially orders, to publish details by which any child appearing before the court can be identified. The atmosphere is generally more relaxed than in adult courts, but the procedure is practically the same.

Juvenile courts have two types of jurisdiction. The first is over criminal charges against a child aged 10 years or over, but under the age of 17. A child under the age of 10 cannot be tried on criminal charges. A child over 10 but under 14 must be tried in the juvenile court unless he is charged with homicide, in which case he must be tried by jury at Assize, or unless he is charged jointly with an adult, in which case he may be tried by an ordinary court. So-called 'young persons'—those from 14 to 17—are generally tried in the juvenile courts but have the right to elect trial by jury if the offence is one other than assault and is punishable by more than three months' imprisonment.

The second type of jurisdiction is over children (including those under 10) and young persons who are in need of 'care, protection, or control'. If the court finds that a juvenile falls within this category, it may impose certain of the same measures which are available to it in the case of a juvenile charged with a criminal offence, i.e. commit him to an approved school, place him in the care of a fit person (usually the local authority), call upon his parents to enter into a recognizance to exercise proper guardianship, or put him under the supervision of a probation officer. This type of jurisdiction is narrower in England than in the United States. It can only be used when a child is actually abandoned or ill-treated or seriously delinquent. Whenever a specific offence is involved, that must be dealt with as a criminal charge.

As noted earlier, the Home Office has recently recommended substantial changes in the method of handling juveniles. Children under the age of 16 would be kept out of court as far as possible. Their cases would be handled by social workers in consultation and agreement with the parents, and would go before the 'family court' (a special sitting of magistrates) only if the facts were disputed or agreement could not be reached. This procedure would be substantially similar to the 'intake service' found in the Family Court of New York. Persons between the ages of 16 and 21 would be dealt with separately in a manner to be described later.[1]

[1] Cmnd. 2742.

Juvenile Courts in the United States

In the United States there is legislation pertaining to juveniles in every state.[1] Most of the states now provide that a juvenile court shall have jursidiction over children under 18 (this is the generally recognized limit), although in some states the upper limit is only 16 or 17, and in a few it has been raised to 21. Without formally drawing a distinction between 'children' and 'young persons' as is done in England, nearly all the states provide for concurrent jurisdiction in the ordinary criminal courts over older juveniles, e.g. those from 16 to 18 or over certain serious offences. In many states facilities are so limited that juveniles who are tried in the ordinary criminal courts are sent to adult prisons, training schools and the like being reserved for those committed by a juvenile court.

The philosophy of American juvenile courts is one which, even more so than in England, stresses the welfare of the child. The jurisdiction of these courts everywhere includes acts done by children which would be crimes if done by adults, but in the proceedings are not regarded as 'criminal' in character, are not in most states subject to the ordinary rules of criminal procedure, and do not generally result in a finding of 'guilty'. Instead, the child is found to be a 'delinquent'. In these proceedings, the practice is to rely heavily on the pre-hearing report of a probation officer.

Juvenile court jurisdiction also generally covers many acts and courses of conduct which are not adult crimes. This type of jurisdiction is like that in England which is exercised over juveniles in need of 'care, protection, or control', but is in most instances considerably broader and exercised with much greater frequency. To a large extent, delinquency in the United States is what the juvenile court says it is, and nearly half the cases in which children are adjudicated 'delinquent' concern trivial acts of carelessness or mischief, truancy, running away, or being ungovernable.[2] One consequence of regarding

---

[1] Sussman, pp. 65–93; Tappan, pp. 387–401.

[2] Handler, 'The Juvenile Court and the Adversary System: Problems of Function and Form', 1965 *Wis. L. Rev.* 15. The scope of delinquency statutes is wide. Most active adolescents commit acts which are 'delinquent' under state law: smoking cigarettes in a public place; using intoxicating liquors; patronizing a public poolroom; using vulgar language in public; disobeying a parent or guardian. See list collected in Rubin, p. 49. Unfettered discretion generally controls the present administration of juvenile justice. For those who commit identical offences, release or arrest frequently depends on the youth's demeanour. Defiance is the quickest way to the juvenile court. Handler, op. cit., pp. 18–19 and n. 52.

juvenile courts as non-criminal in character is that in most states there is no lower age limit to their jurisdiction.[1] Except in a few states, a child of any age may in theory be adjudicated a delinquent for committing a criminal act.

On the other hand, despite the tendency in the United States to regard juvenile courts more as agencies of child welfare than as judicial tribunals, some of these courts are, in practice, little different from the ordinary criminal courts. While there are large cities and a few states where the juvenile court is an independent entity or is part of a family or domestic relations court, in many places it is nothing more than a special sitting of the adult criminal court and commonly the judge in charge devotes only a small part of his time to children's cases. The nature of the proceedings depends to a large extent on the outlook of the individual judge.

Adolescents

It has not been customary in either England or the United States to provide special tribunals (as opposed to special penal institutions) for adolescents over the juvenile court age. In a few American states, the juvenile courts have concurrent jurisdiction with ordinary criminal courts over offenders up to age 21, but such jurisdiction is not much used in practice. A few American cities have established special terms of the ordinary criminal courts in which adolescents are handled separately. New York is the only state which has a specialized form of trial for these young offenders: an adolescent between 16 and 19 may, if the judge so determines on the basis of a probation officer's report, be tried in a special term of the criminal court as a 'youthful offender'. As in the juvenile court, the hearing is private and no finding of 'guilt' results; probation is frequently employed, but the youth may also be committed for three years to a state reformatory. In England, the Home Office has proposed that persons between the ages of 16 and 21 be tried by 'young offenders' courts'—magistrates specially designated as qualified to deal with juveniles, sitting separately from the sessions at which the cases of young children or those of adults are heard. Hearings, however, would be public and there would be no restriction on the publication of the names of persons involved. The procedure in general would be substantially similar to that for adults, but in sentencing great stress would be placed on the welfare and rehabilitation of the offender.[2]

[1] Rubin, pp. 56–57. [2] Cmnd. 2742.

Special sentencing arrangements for young people up to 21, and sometimes up to 26, exist in about nine American states and in the federal courts. In these jurisdictions, an ordinary criminal court tries but does not sentence a youthful offender. Instead it commits him to the custody of a youth authority which, after a period of observation, has the power to place him in an appropriate institution or put him on probation.[1]

Institutions for Young Persons—England

In England, there is a wide range of sentencing options open to a court in dealing with a juvenile or young offender. The court may itself commit him to any one of a number of specialized institutions:[2]

1. Offenders 17 or over who are tried in the ordinary courts may be sentenced to prison, but those under 21 are segregated from the others. Furthermore, before sentencing an offender under 21 to prison, the court must be satisfied that no other form of punishment is suitable. Since 1961, the only prison sentences which can be imposed on persons of this age group are either under six months or over three years. Other methods have entirely replaced medium length imprisonment of those under 21, and the present programme of penal reform in England calls for the ultimate abolition of prison for young offenders as soon as enough alternative facilities for short-term detention become available.[3]

2. England maintains an extensive system of Borstals for the medium length custody of young offenders between 15 and 21 years of age. The term 'Borstal' derives from the locality where the first special institution for young offenders was established. It now covers a wide range of institutions that vary from maximum security to open conditions, although all emphasize vigorous and constructive training based on a close study of the individual by a specially selected staff. Borstal sentences are for a period of two years (three years before 1961) with a minimum of six months' detention. After the minimum

[1] Cmnd. 2742, pp. 109–18.

[2] Elkin, pp. 64–109, 237–68; Home Office, *Prisons and Borstals*, pp. 51–65 (4th ed. 1960); Home Office, *The Sentence of the Court*, pp. 7–31 (1964).

[3] At present, no one under 17 can be sent to prison. Under the Criminal Justice Act, 1948, the Home Secretary can extend this prohibition to cover all persons under 21 if and when he is satisfied that adequate alternatives to prison are available. This would prohibit any court of summary jurisdiction from sentencing any young offender to prison. See Home Office, *Prisons and Borstals*, p. 51 (4th ed. 1960).

period, the prison authorities may release the offender at any time they think he is ready for it. Release is followed by a period of up to two years compulsory after-care supervision. Only Quarter Sessions and Assize Courts can sentence to Borstal training. If a juvenile or magistrates' court feels that an offender requires such a sentence, it must refer the case for sentencing to a superior court. Allocation to a particular Borstal within the system is made by prison authorities at a reception centre.

3. Offenders between 14 and 21 for whom short sentences are considered desirable may be sent to Detention Centres for three to six months.[1] These are residential establishments run by the prison authorities, emphasizing hard work and brisk discipline. Educational arrangements are provided for those of school age. After release, the offender is subject to supervision for a year. Detention Centres were inaugurated under the Criminal Justice Act of 1948,[2] and so far about fifteen have been established. In areas where they are not available, short term imprisonment is still often used. It is contemplated that Detention Centres will ultimately become the standard institutions for the custody of young offenders with little sophistication in crime who are thought to require punishment but not a long period of residential training.

4. For offenders under 17 who are thought to require a long period of close residential supervision, but not Borstal training, there are over 100 approved schools. Some are run by local authorities and some by religious or voluntary organizations, but all are subject to inspection and approval by the Home Office. The management of a school may conditionally release an inmate as soon as he has made sufficient progress, in which case it becomes responsible for providing after-care supervision, usually through the probation service or the children's service of the local authority. There are a great number and variety of approved schools. A juvenile court no longer chooses a particular one. Instead the juvenile is sent to a classifying school or centre, which then allocates him to a suitable training school; but if a classifying establishment is not available, the Home Office selects the training school. Approved schools are used for delinquents under the age of criminal responsibility and for children in need of care and protection, as well as for juvenile offenders.

[1] But if the offender is of compulsory school age the term may, under certain conditions, be for as short a time as one month. Ibid., p. 52.

[2] 11 & 12 Geo. VI, c. 58.

5. A juvenile under 17 whose home surroundings are unsatisfactory, but who does not otherwise require the sort of residential training available in approved schools, may be committed by juvenile court until he reaches the age of 18 to the care of a 'fit person'—which may be, and usually is, the local authority. It then gives the child the benefit of the normal range of services provided for orphans in its care and may board him with a guardian, relative, or friend.

6. An offender under 17 may be committed by a juvenile court to the custody of a Remand Home for up to one month. Such homes are provided by local authorities of counties and county boroughs under Home Office control, primarily for holding and providing reports on juveniles against whom proceedings are pending or who are awaiting transfer to an approved school. Under its present programme, the Home Office has begun to establish a number of Remand Centres to hold before trial those between the ages of 14 and 17 who are too unruly for a Remand Home, as well as untried offenders up to 21 who would otherwise be held in local prisons. It is expected that these Remand Centres will offer diagnostic facilities to which difficult cases can be sent for observation before sentencing.

7. Offenders under 21 for whom the mild measures will suffice can be ordered by a juvenile or magistrates' court to spend up to twenty-four hours of their spare time, in two-hour stretches or so, at an Attendance Centre. These centres are established by the Home Office in large cities. There are now over fifty of them, aimed at deterring offenders by depriving them of some of their leisure time and teaching them the constructive use of such leisure as remains. They are usually run by police officers in their free time, are housed in schools, police premises, and youth clubs, and provide programmes of lectures, physical exercise, and handicrafts.

Various changes in the English penal institutions to which children and young offenders may be sent are in prospect as a result of recent studies and recommendations by the Home Office.[1]

Institutions for Young Persons—The United States

In the United States, as in England, much of the penal effort has been directed towards the provision of specialized facilities for young offenders. However, the American states on the whole have not come close to the diversity of English institutions, and there are many states hardly touched by the tendency towards specialized establishments.

[1] Cmnd. 2742.

Unlike the English movement which produced the Borstal system, the American movement to establish reformatories for young offenders over 16 has not progressed far.[1] Today there are twenty reformatories for boys in eighteen states, taking offenders over 16 or 18, sometimes up to 26, but most of these are scarcely distinguishable from adult prisons. Many of them were established before 1900; most accommodate populations of from 700 to 2,000; and nearly all are built on the plan of a maximum security prison. Conditions in adult prisons are often more relaxed. The federal government and a handful of states, notably California, Michigan, New Jersey, and New York, have recently undertaken extensive efforts to provide proper specialized facilities for youthful offenders. In the forestry camp programme of the California Youth Authority there is a statewide network of institutions roughly comparable to the English Borstal system.

There are more than 350 institutions in the United States to which juvenile delinquents can be committed.[2] Apart from forestry camps in a number of states and diagnostic centres in about a dozen, these are mainly training or reform schools. A few are run locally by county or city governments or under private auspices. Each state usually has at least two publicly managed reform schools, one for each sex. The privately managed institutions, like the English Approved Schools, are licensed and inspected by state departments of social welfare.

In nine states the courts must commit a young offender to the custody of a 'Youth Authority' which then determines how his sentence will be served. In the others, courts commit young offenders to the custody of the state prison or department of correction, so that prison authorities determine the type of institution in which they shall be held. In about a dozen states there are diagnostic or reception centres where a youth can be studied for purposes of allocation. The most serious offenders are usually sent to a state prison, and the rest to a conservation or forestry work camp or a reformatory. In a few states there is a choice of several reformatories, as in New York, where besides one general reformatory for boys and two special institutions for girls aged 16 to 21 there is a vocational institution for tractable types, a special reformatory for those who are academically retarded, and another for especially difficult offenders.[3]

---

[1] Tappan, pp. 648–52.

[2] Blackburn, 'Institutions for Juvenile Delinquents', in *The Problem of Delinquency*, p. 687 (Glueck, ed. 1959).

[3] 2 New York State Committee for the 1960 White House Conference on Children and Youth, *A Decade of Progress*, pp. 94–99 (1960).

As in England, children of juvenile court age in the United States are usually kept out of the ordinary penal system. There is some attempt to provide the same sort of segregation while hearings are pending. Most states require by law that children shall not be housed in the county jails, and most large cities provide one or more separate detention homes along the lines of the English remand homes for children. However, in many places detention homes for juveniles are not available, and it has been estimated that 100,000 children from 7 to 17 years of age are held at least temporarily in the county jails each year.[1]

For a child who is found to be delinquent but not to have committed a specific offence, four types of disposition are generally authorized by law: (1) discharge, (2) probation, (3) placement in a foster home, and (4) commitment to a training or reform school.[2] An informal type of probation is also commonly achieved by continuing a case for a definite or indefinite period without entering a finding of delinquency. Where a child is committed to a training institution, it is often for the duration of his minority,[3] or the institution may be given the power to decide upon the date of release along with responsibility for maintaining supervision until the child reaches 21.

PAROLE AND AFTER-CARE

In the United States the term 'parole' refers to the conditional release of a prisoner at a time earlier than the expiration of his sentence (less automatic remission for good behaviour).[4] It normally entails supervision by a parole officer aimed at ensuring that the conditions of release are observed and guiding the prisoner in his readjustment to community life. This sort of conditional release is provided by law in every state and has assumed great importance in the American penal system.

In England the term 'parole' is usually used to refer to the temporary release of a prisoner for a short period of time—e.g. to attend the funeral of a relative.[5] The power of the prison authorities to release in

---

[1] National Conference on Juvenile Delinquency, *Report*, 29 (1954).

[2] Sussmann, pp. 45–50.

[3] Rubin, pp. 73–74. The Standard Juvenile Court Act (1959) provides that a transfer of legal custody cannot be for more than three years, with a provision for renewal which cannot extend beyond the child's minority.

[4] Tappan, pp. 709–50; Edwards, 'Parole', in Rubin *et al.*, pp. 543–68; Comment, 'Parole: A Critique of its Legal Foundations and Conditions', 38 *N.Y.U.L. Rev.* 702 (1963).   [5] Home Office, *Prisons and Borstals*, p. 37 (4th ed. 1960).

this manner is also often used to grant 'home leave' for five days to a prisoner nearing the end of a long sentence in order that he may make arrangements for settling down upon release. Parole in the American sense has not developed to any great extent in England, possibly because of the fact that English prison sentences tend to be considerably shorter than American ones.

The term 'after-care' in England refers to efforts to aid a former prisoner to readjust to free life, e.g. by helping him to find a home and a job.[1] In the ordinary case it is up to the prisoner whether he wants to accept this sort of aid. Formerly, such help was given by a local voluntary organization known as a Discharged Prisoners' Aid Society. Now all after-care work, both compulsory and voluntary, together with the work done within prisons by welfare officers, is in the process of being taken over by an enlarged and reorganized probation and after-care service.

The English Pattern

In most cases after-care is undertaken only after a prisoner's release at the end of his term (less good-conduct time). There are, however, in England certain categories of offenders who may be released 'on licence' before that time. In these cases after-care is compulsory, and this combination of conditional release with compulsory after-care results in a close approximation of the American parole system.

Thus children and young persons may be released from an Approved School when they are deemed ready for it, and the managers of the school are responsible for their after-care and supervision for a period of two years (or until age 21).[2]

Similarly, a young offender sentenced to Borstal training may be conditionally released at any time after he has served six months, but he is subject to compulsory after-care and supervision for up to two years from that time. After-care in these cases is undertaken by the Central After-Care Association, which uses probation officers to act as supervisors.[3]

An offender under 21 who has been sentenced to prison is entitled like any other prisoner to remission of one-third of his sentence for good behaviour; however, instead of unconditionally releasing the young person at that time, the Home Office may direct that he be

---

[1] Ibid., pp. 74–80.
[2] Home Office, *The Sentence of the Court*, pp. 16–17 (1964).
[3] Ibid., pp. 19–22.

released on licence subject to recall. All young offenders sentenced to three months or more are so released, after-care and supervision being compulsory for them.[1]

An habitual offender in England may be given a special sentence to corrective training or preventive detention, and in either case may earn remission of one-third of his sentence for good conduct. At that point he is released on licence to the supervision of the Central After-Care Association, which may work through the Probation Service or which may, in certain areas, undertake this work directly.[2]

In connexion with preventive detention, which entails a sentence of up to fourteen years, it used to be provided that the prison authorities could release an offender at the end of either two-thirds or five-sixths of his sentence. The prison regulations, in turn, provided for the establishment of Preventive Detention Advisory Boards to decide on who was qualified for early release. This came close to the sort of parole board operation which is common in the United States, but it was found to be unsatisfactory. Prisoners tended to regard the Boards' decisions as arbitrary, and this had a damaging effect on morale. As a result, the Boards were abolished in favour of a standard one-third remission for good conduct.[3] Preventive detention itself may soon be replaced by ordinary long-term imprisonment for habitual offenders.[4]

The American Pattern

In the United States release on parole is permitted in every state and in the federal system.[5] It is normally used only in cases of imprisonment for over one year and rarely where shorter periods in a local jail are involved. The time at which a prisoner becomes eligible to be considered for parole is fixed by law; and after that the question of whether he will actually be released is within the discretion of a parole

---

[1] Home Office, *The Sentence of the Court*, p. 23.   [2] Ibid., pp. 29, 31.

[3] Advisory Council on the Treatment of Offenders, *Report: Preventive Detention*, pp. 12–15 (H.M.S.O. 1963). The Chairman stated that 'our decision at the end is basically a hunch, and often a majority hunch at that'. A study showed that, in the long run, there was little significant difference in the rate of re-conviction between those held in prison and those released early.

[4] Cmnd. 2296, p. 10.

[5] In 1960, 56 per cent. of the 75,000 felony prisoners released from American prisons (both federal and state) were released on parole. State institutions used parole more extensively (in 60 per cent. of the releases) than did the federal institutions (in 34 per cent.). Federal Bureau of Prisons, *National Prisoner Statistics: Prisoners Released from State and Federal Institutions*, p. 14 (1960).

board. In most states the board interviews a prisoner at or near the time of his eligibility for consideration. It also receives information from a special staff in the prison who operate either under the prison authorities or the parole board itself. There is great diversity in the organization of parole boards.[1] In some jurisdictions, the board consists of full-time members, while in others it is composed of part-time members (such as a lawyer or psychiatrist) or *ex-officio* members (e.g. prison authorities, the Attorney-General, judges, etc.). In still others it consists of the governor assisted by an advisory board; and in a few states where prisons are locally managed each institution has its own parole authority. In most states the parole board is in charge of the staff who work with offenders after they are released. In the few states which have a Youth Authority, that authority is usually in charge of the parole of younger offenders in its custody, and the regular parole board deals only with adults. The federal parole board has three members specially appointed to administer the parole of young offenders.

Among parole boards in the United States there is great diversity in the criteria which guide decisions regarding release on parole. The result is that there are great differences from state to state in the proportion of prisoners who are granted parole. In 1960 Hawaii released 99 per cent. of its felony prisoners on parole, whereas Vermont released only 5 per cent. of such prisoners on parole.[2] The relatively low rate in some states indicates the broad discretion of the parole board exercised commonly upon the idea that only 'good risks' should be paroled. When a 'bad risk' is released upon termination of his sentence, he receives no community supervision.[3] In contrast with this view of parole as an exceptional act of grace bestowed upon the good, another view regards parole as a normal and necessary phase in the transition from imprisonment to freedom. Accepting this theory, the Model Penal Code would make parole mandatory for all released offenders.[4] The advocates of mandatory parole, although they realize that the rate of parole violations will undoubtedly increase, seek a more substantial victory in the decline in the rate of recidivism.[5]

In granting parole, a board may attach conditions to release, such as the proper and almost universal requirement that the offender

[1] Tappan, p. 720.

[2] Federal Bureau of Prisons, *National Prisoner Statistics: Prisoners Released from State and Federal Institutions*, p. 14 (1960).   [3] Tappan, pp. 723–4.

[4] Model Penal Code, § 6.09 A, and comment (Tent. Draft No. 5, 1956). See also § 305.12 and § 305.5.   [5] Tappan, p. 724.

report periodically to a parole supervisor. Some conditions, however, are more questionable, like the prohibition against getting married or operating a motor vehicle without the consent of the parole supervisor. Parole may be revoked at any time for violation of its conditions, with power to recall an offender to prison being lodged in the parole board. In only a few states does the law give the prisoner a right to a hearing before the board to contest the revocation of his parole, although in some he is given a hearing as a matter of grace.[1] Courts have occasionally granted writs of habeas corpus where the actions of parole boards in revoking parole were completely arbitrary, but on the whole the parole process has not been subjected to substantial judicial control.

---

[1] In at least sixteen states no parole revocation hearings are held. Several states by statute deny that a parolee has a right to the hearing. Even when a hearing is provided, the prevailing doctrine is that revocation is at the unhampered discretion of the board. *Model Penal Code*, § 305.21, comment (Tent. Draft No. 5, 1956). The federal parolee, by statute, has been accorded the right to a hearing before final revocation of his parole. See Note, 'Rights of a Federal Parolee Threatened with Parole Revocation', 1964 *Wash. U.L.Q.* 335.

PART II

THE STAGES OF CRIMINAL PROSECUTION

6

POLICE POWERS

In the first part of this book we described the machinery of criminal justice in England and the United States. In this part we observe that machinery in motion, comparing the successive stages through which a criminal prosecution passes in the two countries, starting with the stage when the police are still pressing their investigations.

Before discussing the specific powers of the English and American police with regard to the arrest, detention, interrogation, and search of suspects, it will be helpful to set that discussion in perspective with a few remarks on public attitudes towards police power in the two countries and on the nature of American as contrasted with English law on police powers.

THE PUBLIC DEBATE

There is at present in both countries considerable public concern over the question of how far police powers ought to extend. It is impossible to give a satisfactory account of all the reasons for this concern, but we may suggest a few.

Concern over police powers is a particular instance of a broader concern over criminal justice in general, reshaping some of the institutions discussed in Part I. The Anglo-American criminal trial itself is not likely to be altered too drastically by these pressures for reform, for it seems to be settled for the time being along lines generally considered satisfactory. But the two stages at either end of the trial—the police stage on the one hand, and the sentencing stage on the other—

are ripe for fundamental change. Both are areas of loosely controlled discretion, and there is mounting feeling that both ought to be subjected to stricter controls of some sort. Of the two, the police stage, involving a dramatic confrontation between the state and citizen, has attracted special public attention.

Public concern over police powers is stimulated also by the rising rate of crime in both countries. Because of it, the police claim that they need all of the powers they have traditionally possessed to cope with the problem. On the other hand, by focusing more attention on police practices, the increase of crime also illuminates instances of the abuse of police powers. This, in turn, encourages people who are temperamentally opposed to the police to claim that they ought to be more severely limited than they now are. Thus far, no causal relationship has been demonstrated between the limitations recently imposed by judicial decision upon police powers and the rising rate of crime, but there is certainly a coincidence in point of time between the two phenomena.

The search for abuse of police power has been pursued more vigorously in the United States than in England. Perhaps this is because there are more police abuses to be found in the United States, or possibly it is because England, with a generally homogeneous society, has been able to afford the luxury of thinking that civil liberties somehow take care of themselves. Civil liberties in the United States have long been viewed as a matter of rights actively asserted for the nation's minorities against the majority, as manifested in the 'Negro revolt' and the 'war against poverty'. Such movements are directly connected with the question of police power in America, since it is on the Negro and the indigent that police abuses are claimed most often to be practised.

Further, the United States has a tradition of empirical inquiry into police activity, which began during the Prohibition era. Over a hundred surveys into crime and the breakdown of law enforcement were launched at the time, resulting in a depressing picture of police malpractice. The report of the national Wickersham Commission in 1931 is generally credited with causing the United States Supreme Court, by way of reaction, to begin applying constitutional standards of criminal procedure to the states. In a sense, therefore, the current American preoccupation with police power is a fruition of the work of an earlier decade.

For these reasons, among others, concern with police power in the

United States is more intense than in England, and the opposing viewpoints more sharply antithetical. They are sharp enough for the Attorney-General to condemn 'blindness and bitterness' on both sides. The differences of viewpoint, he said, have become so corrosive as to be 'not only profitless, but damaging'.[1]

One vice in this sort of intemperate debate is that neither side pays much attention to the claims of the other. Critics of the police in the United States almost go so far as to say that crime is preferable to police action. They make the police seem at best a necessary evil. At the other extreme, supporters of the police almost regard their critics as people who would like to see society subverted. They feel that the social danger from widespread criminal activity is so great that all doubts about the extent of police power ought to be resolved in favour of the police.

On neither side are the assumptions entirely untenable. Critics of the police are right in stressing that a society is to be judged by the liberty it allows to the individual and that the police (and the courts) make mistakes which ought to be minimized; and they are soundly sceptical of the uses to which the criminal law is sometimes put. On the other hand, supporters of the police are right in stressing that widespread crime is itself a restraint on liberty which ought to be dealt with forcefully and efficiently, and that it is undesirable for criminals to escape through technicalities which are useless as safeguards to liberty and which only serve to make conviction a matter of chance.

The American disputants are apt to think in stereotypes, which make the claims of one side appear irrelevant or silly to the other. Each side tends to talk about a different case. To critics of police action, the typical police investigation consists of a collection of uniformed toughs, in a small sound-proof interrogation room, beating a false confession out of an abject, ignorant, poverty-stricken drifter. Supporters of the police are more likely to think in terms of an arrogant, astute, and wealthy member of the Mafia being patiently questioned by a high-minded plain-clothes agent in a car *en route* to a prompt hearing before the nearest magistrate, while the lawyer for the accused is arranging bail and thinking up a defence that will eventually result in acquittal.

This tendency to talk in extremes is also seen in American arguments on the question of the balance of advantage as between prosecution and defence. Critics of the police stress the resources in staff,

[1] *N.Y. Times*, 4 Dec. 1964, p. 23.

facilities, and money possessed by the prosecution. They speak of the 'awesome power' of government and, by contrast, of the isolation and poverty of a majority of defendants.[1] They point out that despite all the restrictions on police and prosecution, the vast majority of accused persons plead guilty. Supporters of the police stress the increasing education and sophistication of professional criminals. They speak of the obstacles put in the way of effective police investigation and the heavy burden of proof which the prosecution bears.[2] They point to the mounting rate of crime and the fall in the proportion of crimes cleared by arrest.

England has thus far managed to avoid the hysteria and melodramatic assumptions of much of the American argument. Lately, however, the Metropolitan Police Commission has taken to speaking of a growing feeling among the police 'that the odds are against them and that the barriers protecting the suspected or accused persons are being steadily reinforced',[3] and Lord Shawcross has urged that English law must stop considering criminal justice as a game in which the criminal has all the advantages.[4] Nevertheless, for the most part, the English argument has been tame. Even writers who criticize police activities and what they consider the complacent Establishment attitudes about law enforcement raise no serious doubts about the need for a compromise between the demands of liberty and the demands of order. Such writers do not reflexively oppose every proposal to increase police powers, nor do their opponents treat every criticism of the police as evidence of treason. Both sides are prepared to consider the prosecution and defence as each having advantages and disadvantages of an incommensurable sort, and to seek a fair balance between them.

While this kind of middle position is also common in the United States among large but inarticulate segments of the public, it tends to be under-represented in legal literature and in judicial decisions.

The cooler approach of the English is not an unmixed blessing. Strong passions and prejudices in the United States have resulted in great intensity of thought about the problem of police power, whereas among English lawyers there seems to be a lack of enthusiasm for rigorous thinking about police power.

[1] Goldstein, 'The State and the Accused: Balance of Advantage in Criminal Procedure', 69 *Yale L.J.* 1149 (1960).

[2] See, e.g., *United States* v. *Garsson*, 291 Fed. 646, 649 (S.D.N.Y. 1923) (L. Hand, J.).   [3] *N.Y. Times*, 17 July 1964, p. 3, col. 5.

[4] Shawcross, 'Police and Public in Great Britain', 51 *A.B.A.J.* 225, 227 (1965).

THE NATURE OF ENGLISH AND AMERICAN RULES REGULATING POLICE ACTIVITY

English law on police power is simpler than American law on the same subject in several respects.

The Judges' Rules

England has a concise and authoritative statement of some of the essentials of police conduct in the 'Judges' Rules'. These regulate police interrogation by outlining the circumstances in which suspects must be cautioned as to their rights before being questioned, and those in which they may not be questioned at all. They were first promulgated in 1912 when conflicting judicial decisions led the police to ask the Queen's Bench judges to agree on proper methods of interrogation which would insure the admission into evidence of confessions legitimately obtained. They were added to in 1918, revised in 1930 and again in 1964, and they are issued with the approval of the Home Office, thus making them in effect administrative regulations for all police forces in England.[1] While they do not purport to cover police activity in general and while they are not entirely free of ambiguity, they provide in compact and generally clear form a practical guide to police conduct in one of its central and crucial aspects.

No close equivalent to the Judges' Rules exists anywhere in the United States. Instead, the rules governing police conduct are scattered through statutes, administrative regulations, judicial decisions, and official and unofficial manuals of bewildering variety and complexity and awesome bulk. The result is that police officers in the front line of law enforcement are too often unsure of what the law is with respect to their duties and responsibilities.[2]

---

[1] Abrahams (1964).

[2] Manuals of instruction issued by police departments for the training and instruction of their officers are frequently inadequate. Their analysis of the law on such typically difficult problems as arrest and search and seizure tends to be over-generalized and imprecise. See LaFave, p. 211 n. 14. Even large metropolitan departments are seldom provided with legally trained personnel of their own, to construct and revise the manuals. See LaFave & Remington, 'Controlling the Police: The Judge's Role in Making and Reviewing Law Enforcement Decisions', 63 *Mich. L. Rev.* 987, 1005, 1007–8 and n. 91 (1965). Opinions of appellate courts, even if available to police officers, may be of little assistance in informing them of current law, because they are typically not written in a form understandable by laymen. The Attorney-General has asserted that the result of confusing and uncoordinated judicial opinions leads to a situation where police officers, district attorneys, and judges are unsure of what the law is with respect to their duties. See *N.Y. Times*, 5 Aug. 1965, p. 1, col. 3.

Written Constitutions

England operates without a written constitution, whereas all of the American states and the federal government work within the framework of written constitutions, amendable only by special procedures which are different and much more difficult than those required to change ordinary legislation. State constitutions all embody a 'bill of rights', limiting to some extent the manner in which the state may enforce its criminal law. Similarly, law enforcement by the federal government is limited by the Bill of Rights which was added to the federal constitution in 1791.

The provisions of the federal Bill of Rights which bear on criminal procedure are as follows:

AMENDMENT 4

The right of the people to be secure in their persons, houses, papers, and effects, against unreasonable searches and seizures, shall not be violated, and no Warrants shall issue, but upon probable cause, supported by Oath or affirmation, and particularly describing the place to be searched, and the persons or things to be seized.

AMENDMENT 5

No person shall be held to answer for a capital, or otherwise infamous crime, unless on a presentment or indictment of a Grand Jury, except in cases arising in the land or naval forces, or in the Militia, when in actual service in time of War or public danger; nor shall any person be subject for the same offence to be twice put in jeopardy of life or limb; nor shall be compelled in any criminal case to be a witness against himself, nor be deprived of life, liberty, or property, without due process of law; nor shall private property be taken for public use, without just compensation.

AMENDMENT 6

In all criminal prosecutions, the accused shall enjoy the right to a speedy and public trial, by an impartial jury of the State and district wherein the crime shall have been committed, which district shall have been previously ascertained by law, and to be informed of the nature and cause of the accusation; to be confronted with the witnesses against him; to have compulsory process for obtaining witnesses in his favor, and to have the Assistance of Counsel for his defence.

AMENDMENT 8

Excessive bail shall not be required, nor excessive fines imposed, nor cruel and unusual punishments inflicted.

There are comparable guarantees, although with variations, exceptions, and additions, in each of the state constitutions. They are not merely declarations of principle, but provisions which confer legal rights. They are enforceable by the courts, even as against acts of the Legislature. The state provisions have not, on the whole, been as broadly interpreted or stringently enforced as the federal provisions, but even so, they add to the judicial control of police power a dimension which is lacking in England.

Dual Sovereignty

England does not suffer from the complications of dual sovereignty. It has a single system of courts administering a single body of substantive and procedural criminal law, and an integrated system of police forces. In the United States, on the other hand, each of the fifty states has its own body of law, its own system of courts, and its own set of police forces. Superimposed upon these are a body of federal criminal law, a system of federal courts, and a set of federal police forces. The result is that in every state there are two sets of criminal courts, two bodies of criminal law, and two sets of police forces governed by separate rules. American states are limited in their manner of law enforcement not only by their own constitutions, but by the federal constitution as well. They are not directly bound by the federal Bill of Rights, which applies of its own force only to activities of the federal government, but they are bound by Article 1, Section 10 of the original constitution which contains a prohibition against bills of attainder and *ex post facto* laws, and, far more important, by the Fourteenth Amendment, added in 1868. That Amendment contains these words: 'No State shall make or enforce any law which shall abridge the privileges of immunities of citizens of the United States; nor shall any State deprive any person of life, liberty, or property without due process of law; nor deny to any person within its jurisdiction the equal protection of the laws.'

In consequence of this provision, federal courts have power to review state criminal proceedings in order to determine whether 'due process of law' was denied to an accused. On this foundation a large body of precedent has been built by the Supreme Court of the United States. The tendency of the Court has been to find in the Fourteenth Amendment more severe limitations on police powers than most of the state courts are willing to find in that Amendment or in their own law. Justices of the Supreme Court have disagreed on whether the

Fourteenth Amendment should be interpreted to apply to the states all of the specific guarantees of the Bill of Rights, which applies of its own force only to the federal government.[1] A majority in all cases thus far have held that it should not be so interpreted as a general proposition. But in many particular instances, the Court has held that the states are limited by the Fourteenth Amendment in precisely the same way that the federal government is limited by specific provisions of the Bill of Rights. In particular, the states have been obliged to observe the whole of the Fourth Amendment on search and seizure,[2] the Fifth Amendment privilege against compulsory self-incrimination,[3] the Sixth Amendment guarantee of the assistance of counsel[4] and of confrontation of witnesses,[5] and the Eighth Amendment prohibition against cruel and unusual punishments.[6]

Fairness v. Constitutional Rights

One should not conclude that nothing more than the Judges' Rules, case law, and statutes limit the English police. They are limited in a very real sense by the informal opinion of the judges and of the public.[7] Pressures of this sort create a type of control which hardly exists in the United States because of the tendency there to rely so heavily on constitutional restrictions. Even the powers of the British Parliament are limited by principles which are not written down and not judicially enforced, but which are recognized as authoritative by the people as a whole.[8] It is hard to imagine, to take only one example, that any Parliament in Britain would in peacetime consider itself constitutionally capable of abolishing the writ of habeas corpus.[9] These kinds of pressures and conventions are potent in England, and their result is often not much different from what would be reached on the basis of a judicially enforceable bill of rights.

[1] Black, pp. 77–80 (1963); Freund, pp. 45–51; Brennan, 'The Bill of Rights and the States', 36 *N.Y.U.L. Rev.* 761 (1961); Frankfurter, 'Memorandum on "Incorporation" of the Bill of Rights into the Due Process Clause of the Fourteenth Amendment', 78 *Harv. L. Rev.* 746 (1965); Henkin, ' "Selective Incorporation" in the Fourteenth Amendment', 73 *Yale L. J.* 74 (1963).

[2] *Mapp* v. *Ohio*, 367 U.S. 643 (1961).

[3] *Malloy* v. *Hogan*, 378 U.S. 1 (1964). The Fourteenth Amendment also prohibits comment by the prosecutor on the defendant's failure to testify. *Griffin* v. *California*, 380 U.S. 609 (1965).

[4] *Gideon* v. *Wainwright*, 372 U.S. 335 (1963).

[5] *Pointer* v. *Texas*, 380 U.S. 400 (1965).

[6] *Robinson* v. *California*, 370 U.S. 660 (1962).

[7] Devlin (1960), pp. 12–13, 22–23.

[8] Goodhart, p. 55.   [9] Ibid., p. 57.

While England sometimes tolerates interferences with liberty 'in circumstances where it is inconceivable that the courts in America would stand aside',[1] there is little doubt that, generally speaking, current English law is in keeping with principles 'so rooted in the traditions and conscience of [the] people as to be ranked as fundamental'.[2] These words are the traditional interpretation of what the Fourteenth Amendment imposes on the American states. 'Due process of law', in other words, simply requires a state to observe 'fundamental fairness',[3] following procedures which are 'of the very essence of a scheme of ordered liberty'.[4] Since England also aims at a scheme of ordered liberty, there should be little difference between the effects of English constitutional convention and of American constitutional law. But in fact, the Supreme Court of the United States has interpreted 'fundamental fairness' to be more demanding than the English sense of fair play. This is obviously not because Americans have sensitive consciences while Englishmen have blunt ones, but seems to be due primarily to the fact that American judges are expounding a written constitution.

A constitutional text affects the quality of thought about civil liberties.[5] It stimulates fine distinctions and litigation in which such distinctions can be drawn. It encourages judges to view their work as embodying a measure of national policy, vesting them with authority and responsibility to be bold in their pursuit of justice.[6] Sometimes, however, it leads Americans to formulate problems of police power in terms that seem far-fetched in England. On the face of it, the Bill of Rights touches the police only in the Fourth Amendment, but the Supreme Court has recently held in a landmark decision that the Fifth Amendment's prohibition against a person's being compelled in any criminal case to be a witness against himself comes into play as soon as a man is taken into police custody and imposes severe limitations upon the power of the police to interrogate him.[7]

Concentration upon a text may also help to explain an American rule which presents one of the most significant contrasts between English and American law regarding police powers—that which holds that courts are obliged to exclude any evidence obtained,

---

[1] Street, p. 285.   [2] *Snyder* v. *Massachusetts*, 291 U.S. 97, 105 (1934).
[3] *Lisenba* v. *California*, 314 U.S. 219, 236 (1941).
[4] *Palko* v. *Connecticut*, 302 U.S. 319, 325 (1937).
[5] See Street, pp. 283–9.
[6] Cahn, 'The Parchment Barriers', Winter 1962–3, *The American Scholar*, p. 21.
[7] *Miranda* v. *Arizona*, 34 U.S.L. Week 4521 (U.S. 14 June 1966).

directly or indirectly, as a consequence of constitutionally unlawful arrest, interrogation, search, or seizure. We shall discuss the exclusionary rule more fully in connexion with the specific police practices on which it bears, but for the moment, two points should be noticed. First, the rule does not allow the trial judge any discretion: he cannot admit illegally obtained evidence on the ground that it is in the interests of justice to do so, but must exclude it. Second, if such evidence is improperly admitted and the accused is convicted, his conviction will be reversed.[1] While an American appellate court feels more justified in reversing a conviction than does an appellate court in England because of the possibility of a new trial, the point here is that in a constitutional case an American court does not ask whether the miscarriage of justice was substantial or whether any other verdict was possible; it reverses without further inquiry. In the respects just noted, the American rule differs markedly from the limited exclusionary doctrine which the English courts follow with regard to improperly obtained confessions.

English law contains the seeds of an exclusionary doctrine, for where the accused's confession is offered in evidence, an English court will not allow it to be used unless it is shown to have been made voluntarily.[2] This is a common-law rule of evidence (and as such it has been essentially adopted in every American state quite apart from constitutional considerations) based upon the idea that involuntary statements are untrustworthy. The rule excluding involuntary confessions because they are unreliable differs significantly from the rule excluding illegally seized physical evidence. When objects have been unlawfully obtained, there is usually no question of their probative value. But in England as well as in the United States there are grounds for excluding evidence which go beyond the common-law rule on involuntary confessions. These grounds are irregularities in police conduct, warranting the exclusion of evidence not because it is unreliable but because it has been unlawfully obtained. The rationale is found in the Judges' Rules which are said to be an expression of a general power in the English judges to exclude any evidence which is

---

[1] The practice of the Supreme Court is to reverse any conviction obtained by violation of the defendant's constitutional rights. In one case considered by the Court after its decision in Mapp, the state argued that the effect of admitting illegally seized evidence caused only harmless error not sufficient for reversal. This issue was not decided by the Court since the majority found the error prejudicial. *Fahy* v. *Connecticut*, 375 U.S. 85 (1963).

[2] Abrahams, pp. 7–9, traces the leading cases.

unfairly or oppressively obtained.[1] In principle, a judge can reject evidence obtained unfairly even though there is no rule which specifically prohibits its admission, just as he can admit evidence even though there was some technical breach of the Rules in obtaining it. This broad power would extend as a matter of logic to the fruits of an unlawful search and seizure, as well as to confessions unfairly obtained,[2] but the power seems to be so narrowly exercised with respect to physical objects that England may be considered in practice to have wholly rejected any exclusionary rule with respect to unlawfully seized evidence.[3]

With this background, we now turn to a fuller discussion of specific limitations on police power in England and the United States.

ARREST

The English law of arrest is less explicit and detailed than American law on the subject, being almost entirely the product of sporadic suits for false imprisonment and of prosecutions for resisting arrest. There are no other occasions on which questions concerning powers of arrest can be brought into issue, for the illegality of an arrest does not affect a court's jurisdiction over the defendant. This rule likewise obtains in the United States; but the question of the lawfulness of an arrest can also be raised in the context of the rule requiring the exclusion of illegally acquired evidence. It often happens that evidence is suppressed because it was obtained incident to an arrest which the courts find to be unlawful. The adoption of an exclusionary rule has therefore meant that American courts have had far more occasions than courts in England to pass on questions regarding the law of arrest.

Warrants of Arrest

In both countries, a warrant ordering the arrest of the person named in it can be issued by any superior judge, but it is usually issued by a justice of the peace or by one of the professional magistrates who

---

[1] Devlin (1960), p. 35; see Abrahams, pp. 10–12.

[2] Smith, 'The New Judges' Rules—a Lawyer's View', 1964 *Crim. L. Rev.* (*Eng.*) 176, 182; Williams, 'Police Interrogation Privileges and Limitations under Foreign Law—England', 52 *J. Crim. L., C. & P.S.* 50, 51–52 (1961).

[3] See *Kuruma* v. *The Queen*, [1955] A.C. 197 (P.C.) (E. Afr.); Williams, 'The Exclusionary Rule under Foreign Law—England', 52 *J. Crim. L., C. & P.S.* 272 (1961); cf. Martin, 'The Exclusionary Rule under Foreign Law—Canada', 52 *J. Crim. L., C. & P.S.* 271 (1961).

have replaced justices in the larger cities. Formerly in England a warrant issued by a justice could be executed only within the area of his jurisdiction, unless it was 'backed' (endorsed) by a justice of the district in which the defendant was found; but now the warrant can be executed anywhere in the country.[1] While some American states still follow the older English idea of requiring a warrant issued by a justice of the peace in one community to be endorsed by another if it is to be executed in a different community, other American states dispense with this requirement so long as the warrant is served within the state borders;[2] similarly, the warrant of a United States Commissioner, who is the federal equivalent of a state or English magistrate, can be executed anywhere within the United States. But a warrant issued in one American state has no force in another. To bring a fugitive across state lines requires a procedure akin to extradition between independent countries.[3]

In England a warrant is obtained by presenting an 'information' to a justice to the effect that the accused has committed an offence or is reasonably suspected of having committed one. The information must be in writing, and not in merely formal or general terms.[4] American procedure is similar.[5] The Fourth Amendment to the federal constitution provides that 'no warrants shall issue, but upon probable cause, supported by oath or affirmation, and particularly describing . . . the persons or things to be seized'. 'Probable cause' means the same as 'reasonable grounds to believe that an offence has been committed', which sounds like something more than the English concept of 'reasonable grounds of suspicion'.

In theory the requirement of 'probable cause' might make it more difficult to obtain warrants in the United States, but in fact they are obtained more easily than in England, chiefly because of a difference between the two countries in the atmosphere surrounding the issuance of warrants. In both countries, the procedure for obtaining warrants is supposed to be a judicial check on police power, but in the United States, this is largely a fiction. In rural districts justices of the peace

---

[1] Kenny, p. 562.   [2] Orfield (1947), p. 13; Puttkammer, p. 62.
[3] See Puttkammer, pp. 160–2.   [4] Devlin (1960), p. 70.
[5] The information in the warrant application must be sufficiently detailed for the judicial officer to make an independent determination of probable cause. *Giordenello* v. *United States*, 357 U.S. 480 (1958). The Supreme Court has recently held that this case has a constitutional foundation and is applicable to the states under the Fourteenth Amendment. *Aguilar* v. *United States*, 378 U.S. 108 (1964). For a general discussion of the issuance procedure, see Puttkammer, pp. 60–61.

are on the whole much inferior to those in England, and are unlikely to assert themselves against the wishes of the police. In urban districts American magistrates generally have abdicated their authority over warrants to their clerks (who are not, as in England, legally trained) signing anything the clerks present or even leaving warrants signed in blank with them. In a city of any size, the issuing of warrants is likely to be a specialized function,[1] with a particular magistrate being designated for a period of time to hear applications, and a clerk assigned to look over complaints before their presentation to the magistrate. Even in this situation, however, there seems to be a tendency on the part of most magistrates to leave decisions to their clerks.

In America there is also a district attorney whose advice the police are likely to seek before obtaining a warrant of arrest. A few states even provide that a warrant may be issued by the district attorney himself or that his approval is required prior to its issuance by a magistrate. This generally reflects the situation even in states which do not have such provisions, for the American warrant serves chiefly as a symbol of the district attorney's decision to prosecute. In some cases, it precedes arrest, but in many, the accused has already been arrested without a warrant, and the warrant is subsequently obtained as a matter of form to reflect the prosecutor's confirmation of police action.[2]

In England warrants are used only in a very small percentage of cases[3] and then only after a genuine exercise of judicial discretion. Partly this is due to the high quality of the English magistracy and to the English tradition of playing by the rules. But also the English magistrate has two collateral decisions to make on an application for an arrest warrant which the American magistrate does not and which force him to think carefully about what he is doing. First, he must decide whether or not to endorse the warrant for bail. We shall come back to this in the next chapter, but here the point to notice is that while in the United States questions of bail do not ordinarily arise until after the accused is arrested, in England they are built into the warrant procedure. Second, in England a summons is frequently used in lieu of arrest, while this is generally not so in the United States. Hence, in England, even in the case of a serious crime, justices may deny a

---

[1] Puttkammer, pp. 59–60.

[2] For a study of the prosecutor's control over the issuance of arrest warrants, see Miller & Tiffany, 'Prosecutor Dominance of the Warrant Decision: A Study of Current Practices', 1964 *Wash. U.L.Q.* 1.   [3] Kenny, pp. 561, 567.

warrant on the ground that a summons will suffice to insure the defendant's appearance. This sort of choice encourages the justices to take their task seriously. In America, where virtually all the magistrates do is confirm the police in their decisions to arrest, they are prone to regard the issuance of warrants as too unimportant to bother about.

Arrest without Warrant

In both countries there is some pressure on the police to seek a warrant of arrest, if they have time to do so, even when one is not necessary.[1] A warrant will protect the officer against an action for assault or false imprisonment—a matter of some importance in England, where the fear of civil suit is thought to have some effect on police conduct. In the United States, where the exclusionary doctrine is in effect, a warrant will improve the chance of admission of evidence obtained in the course of what might otherwise be an arrest of doubtful legality. Nevertheless, in neither country is there any compulsion on the police to seek a warrant if arrest can be made without one.

Citizen Arrests

In both countries not only police officers, but private citizens as well, can arrest without a warrant in certain circumstances.[2] (A private citizen can also apply to have a warrant issued, although it ordinarily must be executed by a policeman.) Much of the law on this subject survives from a time before the rise of police forces. The common law then obliged a private citizen to report to the authorities any felony which came to his notice, and his failure to do so was made the offence of 'misprision of felony'. Furthermore, the common law required a private citizen to arrest any person who in his presence committed a felony, or, broadly speaking, a dangerous breach of the peace; and in addition, it permitted him to arrest any person whom he reasonably suspected of having committed a felony, provided the felony was actually committed. This is still basically the law in England, supplemented by a few modern statutes which extend a citizen's right to arrest for particular crimes and in particular circumstances. Most American statutes retain the common-law principles; a few states have extended the citizen's power of arrest to include cases

---

[1] LaFave, pp. 36–51, classifies recurring situations in which warrants are used even though not strictly required by the law.
[2] Orfield (1947), pp. 15–17.

of reasonable belief that a felony was committed, although it was not; and an equal number have narrowed it to require actual commission of the felony by the person arrested.

Police Arrests

In both countries a police officer is in a more favoured position to make an arrest than a member of the general public. A citizen who may be in error as to the facts of a case is ill-advised to attempt an arrest, for he may find himself liable for damages if he is mistaken. Even apart from that danger, however, most citizens are content to leave law enforcement in the hands of professional police forces. Sometimes, indeed, they refuse outright to co-operate with the police. In both countries there is a tendency to treat crime as a spectator sport. In the United States sporadic efforts have been made to reverse this trend by the patrolling of the big city neighbourhoods at night by groups of local citizens.

For a policeman arresting without warrant in either country, the distinction between a felony and a misdemeanour is of prime importance.[1] In both England and the United States, an arrest may generally be made for a felony whenever a police officer has reasonable grounds to believe that a felony has been committed and that the person he arrests has committed it. Some American statutes preclude tort liability on the part of a police officer whenever the arrested felon turns out to be guilty, seeming to say that he can arrest anyone who has in fact committed a felony, whether he had reasonable grounds to believe so or not. However, the Fourth Amendment, which prohibits the issuance of warrants without probable cause, has often been assumed to mean also that arrest without a warrant must be justified by probable cause, i.e. reasonable grounds to believe that an offence has been committed. If this is so, no state can constitutionally authorize arrest on any lesser ground.

With regard to misdemeanours, the general English rule is that an officer can arrest without a warrant only if a breach of the peace is committed in his presence. What constitutes a breach of the peace, however, has never been authoritatively defined; it may mean any crime or it may mean an actual public disturbance. A number of statutes have enlarged the English policeman's powers with respect to particular offences, and in London a constable may by statute arrest any 'loose', 'idle', or 'disorderly' person whom he reasonably

[1] Devlin (1960), pp. 70–71; LaFave, pp. 17–21; Orfield, pp. 14–15.

suspects of having committed any indictable offence.[1] In the United States most state statutes provide that an officer can arrest for any misdemeanour committed in his presence, although a few say that the misdemeanour must be a breach of the peace in the literal sense. A few others allow a policeman to arrest whenever he has reasonable grounds to believe that a misdemeanour has been committed, sometimes requiring him to show that the arrest was reasonably necessary in the circumstances.[2] As in England, the general rules are often supplemented by specific legislation giving greater powers with regard to particular offences.

In May 1965 the Criminal Law Revision Committee of England rendered a report recommending the abolition of the distinction between felonies and misdemeanours, particularly because of the obscurity and confusion caused by those terms in the law of arrest.[3] If its recommendations are enacted into law, the essential distinction will be between 'arrestable' offences—meaning those which carry a maximum penalty of five years or more—and non-arrestable offences —those carrying a lesser maximum penalty. The basic rule will then be as follows: 'The powers of summary arrest conferred by the following subsections shall apply to offences for which the sentence is fixed by law or for which a person may under or by virtue of any enactment be sentenced to imprisonment for a term of five years, and to attempts to commit any such offence; and in this Act (including any amendment made by this Act in any other enactment) 'arrestable offence' means any such offence or attempt.'[4]

Advising the Accused of the Charge against Him

In England the rule is firmly established that on an arrest without a warrant, the accused must be told of the substance of the charge against him, unless it is self-evident or unless he makes it practically impossible for this to be done, as by attacking the policeman or running away.[5] If he is not informed at the time of arrest, he has an action

---

[1] See *Bowditch* v. *Balchin*, 14 J.P. 449 (Ex. 1850), construing a provision in the City of London Police Act, 1839, 2 & 3 Vict. cap. xciv, § 18.

[2] For example, in Wisconsin an officer may arrest without a warrant for a misdemeanour committed outside his presence if he has reasonable grounds to believe the suspect committed the offence and that he will not otherwise be apprehended, or personal or property damage will result unless the suspect is immediately arrested. *Wis. Stat. Ann.* § 954.03 (1) (1958).

[3] Criminal Law Revision Committee, *Seventh Report*, Cmnd. 2659, pp. 3–7 (1965).   [4] Ibid., p. 24.

[5] Devlin (1960), p. 71; Kenny, p. 566; Street, pp. 14–17.

for damages for false imprisonment. He even has an action if the arrest cannot be justified on the ground claimed for it at the time, even though it later turns out to be justifiable on some other ground.[1]

American police practice does not ordinarily include telling the accused of the reason for his arrest at the time the arrest is made. Whereas the English police delay making an arrest until they have built up a case against the accused, the American police until very recently tended to arrest at an earlier stage, when they were not yet in a position to justify a charge.[2] They then completed their case after arrest, often on the basis of admissions made by the accused; but if no case could be made out, they released the accused. It was once estimated that one out of every three persons arrested was released in this manner.[3] Recent rulings by the Supreme Court have gone a long distance toward discouraging such unlawful arrests, but it is probable that some are still being made.

Summons instead of Arrest

In England a magistrate has discretion to issue a summons instead of a warrant for arrest, and in most situations he prefers the summons. In theory he can use a summons even if the charge is murder, and recent statistics indicate that a summons is, in fact, used even in many serious cases, although not in homicide cases.[4]

The summons is widely used in the United States for securing the appearance of traffic law violators, but has rarely been used in other types of cases; twenty-eight states allow it to be generally substituted for a warrant of arrest, but even in these, it is almost entirely unused. It is a tradition, based on nothing more than force of habit, to issue a warrant of arrest as a matter of course, even where a summons could just as well be used. However, a landmark experiment in the use of the summons has recently been launched in New York City.[5] Under it an offender is taken to a police station, but instead of being charged and held in custody to appear before a magistrate, he is interviewed by volunteer workers who determine the likelihood of his appearing for trial if a summons is issued to him. On the basis of their recommendations, the police decide whether to release the offender on summons or not. In English terms this is not a summons at all, for

[1] *Christie* v. *Leachinsky*, [1947] A.C. 573 (1946).
[2] LaFave, p. 188; Orfield (1947), pp. 35–36.
[3] Hall, 'The Law of Arrest in Relation to Contemporary Social Problems', 3 *U. Chi. L. Rev.* 345, 359, 362 (1936).   [4] LaFave, p. 170 n. 7.
[5] The project is described in Freed & Wald, pp. 72–73.

the accused has in the first instance been arrested. It comes closer to the English practice—entirely unknown in America—by which the police desk officer, upon a person's being arrested without a warrant, may release him on bail, and must do so if he cannot be brought before a magistrate within twenty-four hours.[1] The American experiment grows out of and is closely related to the movement to reform bail practices and to decrease the number of persons who are kept in jail while awaiting trial.

DETENTION

Neither English nor American law specifically recognizes a distinction between 'arrest' and 'detention'. The traditional view in both countries is that the police have no power to detain anyone for the purpose of questioning unless they arrest him. Police officers are free to ask questions of anyone, and to request whatever co-operation they need, but whenever they take a person into custody or restrict his full liberty of movement, their action either constitutes a lawful arrest, sustainable by reference to the law concerning their powers of arrest without warrant, or a false imprisonment.

In both countries the police are not very happy with this view. There are two situations in which they claim that without making an arrest, they ought to have the power to compel a person to stand still and listen to, if not answer, questions. The first is the situation where a policeman has his suspicions aroused by the general appearance and actions of a person, usually in a street or other public place and usually at night. He is not prepared to take the definitive step of arrest, but he would like to question the suspect as to what he is doing. The second situation is where the police would like to take a suspect to the station house for questioning. They think he has some connexion with a crime they are investigating, but cannot be sure until they have spoken to him. They might ask their questions on the street or in private premises, but they would prefer to take him to a station house where he would be less likely to be distracted and where he could be held while they checked his answers.

On-the-Street Detention

With regard to the first situation, there are traces in England of a common-law doctrine which authorizes watchmen to demand that

---

[1] Magistrates' Court Act, 1952, 15 & 16 Geo. VI and 1 Eliz. II, c. 55, § 38 (1).

suspicious persons abroad at night give an explanation of what they are doing. However, no modern English decision deals with this doctrine, and it is widely assumed that, apart from special statutes conferring it, constables today have no such power.[1] Nor could a suspect's refusal to stop and answer ordinarily furnish the constable with grounds for arresting him.[2]

In the United States a small number of state courts have upheld the lawfulness of on-the-street detention,[3] while an almost equal number have denied it. There is little doubt that everywhere the police in fact stop and question suspects whom they would not have power to arrest, but in most states it is uncertain whether this practice is lawful.

Sometimes specific statutes give policemen power to detain people temporarily for a particular purpose. In both England and the United States, for example, statutes allow the police to stop the driver of a motor vehicle for the purpose of examining his operator's licence.[4] In England there are also a number of statutes, applicable to particular cities, which give the police power to stop people or vehicles on reasonable suspicion that they are carrying stolen goods.[5] The first and most important of these statutes is the Metropolitan Police Act, 1839, Section 66, which allows the London police to 'stop, search and detain . . . any person who may be reasonably suspected of having or conveying in any manner any thing stolen or unlawfully obtained'.[6] Section 69 of the Act requires the detained person to be taken before a magistrate. The provisions are superfluous with regard to thefts that constitute felonies, as to which there is power to arrest on reasonable suspicion anyway. It seems that the point of the statute was to authorize arrests without warrant for what in England may be only a misdemeanour—unlawfully obtaining or possessing stolen goods in

[1] Devlin (1960), p. 68; Williams, 'Police Detention and Arrest Privileges under Foreign Law—England', 51 *J. Crim. L., C. & P.S.* 413 (1960).

[2] Williams, op. cit., p. 414.

[3] Remington, 'The Law Relating to "On the Street" Detention, Questioning and Frisking of Suspected Persons and Police Arrest Privileges in General', 51 *J. Crim L., C. & P.S.* 386, 391 (1960); Comment, 39 *N.Y.U. L. Rev.* 1093 (1964). Several states have passed 'stop and frisk' statutes which permit on-the-street detention without probable cause. Comment, 39 *N.Y.U. L. Rev.* 1093 (1964); 78 *Harv. L. Rev.* 473 (1964).

[4] Remington, op. cit., p. 390; Williams, op cit., p. 148; Note, 'The Driver's Licence "Display" Statute: Problems Arising from its Application', 1960 *Wash. U. L. Q.* 279.

[5] Williams, op. cit., p. 148; see Whitaker, p. 57.

[6] 2 & 3 Vict., c. 47.

circumstances not amounting to larceny. But Section 66 has at times been made the basis for the London police stopping and questioning people at night in circumstances where there is no suspicion of theft at all, but only something in someone's dress or demeanour or in what he carries, to raise the possibility that he may not be a harmless citizen.[1]

Most citizens so stopped probably do not have the prickly anti-police reaction that characterizes some Americans, and are glad to think that their city is so well patrolled. Nevertheless, if the American exclusionary doctrine applied, the police might be challenged more often. Complaints about use of the act have been frequent enough so that Parliament is unwilling to extend like powers to cities which do not now have them. As a result, most large cities are without such special powers.

In the United States a Uniform Arrest Act (proposed in 1941) provides that a police officer may stop any person abroad whom he reasonably suspects of committing a crime, and may demand his name, address, business abroad, and where he is going. Any person so questioned whose answers are unsatisfactory may be detained for further questions and investigated for a period of two hours or less, at which time he must either be charged with a crime and arrested or else released.[2] This Act, however, has been adopted in only three states: Delaware, New Hampshire, and Rhode Island. Massachusetts and Hawaii have roughly analogous provisions, and as we have indicated, several other states by judicial decision allow the stopping and questioning of vaguely suspicious persons. A similar statute was enacted in New York in 1964[3]—the so-called 'stop and frisk' law, under which a police officer may stop any person abroad in a public place whom he reasonably suspects of committing a felony or one of a group of serious misdemeanours, and may demand his name and address and an explanation of his actions. Unlike the Uniform Arrest Act, the New York law says nothing about detaining the suspect while his answers are verified; and unlike the London Act, it does not confer the equivalent of a power to arrest. These limitations are quite deliberate, for it was feared that anything broader would be unconstitutional. Indeed, the constitutionality of even the limited power

---

[1] See Rolph (1962), pp. 11–48, 195–6.
[2] Uniform Arrest Act, § 2, Warner, 'The Uniform Arrest Act', 28 *Va. L. Rev.* 135 (1942).
[3] *N.Y. Code Crim. Proc.* 180 (*a*).

granted is not entirely clear, since the statute allows interference with liberty on less than 'probable cause'.

When the English speak of 'reasonable suspicion', as in the London Act, they are referring to grounds which a reasonable man would regard as justifying a decision to arrest. Americans use the formulae 'probable cause' or 'reasonable grounds to believe' for that situation. 'Reasonable grounds to suspect' in the United States refers to a state of mind which would not generally be thought to justify an arrest. The constitutional argument against the New York law assumes that the Fourth Amendment requires all interference with liberty of movement to be justified by a degree of belief strong enough to warrant arrest. 'Reasonable suspicion' in its American sense is not enough. Whether the Fourth Amendment requires this interpretation has not been clearly settled by the Supreme Court of the United States.[1]

A second section of the New York law provides that when he has stopped a person for questioning, a policeman may, if he reasonably suspects he is in danger of life or limb, search for a dangerous weapon (concealment of which is a crime in New York). A similar provision is contained in Section 3 of the Uniform Arrest Act, which requires, however, that the officer reasonably *believe* himself to be in danger. Other states which have recognized a right to stop and question usually also recognize the right of the officer to search the suspect for a concealed weapon.

Until recently there was no explicit English authority for searching a suspect who was thought to be armed, although it had been claimed that this power was so obviously necessary that it would not be denied by the courts.[2] A Bill recently passed now makes it an offence to have 'a firearm or imitation firearm with intent to commit an indictable offence, to resist arrest or prevent the arrest of another' and gives the police power to stop and search persons in public places on reasonable suspicion that they are in unlawful possession of a firearm. Given the English meaning of 'reasonable suspicion' this last provision operates to extend the usual grounds of arrest in felony cases to a particular misdemeanour. In the United States the same words would be interpreted to allow the police to act on grounds which normally

---

[1] See *Rios* v. *United States*, 364 U.S. 253 (1960); Remington, op. cit., pp. 389–92. The constitutional problems involved in drafting legislation to permit police to detain and question or stop and frisk on 'reasonable suspicion' are discussed in Foote, 'The Fourth Amendment: Obstacle or Necessity in the Law of Arrest?', 51 *J. Crim. L., C. & P.S.* 402 (1960).

[2] Williams, op. cit., p. 418.

would not justify their arresting even had a felony been concerned. As we shall see in a later section of this chapter, allowing the police to search on grounds which would not justify arrest has been held in the United States to violate the Fourth Amendment.

Detention for Questioning

Under Section 2 of the Uniform Arrest Act or its equivalent in five American states, the police may detain people for a few hours while they are questioned and while their answers are verified. However, judicial decisions in these states have interpreted this as requiring the same degree of belief for detention as would be needed to justify an arrest.[1] This avoids possible conflict with the Fourth Amendment, but does so at the cost of depriving the rule of the effect it was intended to have.[2]

The Uniform Arrest Act provision was drafted to make lawful what the police did anyway—namely, detain people for questioning for a reasonable period of time. California is the only state where the courts have allowed this. The general American view is that prolonged detention for questioning is invalid, that if the police wish to detain, they must arrest, with all the consequences of arrest. This view is also taken in England.[3]

Nevertheless, it is clear that the police of both countries upon occasion do hold suspects in investigative detention. In England this is done more politely than in the United States, so that in most instances of detention for questioning, it is not clear whether the suspect voluntarily complied with a police request or involuntarily yielded to police pressure. There have been a few cases in which a suspect is kept under questioning in a police station for three or four days without a charge being brought against him, although this is rare. In any event investigative detention in England is usually conducted in such a manner as to forestall complaints about the abuse of police power.

We shall see in the next section that upon arrest in England police questioning is required to end. It follows that if the police intend to ask questions of a suspect, they must do so before arresting him. In the United States, on the other hand, there is no rule requiring that questioning should stop on arrest, although we shall see that other

---

[1] Cases are collected and discussed in *District of Columbia Report and Recommendations of the Commissioner's Committee on Police Arrests for Investigation* 71–76 (1962).   [2] See Foote, op. cit., pp. 402–3.

[3] Devlin (1960), p. 48; Williams, op. cit., pp. 413–14.

rules are beginning to combine to produce that result. Increasingly it is becoming necessary for the American police to carry on interrogation before arrest. Up to now, however, they have not generally done so, but when they have wanted to question someone, they have arrested him despite the lack of grounds sufficient to justify their doing so on a specific charge.[1] This practice of 'arrest on suspicion' is conducted on a wide scale, and the suspect may be held for a prolonged period while being questioned to determine whether a specific charge against him can be supported. This is one of the practices which has helped to feed anti-police feeling in the United States. It may be that the police have a valid claim to a limited period in which to question a suspect without taking the more serious step of arrest, but many police critics find it impossible to consider such a claim dispassionately. They take present practices to demonstrate that the police cannot be trusted.

Akin to arrest on inadequate grounds as a cover for police questioning is the practice of holding suspects on some trivial charge while their connexion with a more serious offence is investigated. This tactic is not unknown in England,[2] but has been widespread in the United States, often taking the form of arresting a suspect on a charge of vagrancy.[3] The vagrancy charge is used to justify detention while the suspect is interrogated or while the police seek the evidence of his complicity in the major crime.

Another tactic occasionally used in the United States is the holding of a suspect as a 'material witness'.[4] Nearly every state allows a witness whose testimony is material in a pending criminal proceeding to be held in custody or on bail awaiting trial. In some states bail is set at such a prohibitive figure as to ensure his detention. This procedure has some justification in cases where it is feared that an essential witness may leave the jurisdiction or be harassed or tampered with by an accused. But there have also been cases where a person was detained as a material witness when the real purpose was to interrogate him in hope of justifying a charge against him. In such cases the requirement of a pending proceeding has sometimes been met by the

---

[1] See Trebach, pp. 4–7.   [2] See e.g. Kennedy, pp. 73–74.

[3] Douglas, 'Vagrancy and Arrest on Suspicion', 70 *Yale L.J.* 1, 9 (1960); Foote, 'Vagrancy-Type Law and Its Administration', 104 *U. Pa. L. Rev.* 603, 649, 1956; Comment, 'The Vagrancy Concept Reconsidered: Problems and Abuses of Status Criminality', 37 *N.Y.U. L. Rev.* 102 (1962).

[4] See comment, 'Material Witness and "Involuntary Confessions" ', 17 *U. Chi. L. Rev.* 706 (1950).

dubious device of issuing a warrant for the arrest of culprits un-known.[1]

English law also makes provision for ensuring the appearance of a witness at the trial of an indictable offence. He is ordered by the examining magistrate to appear, under penalty of his disobedience being punished as contempt of court by a fine or maximum of three months imprisonment. Upon proof of the probability that he will dis-obey such an order, as by fleeing the country, a judge of the High Court may issue a warrant for his arrest. However, this procedure is avail-able only after a preliminary examination has been held, the witness has testified at it, and the accused has been committed for trial. It cannot be abused in the same way the American procedure for detaining a material witness is abused.

England has a device for legitimately holding a defendant in cus-tody while the police build up their evidence against him, assuming there has been a valid arrest.[2] After such arrest, the police bring the defendant before a magistrate and ask for an adjournment of the preliminary hearing in order that they may fully prepare their case (not from the mouth of the accused, but from other sources). Then, in the discretion of the magistrate, the accused may be released on bail or held without bail, but not for more than eight days at a time without judicial renewal.[3] This is frequently done, but only in circum-stances where the police are reasonably confident that they will get enough evidence in the end. There is no formal American equivalent to this sort of remand in custody in the majority of states.[4] We shall see that, in theory at least, it is not permitted in the United States to hold an accused in custody on any but a capital charge without allow-ing him the opportunity to furnish bail as an alternative. It is, how-ever, always possible, as in the case of the material witness, to make bail so onerous that the defendant cannot afford it. Other practices,

---

[1] See, e.g., *People* ex rel. *Nuccio* v. *Warden*, 182 Misc. 654, 45 N.Y.S. 2d. 230 (Sup. Ct. 1943).

[2] Devlin (1960), pp. 78–80.

[3] Magistrates' Court Act, 1952, 15 & 16 Geo. VI and 1 Eliz. II, c. 55, §§ 6, 105.

[4] The three states that have substantially adopted the Uniform Arrest Act have statutes which, although requiring the arrested person to be brought before a magistrate for formal charge within twenty-four hours of arrest, permit the judge for good cause to extend this time for another forty-eight hours, during which the police presumably may conduct in-custody investigations and build their case. LaFave, 'Detention for Investigation by the Police: An Analysis of Current Practices', 1962 *Wash. U.L.Q.* 331, 333 and n. 20. This practice appears to be comparable to the English remand procedure, ibid., p. 333 and n. 22.

legitimate and illegitimate, have made remanding in custody less necessary in the United States than in England.

INTERROGATION

In both England and the United States one form of restriction on police questioning which has long existed is the common-law rule of evidence which precludes the use at trial of involuntary statements. This rule indirectly limits the police by frustrating their efforts when they resort to methods that produce what will be held to be an involuntary statement.

The rule does not require that the statement of an accused person be spontaneous; and it does not render inadmissible a statement merely by reason of its having been obtained through police questioning.[1] All the common law requires is that the statement shall not have been induced by force, threat of force, or promise of leniency from a person in authority, for if it has been so obtained, it is considered 'involuntary' and excluded.[2]

In England the common-law rule has been extended to 'admissions' which fall short of confessing guilt, so that any statement made by an accused must be voluntary if it is to be admitted at the trial. American states split on this point, some holding that admissions can be received in evidence without regard to whether they are voluntary or not, but others recognizing that the grounds for excluding involuntary confessions apply equally to admissions.

English courts have not been much concerned with confessions induced by force, for the police in England in modern times have seldom been accused of physical violence.[3] English cases have been more concerned with statements procured by relatively mild inducements, such as threats that bail will be refused, or promises that it will be granted. It is not clear to what extent English police use methods of interrogation designed to trap an unwary suspect into confessing without actually threatening him. If they do, at least they have the discretion not to boast about it. The American police, on the other hand, have used such methods extensively and these have been widely publicized. Hence there have been many occasions for application of the rule.

In both nations, however, restrictions upon police interrogation

[1] See, e.g., Abrahams, pp. 7–9; McCormick, pp. 231–3.
[2] *Ibrahim* v. *Rex* (1914), A.C. 599, 604 (P.C.).
[3] See Whitaker, p. 147.

have gone far beyond the common-law rule against involuntary statements. In England the extension has resulted from the Judges' Rules, whereas in the United States it has taken place as the result of decisions by the Supreme Court of the United States. The two distinct lines of development tend to converge, as we shall see.

The Judges' Rules on Interrogation

Before 1964 the Judges' Rules[1] imposed essentially two limitations on the police. First, they required that whenever a police officer had made up his mind to charge a person with a crime, he should, before asking any questions, caution the suspect in these words: 'Do you wish to say anything in answer to the charge? You are not obliged to say anything unless you wish to do so, but whatever you say will be taken down in writing and may be given in evidence.'[2] Second, the Rules required that persons in police custody should not be questioned at all.[3]

While questioning without a proper caution, or questioning a suspect in custody would render a resulting statement improper, judges could exercise their discretion to admit the statement in evidence anyway; and over the years they fluctuated in the rigour with which they enforced the Rules. Some writers have suggested that there was a tacit agreement between the judges and the police that the old Rules were unworkable. The police were not happy with them, for they felt that the caution dried up useful sources of information, and that the cessation of all questioning when a suspect was taken into custody was an unreasonable hindrance to police investigation. In practice there were occasions when the latter requirement was ignored.

Against this background the revised Rules of 1964 were prepared.[4]

---

[1] For a general discussion of the rules, see Abrahams; Devlin (1960), pp. 26–51; Rolph (1961), pp. 84–95; Street, pp. 24–31; Williams, 'Police Interrogation Privileges and Limitations Under Foreign Law—England', 52 *J. Crim. L., C. & P.S.* 50 (1961).   [2] Abrahams, pp. 17–18.

[3] This requirement did not clearly appear on the face of the rules, and it was not clear whether it was originally intended when they were drafted in 1912. One of the original rules stated that 'persons in custody should not be questioned without the usual caution being first administered', seeming to imply that such questioning was permitted. In 1930, however, it was settled in a Home Office circular (No. 536053/23), that this rule referred only to questions designed to clear up an ambiguity in an earlier spontaneous statement, and did not apply to questioning designed to elicit fresh information. Such questioning became improper once a suspect had been taken into custody.

[4] *Judges' Rules and Administrative Directions to the Police*, Home Office Circular No. 31/1964 (1964).

The most important new provision is that which allows the police to interrogate a suspect 'whether or not the person in question has been taken into custody so long as he has not been charged with an offence or informed that he may be prosecuted for it'.[1] On its face this rule is ambiguous. In view of the English requirement that an arrested person must be told immediately of the reason for his arrest, it would seem that anyone held in custody against his will is under arrest and 'charged'. If such informal notice is the 'charge' referred to in the new rule, then the questioning of persons in custody is still prohibited. However, it seems more likely that the intention of the new rule is to allow questioning after arrest. The 'charge' referred to may be the formal charge made by the desk officer at a police station. On this interpretation the new Rules allow a period of questioning after arrest, and answers given by an accused during that period are admissible in evidence.[2]

It seems to follow from the new Rules that if the police detain a suspect for questioning against his will without making a specific charge, the answers he gives are admissible in evidence. In effect this gives recognition to the practice of detention for questioning, although in some situations the police may still be liable for false imprisonment if they hold a man without a specific charge. A prefatory statement to the 1964 revision states that the new Rules do not affect the principle 'that police officers, otherwise than by arrest, cannot compel any person against his will to come to or remain in any police station'. There are, however, a number of conceivable instances in which the police may feel they must act before making a specific charge, such as when several people are taken into custody during a raid on premises where illegal activities are being carried on, but where questioning is necessary to establish the complicity of any particular individual. In such a situation, there is no longer any rule which prevents the police from asking questions. The only limitations are the general requirement that the police must bring arrested persons before a magistrate within twenty-four hours[3] and the possibility that at some point in the interrogation a caution will have to be administered.

While the new Rules allow questioning for a longer period of time than did the old Rules, they may require a caution at an earlier stage

[1] Ibid., p. 5 (Rule I).
[2] Cf. *Regina* v. *Collier*, *The Times* (London), 2 July 1965.
[3] See Abrahams, p. 36.

of investigation than before. Under the old Rules the caution had to be given 'whenever a police officer has made up his mind to charge a person with a crime'. If this was read literally the need for a caution depended subjectively on the state of the individual policeman's mind, although in practice the judges tended to make their own assessment of the information available to him and to decide independently whether it was enough to justify a charge. The new Rules embody a more clearly objective test, requiring (in Rule II) that the caution should be administered 'as soon as a police officer has evidence which would afford reasonable grounds for suspecting that a person has committed an offence' and (in Rule III (a)) that a second caution should be administered 'where a person is charged with or informed that he may be prosecuted for an offence'. The first requirement is not entirely clear, for there may be differences of opinion as to what evidence constitutes 'reasonable grounds for suspecting'. It is even possible that the words may refer to the 'reasonable grounds of suspicion' which are required in England to justify an arrest—in which case the caution, like that under the old Rules, need not be given until grounds for arrest are apparent. On the other hand, it seems more likely that Rule II refers to a situation where arrest is not yet justified, but there are grounds for thinking that it may become justified if questioning is pursued. In such a situation the new Rules require a caution whereas the old Rules did not.

As under the old Rules, 'clearing up' questions, designed to resolve ambiguities in a statement made earlier, can be asked after the period of lawful initial interrogation has expired. The new Rules require a *third* caution at this point, in substantially the same terms as the first two, telling the accused that he is not obliged to say anything but that if he does the answers will be taken down and may be given in evidence. The effect is that as long as the police continue to ask questions, they must also warn the suspect at regular intervals of his right to remain silent. It is not clear whether all this cautioning serves any useful purpose. English lawyers have long debated the question, but they have assembled nothing concrete to show how the caution works in practice, e.g. whether it prevents innocent people from explaining their actions; whether it cuts off a helpful flood of information; whether its language fully conveys the idea of the right to remain silent. In any event the new Judges' Rules make it certain that the caution will continue to have a prominent place in English police practice.

Another feature of the Judges' Rules is the provision they make for the recording of statements by a suspect. The old Rules provided that a statement should, whenever possible, be taken down in writing and signed by the suspect after it had been read to him and he had been invited to make any corrections he might wish. This requirement was supplemented by a Home Office circular of 1947 which gave meticulous instructions on methods for taking written statements. Under the 1964 revision the Judges' Rules themselves now contain elaborate provisions as to the procedure to be followed by the police in taking statements; and these are again supplemented by Home Office directions which accompany the text of the Rules.[1] The gist of the provisions is as follows: first, an accurate record must be kept of the time and place of any period of questioning preceded by a caution, and of the witnesses thereto; second, in the exceptional case where a person is questioned after having been charged with an offence, the questions and answers must be contemporaneously recorded in full; third, any written record of interrogation conducted after a caution is administered should be accompanied by a statement of the accused that his answers were voluntarily given and that the record reflects what he intended to say; fourth, a statement must be written down in the exact language of the suspect.

These provisions, which have their counterpart in the instructions appearing in many American police manuals, are valuable safeguards, but they do not solve the problem—which exists in both countries—of obtaining a satisfactory record of police interrogation. One aspect of this problem, especially significant in England since it uses the caution so extensively, is that a signed statement often omits admissions made by the suspect during conversations preceding the caution. Once warned, he may balk at allowing such admissions to appear over his signature. In a large number of cases the entries the police officer makes in his notebook, often some time after a conversation, are the sole record of relevant admissions. This sometimes leads to a police officer on the witness stand 'dropping the verbals'— giving embellished or false evidence to the effect that the suspect has made admissions just sufficient to drive the case home—a far more common practice than the wholesale fabrication of complete confessions. The police are tempted to indulge in it when they are confident that they have the guilty person and can offer reliable evidence

[1] *Judges' Rules and Administrative Directions to the Police,* op. cit., pp. 7–9.

sufficient to carry the case almost, but not quite, to the point of conviction.

Another aspect of the problem is that written statements represent only the end product of a period of interrogation. They do not reflect the hints and pressures which the police may have brought to bear on a suspect to make him confess or the extent to which his responses were influenced by the way in which questions were put. Perhaps the only solution would be to make a full, contemporaneous record of all interviews between the police and a suspect. In neither country are the police receptive to this suggestion. Partly this is because of cost, for to have a stenographer present at every interrogation would be exceedingly expensive, especially in view of the limited and shrinking supply of stenographers. Electronic recording devices might be used, but these are easily tampered with. Cost, however, is not the only objection, or the principal one. The police forces of both countries feel that effective interrogation requires informality, which would be destroyed by the overt recording of all conversations. Secret recording would run into difficulties from the point of view of civil liberties and also raise the problem of falsification in a serious form.

United States Supreme Court Decisions

Until recently no close equivalent to the English Judges' Rules existed in the United States. There were no statutory provisions specifically requiring the cautioning of suspects of their right to remain silent,[1] and police practice did not ordinarily include such a caution. Prosecutors tended to give a caution when interrogating a defendant —or at least before taking a written statement—not because they had to do so, but in order to ward off criticism and to anticipate a possible defence that the statement made was involuntary. A few police forces also administered cautions, again as a matter of grace and for much the same reasons.

Similarly, no American jurisdiction had a statutory rule requiring interrogation to cease at a particular point.[1] Questioning took place until the accused was brought before a magistrate and sometimes continued afterward, especially when a prosecutor who had not previously been in on the case wished to take a hand in talking to the defendant.

The lack of statutory rules governing questioning, however, has

---

[1] However, such a rule is proposed in a first draft of a *Model Code of Pre-arraignment Procedure* under consideration by the American Law Institute.

now been supplied by decisions of the Supreme Court of the United States. Two distinct lines of cases, one dealing with prosecutions in the federal courts and the other dealing with prosecutions in the state courts, require separate discussion.

The former group of decisions are based on Rule 5-A of the Federal Rules of Criminal Procedure which provides that an officer 'shall take the arrested person without unnecessary delay before the nearest available commissioner' (committing magistrate). The Supreme Court held that confessions or admissions obtained in violation of this Rule could not be received in evidence in the federal courts.[1] Some differences of opinion developed among lower federal judges as to what constituted 'unnecessary delay', but these have now become largely academic as a result of the *Miranda* case, shortly to be discussed.

The other line of Supreme Court decisions arises out of state cases. The development began in 1936 in a case where a state court failed to exclude confessions obtained after a severe and brutal beating of the defendant, although it clearly could and should have done so under the common law rule against involuntary confessions.[2] The Supreme Court reversed the conviction not on the basis of the common law of evidence, but on constitutional grounds—because the confession had been obtained unfairly. Since that time there has been an extension of the circumstances in which the Court requires the exclusion of a statement on the ground that it was procured unfairly. The Supreme Court said that these circumstances could not be reduced to formulae;[3] it said that 'inherently coercive' questioning was constitutionally prohibited, but maintained that whether a case fell within this prohibition depended on 'the totality of the circumstances'. In holding that confessions should have been excluded it has adverted to such factors as physical maltreatment, deprivation of food and sleep, prolonged questioning, secret detention, failure to warn the defendant of his rights, denial of counsel, use of deception or trickery, failure to comply with statutes requiring prompt production of the accused before a magistrate, and lack of perspicacity on the part of the defendant.[4] The court emphasized psychological as well as physical

---

[1] *Mallory* v. *United States*, 354 U.S. 449 (1957); *McNabb* v. *United States*, 318 U.S. 332 (1943).　　[2] *Brown* v. *Mississippi*, 297 U.S. 278 (1936).　　[3] Spanogle, The use of Coerced Confessions in State Courts, 17 Vand. L. Rev. 421, 422-23 (1964).

[4] For a collection of Supreme Court cases catalogued according to the nature of the coercion used by the police see Nat. Legal Aid and Defender Assoc., Defender Newsletter, *Admissibility of a Confession*, vol. ii, no. 5 (Sept. 1965), pp. 6–7.

coercion, and said that coerced confessions were to be excluded under the Fourteenth Amendment not only because they were likely to be untrue, but because the methods used were objectionable and oppressive.[1]

Both of these approaches received a vast impetus from two recent decisions of the Supreme Court, one in *Escobedo* v. *Illinois*,[2] decided in 1964, and the other in *Miranda* v. *Arizona*,[3] decided in 1966. The first is predicated upon the right to counsel guaranteed in the federal courts by the Sixth Amendment and in the state courts by the Fourteenth Amendment.[4] In this case, the court reversed a state conviction based upon a confession obtained in the following circumstances: the accused was the principal suspect; he had been arrested but had not been warned of his right to remain silent; he asked to consult with his retained counsel who was present in the police station, and was denied this opportunity.

The *Miranda* case carries the restriction upon police questioning much further. Predicated upon the privilege against self-incrimination embodied in the Fifth Amendment, and bolstered by the idea that equal protection requires that indigent persons be offered the same safeguards as those who are able to employ counsel, it holds that no statement taken from the accused while he is in the custody of police —whether a confession or a mere admission—can be used against him unless he has first been advised of his right to remain silent, of the fact that any statement made can be used against him, and that he is entitled to the presence of counsel. Furthermore, if he is unable to employ an attorney he has the right to be furnished one at government expense. Finally, his failure to ask for a lawyer does not constitute a waiver of these rights. If the prosecution wishes to use any statement by the accused, it has a heavy burden of showing that he knowingly waived his right to remain silent or his right to counsel.

The practical effect of this decision may be to halt police questioning in the United States at an earlier time than it is halted in England under the Judges' Rules, for if the accused must be furnished a lawyer before he says anything that can be used against him, it seems highly likely that he will say nothing at all after the moment he is taken into custody. Furthermore, there is language in both the *Miranda* and

---

[1] e.g. *Rogers* v. *Richmond*, 365 U.S. 534 (1961).
[2] 378 U.S. 478 (1964).
[3] *Miranda* v. *Arizona*, 34 U.S.L. Week 4521 (U.S. 14 June 1966).
[4] *Gideon* v. *Wainwright*, 372 U.S. 335 (1963).

Escobedo opinions which disparages a system of law enforcement based upon confessions resulting from incommunicado questioning by the police rather than on extrinsic evidence independently secured through skilful investigation.[1] The decisions seem to rest mainly on the proposition that a criminal trial should be something more than the ratification of a result effectively reached earlier at the police station, but it may also be based in part on an exaggerated notion of the feasibility of police detection by means other than interrogation. There are some crimes in which there is no extrinsic evidence on which a case can be built. The best the police can do, if they can do anything, is to use their knowledge of likely culprits, based on patterns in method or tips of informers, and try to obtain a confession. The alternative is to leave such crimes unsolved. The English generally regard this alternative as undesirable, as do most Americans. But there is a strong minority view in the United States to the effect that failing to solve crimes is preferable to solving them through the use of confessions. This view derives support from the occasional and perhaps aberrational cases in which seemingly voluntary confessions turn out to be entirely untrue.

Perhaps the prejudice against police interrogation will run its course in time, especially if there is a marked improvement in the calibre of police forces. Meanwhile, the police are fearful that the courts will convert the argument against using some confessions into a flat constitutional prohibition against the use of any at all.

SEARCH AND SEIZURE

English and American law follow roughly the same pattern with respect to police powers of search,[2] but they differ sharply with respect to the admissibility in evidence of the fruits of an unlawful search. English law in nearly every instance admits such evidence while American law excludes such evidence.

Just as the police have no general power to detain suspects at their pleasure, they have no general power to compel people to submit to a search of their persons, possessions, or premises. In both countries

---

[1] An interesting state decision which antedated and anticipated the *Escobedo* case is *People* v. *Donovan*, 13 N.Y. 2d 148, 193 N.E. 2d 628, 243 N.Y.S. 2d 841 (1963) in which the New York Court of Appeals held, wholly on the basis of state law, that a confession could not be received in evidence if it resulted from questioning by the police after they refused to allow the accused to consult with his lawyer.

[2] See, e.g., Devlin (1960), pp. 52–59; Puttkammer, pp. 79–86; Street, pp. 20–23.

a police search in order to be valid must be by consent, or in the course of a lawful arrest, or under a search warrant.

In the first situation, where someone genuinely consents to a search, he has no basis for complaining that the police acted unlawfully. In England it is said that search warrants are seldom used because permission to enter premises is usually granted. This is not so obviously true in the United States, although undoubtedly there are many cases where consent is easily obtained. Both countries, however, are faced by the problem of consent induced by a fear of the police in general or a fear that they will search anyway. In England there is no effective remedy in this situation. In the United States the question of whether consent was truly voluntary can be raised in an attempt to exclude from use at the trial any evidence seized in the course of the search.

In the case of a valid arrest the police of either country may search the person of the accused for evidence of crime or for anything which will aid him to escape, such as a concealed weapon. In the United States they may also search his immediate surroundings for the same sort of objects, but various state courts differ as to how far a search of the adjacent premises may extend. The English rule is entirely vague; indeed no English case has squarely settled the point that the police may even search the vicinity of the person they arrest, although it is generally assumed that they may. This is one of the many instances where American law is more detailed and explicit than English law, largely because of the exclusionary rule.

A search warrant is required in either country if the police wish to make a search of premises, the Anglo-American common-law rule being that any forcible entry into premises without warrant is an actionable trespass. In practice, however, the English police have managed largely without warrants, either by reason of obtaining consent to search through threats of doing so anyway or by searching the whole of a house in which a person is arrested on the theory that such search is incidental to the arrest.[1] The Larceny Act, 1916,[2] tried to regularize this situation by allowing a Chief Constable to issue the equivalent of a warrant to search the house of a known thief; but even in that situation the police prefer to take short-cuts and to search without a warrant.[3] In most parts of the United States a similar situation prevailed until 1961, when the Supreme Court held that the

---

[1] See Rolph (1961), pp. 98–101; Street, p. 22; Whitaker, p. 61.
[2] 6 & 7 Geo V, c. 50, § 42.
[3] Rolph (1961), p. 99.

Fourteenth Amendment prohibited the admission into evidence of the fruits of an illegal search.

As in the case of arrest warrants, the protection which search warrants afford depends on the calibre of the magistrates who issue them and the seriousness with which they consider applications.[1] To some extent there is a check on magistrates in the United States because of the fact that the exclusionary rule extends to evidence obtained under a warrant issued on insufficient grounds. On the other hand, the grounds for a search warrant are generally broader in the United States than in England. In England there is no common law power in the magistrates to issue a search warrant except to search for stolen goods or evidence of larceny, but statutes have extended the power to reach such things as dangerous weapons and obscene articles. In the United States the list of objects for which a search warrant may be issued differs from state to state, but in some states there are statutes authorizing search warrants with respect to (*a*) any stolen or embezzled property, (*b*) any contraband, (*c*) any property intended for use in committing a crime, and (*d*) any property which is itself evidence of a crime.[2] Such broad statutes may exceed constitutional boundaries, for the Supreme Court has held that under the Fourth Amendment the only things which can be searched for and seized are: (1) contraband, (2) fruits of a crime, and (3) means for committing crime.[3]

The sweeping language of such statutes reflects the fact that American police are concerned with offences which are not prominent in England. The English law of search and seizure focuses largely on the problem of stolen goods, whereas in the United States most search and seizure cases are concerned with gambling, narcotics, and liquor offences, which typically cannot be prosecuted without a search having first been made. It is largely in these cases (where many people are sceptical about the wisdom of prosecuting at all) that the American doctrine of excluding illegally obtained evidence has been moulded, and it is largely in them also that the common-law powers,

---

[1] Recently the Supreme Court has extended to the states the requirement that the application for the search warrant and the supporting affidavits must be sufficiently detailed and complete to permit the magistrates to make an independent determination of probable cause. See p. 108, n. 5.

[2] *N.Y. Code Crim. Proc.*, § 792.

[3] *Gouled* v. *United States*, 255 U.S. 298 (1921). For law review commentary, see Shellow, 'The Continuing Vitality of the Gouled Rule: The Search for and Seizure of Evidence', 48 *Marq. L. Rev.* 172 (1964); Comment, 'Limitations on Seizure of "Evidentiary" Objects—A Rule in Search of Reason', 20 *U. Chi. L. Rev.* 319 (1952).

if strictly observed, are inadequate. As a result, some state legislatures have tried to broaden police powers by statute. In New York, following a judicial decision that the police could not search for gambling apparatus where there was no certainty that a crime had taken place,[1] a statute was passed empowering arrest and consequently search without a warrant where the police had reasonable grounds to believe it had been committed.[2] Following a judicial decision that the police had to announce their presence when they entered premises under a search warrant, even though in a narcotics case this would enable the suspect to destroy all traces of the drug, as by flushing it down a toilet, a statute was passed empowering the police, on a special warrant, to enter premises without preliminary warning.[3]

Such statutes are indirectly a response to the imposition of an exclusionary rule on the states in 1961. In 1914 the United States Supreme Court held that evidence seized illegally by federal officers was not to be admitted in federal prosecutions,[4] but the holding was limited to federal cases. In 1949 the Court held that the Fourth Amendment prohibition against unreasonable searches and seizures applied to the states as part of the 'due process' which is guaranteed by the Fourteenth Amendment, but that the state courts were free to admit evidence obtained by unlawful search if they chose.[5] The state courts divided sharply on the question of admissibility, somewhat less than half adopting an exclusionary rule, and the others, including New York, following the English reasoning that the manner in which evidence was obtained had no bearing on its admissibility at trial. In 1961 the Supreme Court reversed itself and held in *Mapp* v. *Ohio*[6] that a state conviction based on evidence obtained by unreasonable search and seizure was a violation of the due process of law guaran-

---

[1] *People* v. *Moore*, 11 N.Y. 2d 271, 183 N.E. 2d 255, 228 N.Y.S. 2d 822 (1962).

[2] *N.Y. Code Crim. Proc.*, § 177 (1).

[3] Ibid., § 799. Although federal law requires announcement before entry, that rule has not been applied to the states through the Fourteenth Amendment. *Ker* v. *California* 374 U.S. 23 (1963).   [4] *Weeks* v. *United States*, 232 U.S. 383 (1914).

[5] *Wolf* v. *Colorado*, 338 U.S. 25 (1949). In *Rochin* v. *California*, 342 U.S. 165 (1952), the accused, upon being arrested as a narcotics offender, attempted to destroy evidence of his offence by swallowing the drug. He was rushed to a hospital and the evidence was retrieved by a stomach pump. Today this might be held an unreasonable search in violation of the Fourth Amendment, but since the exclusionary rule had not yet been held to apply to searches by state officers, the conviction was reversed as a violation of general due process under the Fourteenth Amendment. The police activity was regarded as so outrageous as to result in a fundamentally unfair conviction. This reasoning may be of interest to England because, there too, the courts have a doctrine of fairness which can be invoked to exclude evidence obtained through police excesses.   [6] 367 U.S. 643 (1961).

teed by the Fourteenth Amendment. Shortly thereafter it held that the standards evolved in federal cases should govern state courts in determining the constitutionality of state searches.[1]

The American exclusionary rule bars the admission not only of evidence obtained directly by an unconstitutional search, but also evidence obtained through leads supplied by such activity unless it appears that the connexion between the conduct of the police and the discovery of the challenged evidence has 'become so attenuated as to dissipate the taint', or unless the prosecution shows that it learned of the evidence 'from an independent source'.[2] If neither of these circumstances is shown, the evidence is barred from use in court as 'the fruit of a poisoned tree'.[3]

SURVEILLANCE AND WIRE TAPPING

Related to the problems of search and seizure is police use of espionage systems to give them surveillance over probable sources of criminal activity. The detective in disguise, the 'stool pigeon', and the paid informer represent methods of eavesdropping which have come to be accepted in both countries without much public outcry, even though they probably involve just as serious an invasion of privacy as beating down doors and rummaging through pockets. However, one method of eavesdropping which has given rise to dispute in both countries is wire tapping.

On this, both England and the United States have reached uneasy compromises. In England a public outcry in 1957 led to the appointment of a committee of Privy Councillors to investigate existing law and future policy. It concluded that the Home Secretary had power to authorize telephone tapping, and it approved the terms of a declaration which he had issued to the police in 1951 stating that he would grant permission only in cases where espionage and similar offences were suspected, or to deal with criminal gangs, or to track escaped prisoners and persons evading arrest on serious charges, or to detect receivers of stolen property.[4] Wire tap evidence has never been offered in an English court, but has been used only to obtain leads; and

[1] *Beck* v. *Ohio*, 379 U.S. 89 (1964); *Ker* v. *California*, 374 U.S. 23 (1963).

[2] *Nardone* v. *United States*, 308 U.S. 338, 341 (1939); *Silverthorne Lumber Co.* v. *United States*, 251 U.S. 385 (1920).

[3] Confessions and admissions as well as real and documentary evidence may be excluded from evidence if procured as a result of unlawful arrest or unreasonable search and seizure. *Wong Sun* v. *United States*, 371 U.S. 471 (1963).

[4] *Report of the Committee of Privy Councillors appointed to inquire into the Interception of Communications*, Cmnd. 283, pp. 16–18, 24–26 (reprinted 1963).

English lawyers are not agreed on whether such evidence would be admitted if offered.

In the United States the Supreme Court held in 1928 that the Fourth Amendment's prohibition against unreasonable search and seizure did not apply to information obtained by wire tapping.[1] In 1934 a federal statute made it an offence (without, however, providing a penalty) to intercept and divulge a telephone communication, unless authorized by the speaker. This was held to preclude the admission in federal courts of wire tap evidence. As for state courts, however, the Supreme Court held that they were free to receive wire-tap evidence.[2] Conceivably federal criminal proceedings could be brought against the state police, but this does not happen in fact. Six states, including New York, have statutes which affirmatively allow wire tapping by the police pursuant to court order. Even in these states, however, the trend is to imitate the English practice of using only leads obtained through wire tapping without attempting to introduce the intercepted conversation in evidence. This is partly on the theory that no federal offence is committed by interception until there is a divulgence, and partly to avoid precipitating a new decision by the Supreme Court which might overrule past cases and hold wire tapping unconstitutional.

That the Supreme Court might move in an appropriate case to curtail the use of wire tap evidence by the states is apparent from the thrust of recent decisions discussed earlier. Another recent case, not concerned with police powers, may also be pertinent though it seems remote. In *Griswold* v. *Connecticut*,[3] the Court held unconstitutional a statute prohibiting the distribution and use of birth control devices on the ground that it interfered with a married couple's right to privacy—a right which is nowhere explicit in the Bill of Rights but which was said to be implicit in several of its provisions. If the Court is prepared to establish a constitutionally protected right to privacy, it can be argued that wire tapping is no longer permissible, and that the Court should treat all issues of personal liberty raised by modern technology not merely in terms of the traditional guarantees of the Bill of Rights but in terms of its concept of what a free and democratic society requires. If so, this approach would assume great importance as law enforcement agencies increasingly avail themselves of scientific and technological devices for electronic surveillance and other forms of eavesdropping.

---

[1] *Olmstead* v. *United States*, 277 U.S. 438 (1928).
[2] *Schwartz* v. *Texas*, 344 U.S. 199 (1952).   [3] 381 U.S. 479 (1965).

7

PROCEEDINGS BEFORE TRIAL

IN both England and the United States, when the police arrest a suspect they are required to take him promptly before a judicial officer. (In this chapter we shall refer to him as 'the magistrate', although in England two or more magistrates may act together, and in the United States the official may be called by some other name.) Similarly, when a prosecution is begun by the issuance of a summons, as it is in many cases in England and a few in the United States, the accused is directed to appear before a magistrate.

In either event this is the time when the magistrate deals with a number of matters which have to be attended to before the case can be tried. It is at this point that the accused is first formally advised of his right to counsel, to remain silent, to have bail fixed, and of the various courses which the case may take from then on. If the case is one which can be tried in the magistrates' court, the accused may be asked to plead to the charge, not always with the expectation of immediate trial but sometimes in anticipation of trial a few days or weeks later. If the case is one which will have to be tried in a higher court, the accused may be asked whether he wishes to have a preliminary examination or waive it (as he may do in the United States, though not in England). In the larger urban courts this 'first appearance' is usually attended to in special divisions of the court, by magistrates who while sitting in those divisions do nothing else.

In England the 'first appearance' is not formally recognized as a distinct substage of criminal procedure, but it exists in practice. Often a trial or preliminary inquiry in a magistrates' court cannot begin at once, because in the larger cities court congestion may, as in the United States, make necessary a delay of days or weeks. Also, where a preliminary inquiry must be held, it sometimes happens that the police are still investigating and are not ready to present their evidence. In this situation the proceedings are not unlike the American 'first appearance', for they are adjourned almost as soon as they have opened.

BAIL

When the accused is brought before a magistrate, the possibility of bail is one of the first matters to be considered. Even if the magistrates' court has jurisdiction to try the case forthwith, often it will not do so. The prosecution or the defence may want more time to prepare, or the court may be overburdened with cases. Thus the question of release on bail until the trial arises. Similarly, if the magistrates' court cannot try the case, but is only empowered to conduct a preliminary examination, there still may be an adjournment or continuance and, hence, a demand for bail. After the accused is held for trial or for appearance before a grand jury, and after indictment by a grand jury, there is also a choice between custody and bail.

The English Bill of Rights, like the Eighth Amendment to the United States Constitution, provides that excessive bail shall not be required. This has never been thought in England to accord a right to bail, but only to require that bail should not be excessive in those cases where it was appropriately granted. Apart from the absolute right to police bail (in cases where the offence is not serious and the accused cannot be brought before a magistrate within twenty-four hours), the granting or refusing of bail in England is entirely discretionary.

In the United States the federal constitution provides only that bail should not be excessive, but the constitutions of over forty states provide explicitly that defendant has a right to be granted bail before trial or conviction in all but capital cases.[1] A few more states provide this right by statute. Similarly the Federal Judiciary Act of 1789—which antedated the federal Bill of Rights—gave a right to bail in all except capital cases, allowing the judges in capital cases to grant bail in their discretion.[2] This is still the law in the federal courts.[3] Only four states retain the English common law and allow the judiciary complete discretion with regard to bail in all cases.[4] Finally, there are three states, of which New York is one, which by statute give a right to bail before trial in misdemeanour cases but permit the discretionary denial of bail in felony cases.[4] This provision has been upheld as against the argument that the constitutional prohibition of excessive bail necessarily implies a right to be granted bail in all cases.

---

[1] Freed & Wald, p. 2, n. 8; Sullivan, 'Proposed Rule 46 and the Right to Bail', 31 *Geo. Wash. L. Rev.* 919, 921 (1963); Note, 'Bail: An Ancient Practice Re-examined', 70 *Yale L.J.* 966, 977 (1961).   [2] 1 Stat. 73 (1789).
[3] Fed. R. Crim. P. 16 (a).   [4] Freed & Wald, p. 3, n. 8.

In most of the United States, therefore, the magistrates cannot deny bail altogether. They must at least go through the motions of fixing bail. But this does not prevent them from requiring monetary security in amounts which a defendant cannot possibly obtain whenever they think it likely that he will fail to appear for trial. The setting of impossible surety requirements results, in effect, in a denial of bail; but this practice has been held to be constitutionally permissible where the only alternative would be the accused's disappearance. Thus the existence of a right to bail in the United States has been generally less important than prevailing practices with regard to the nature and amount of bail.

Where England and the United States differ most sharply is in the type of security a defendant is required to offer before he can be released on bail. In England bail can be and often is granted to a defendant on his own recognizance, i.e. a promise by which he undertakes to appear for trial or else forfeit a stated sum of money. Where this is thought insufficient, one or two sureties may be required to enter into similar recognizances on the accused's behalf. The accused on arrest is usually asked to put down the names of friends or relatives he thinks will act as sureties. The police investigate them and report on whether they consider these persons acceptable in the light of their character and financial status. No deposit of cash or pledge of property is required at the time the recognizance is entered into.

In some American states the magistrate in setting bail may require a cash deposit or the pledge of specified property, but this seldom happens. Ordinarily the magistrate relies on the promise or 'bond' of a financially responsible surety to pay a stated sum of money if the accused fails to appear. The United States differs critically from England, however, in not demanding that the surety stand in a personal relationship to the accused. This has permitted the growth of a bail bond industry in which persons make a business of giving surety for bail and charging the accused a fee for the service. The bondsman secures his investment by an indemnity agreement with the accused and by exacting pledges of collateral property—such as the deed to the accused's home—sufficient to cover all or part of his loss should the accused fail to appear. In England such a profession is impossible. Contracts to indemnify a surety are unenforceable; and the furnishing of bonds for profit is a criminal offence.

Some states have attempted to regulate the bail bond business by such measures as limiting premiums, licensing bondsmen, and restricting the trade to those with insurance company backing. But many abuses have persisted which do not respond to regulation. First, only people of some means or well-capitalized rackets can afford the fees and find the collateral which a bondsman demands. A bail system based solely on financial security for appearance at trial is useless for the great number of accused persons who are truly indigent. Second, the bondsman rather than the judge effectively decides whether an accused is to be at liberty, by granting or withholding a bond; and he does so by reference to criteria which are quite different from those ordinarily considered significant to a bail decision. The bondsman, for instance, is prone to charge inordinately high fees to a first offender despite the good chance of his appearing in court, while he is willing to take risks with a professional criminal who furnishes him with steady business.[1] Third, the bondsman is often the first person with any experience of the criminal courts to be encountered by the accused and his family. In this capacity he is likely to select a lawyer for the defendant, promise favours from the court—which he may or may not be able to produce—and otherwise play a generally shady role. It is not surprising that one of the goals of current law reform in the United States is to find a way of dispensing with the professional bondsman.

In England, the tendency has generally been readily to admit to bail all but the most serious offenders and to do so on mild terms, frequently without any surety at all. In most cases, an accused person is able to obtain the modest bail once it is set. Where bail is not obtained, it is usually because the court has refused to allow it at all. Bail-jumping has been of minor proportions in England, and when it does occur, the court is likely to remit or modify the obligations of the sureties.

In the United States, the tendency has been to require substantial bail, with substantial surety requirements, and to do so in a somewhat mechanical fashion according to the technical classification of the offence involved. Thus, if a felony is charged—even a non-violent theft of a comparatively small amount—the minimum bail is apt to be $1,000, where an English court might require only a few pounds,

---

[1] Paradoxically, the judge may set bail much lower for some types of professional criminals than for first offenders accused of relatively minor crimes. LaFave, p. 179, cites this example: 'A numbers writer was brought before the magistrate for the setting of bail. Without inquiry into any of the specific facts of this case, the magistrate immediately set an extremely low bail. "These people would not leave town if an atomic bomb were dropped on it", he remarked.'

which would be forfeited only if and when the accused failed to appear. If he appeared for trial, he would lose nothing. The American defendant, however, has to furnish a bond for the full amount of bail, and unless he or his friends have assets of over $1,000, he has to pay a bondsman $50 to $100 as the premium on the $1,000 bond. Needless to say, this money is not refunded. Since a majority of criminal defendants are virtually penniless, there are great numbers of them in American jails awaiting trial who have had bail set but are unable to make it. In New York City there are more defendants imprisoned before trial than after. It has been asserted upon the basis of a statistical study that their defences suffer thereby, that their chances of conviction are greater, and that their sentences are apt to be more severe than those of defendants at liberty.[1]

For the most part, too little responsible thought has been given by American magistrates to the consequences of their bail decisions. Bail is usually set, as we have said, by mechanical criteria. There are some magistrates who deliberately fix an impossible bail to assure that there will be no delay in the accused's experience of his deserved punishment. Theirs is the philosophy that it will do the offender good to have an immediate 'taste of jail'. This is clearly a misuse of bail. Denial of bail in England for this reason is not unknown, but is uncommon.

Preventive Detention

Denial of bail is often and legitimately used in England as a method of preventive detention where there is ground for thinking that the accused will commit crimes or tamper with witnesses if he is left at liberty. The Court of Criminal Appeal has stressed, apparently against the inclinations of some magistrates, the desirability of refusing bail to defendants with bad criminal records because of the likelihood they will continue to engage in crimes so long as they are free, partly to meet legal costs, partly to provide for their families against the chance of a jail sentence, and partly because of a 'last fling' attitude.

In the United States such a denial of bail is in theory unlawful. The American magistrate is not entitled to speculate on the possibility of the accused committing crimes while at liberty or on the dangers of his suppressing evidence. The sole consideration in setting bail is

[1] See Wald, 'Pre-trial Detention and Ultimate Freedom: A Statistical Study', 39 *N.Y.U. L. Rev.* 631 (1964).

supposed to be whether the accused will appear for trial. This theory, however, does not always square with practice. As in England, bail determinations in the United States are not infrequently influenced by an assessment of what the accused will do if released.

Reform

In England some members of the legal profession were shocked to learn how many persons who had been refused bail were later acquitted or, if convicted, sentenced to some lesser penalty than imprisonment.[1] Nevertheless, there are no present signs in England of far-reaching dissatisfaction with the bail system as such.

It is quite otherwise in the United States, and rightly so. Studies of American bail practices, going back at least to 1927, have clearly shown that far too many people are held in jail before trial when they should be at liberty. The movement for bail reform gained great impetus from the Manhattan Bail Project in New York City, which demonstrated dramatically the possibility of releasing many defendants on their own recognizance after systematic inquiries into their circumstances demonstrated that they had such roots in the community that they were unlikely to disappear[2]. The operation has now been taken over by the City of New York as a regular part of its criminal court system. Other experiments have been started, notably in Illinois, in the use of refundable cash deposits by accused persons, a system which tends to transfer the bail bond business from professional bondsmen to the courts. There are also experiments in release on conditions other than monetary ones, such as supervision by probation or parole officers, release in the custody of the accused's attorney, and day-time release from a lock-up where the accused is required to sleep. (In England conditions of residence in a particular place and of periodic report to the police are often incorporated in bail terms.) The United States Department of Justice, which has actively encouraged the federal courts in similar experiments, convened a National Conference on Bail and Criminal Justice in May 1964 to promote bail reform throughout the country.[3] It is reasonable to expect that within a few years bail practices over a great part of the United States will change materially. It is even possible that English

---

[1] *Report of the Interdepartmental Committee on the Business of the Criminal Courts*, Cmnd. 1289, p. 5 (1961).

[2] Ares, Rankin, & Sturz, 'The Manhattan Bail Project—An Interim Report on the Use of Pre-Trial Parole', 38 *N.Y.U. L. Rev.* 67 (1963).

[3] See Freed & Wald.

reformers will be looking to American experience for some modifications of a system with which they have thus far been satisfied.

Mechanics

In both England and the United States bail before trial is usually fixed in the magistrates' courts. In England an exception is made in treason cases, in which the accused must make application for bail to a High Court judge. Similarly, in some American states it is provided that only the judge of a superior court may admit a defendant to bail in capital cases.

In England, when bail is refused by the magistrate, the accused may make a second application to a judge of the Queen's Bench Division of the High Court, one of whom sits regularly in chambers to hear such applications. Few such applications are successful. This procedure is not available to secure a reduction of the amount of bail set by the magistrates, which can be done only through a writ of habeas corpus sought on the ground that the bail fixed is so excessive as to result in the unlawful imprisonment of the accused. Habeas corpus is likewise the customary procedure in the United States by which to challenge a magistrate's decision regarding bail. It is also possible, in a number of jurisdictions, to make a motion before a judge for the reduction of bail (and to appeal from an order denying the motion). But such procedures are seldom successful.

In both countries it is sometimes claimed that the magistrates exercise little independent discretion in the matter of bail, and that they have tended to give undue weight to the recommendations of the prosecution. In the United States this means the opinion of the district attorney, in England that of the police. It has been estimated that in each country the prosecutor's opinion is accepted in ninety-five per cent. of bail decisions. This is to some extent inevitable, for the courts usually have no other source to consult regarding the defendant's background. As indicated earlier, New York City is now experimenting with the use of probation officers to furnish information relevant to a grant of bail. This is costly, but it avoids the reproach of excessive prosecution influence.

Early and Late Bail Decisions

While the problem of bail arises most commonly in connexion with the defendant's first appearance before a magistrate, it can also arise at an earlier or later stage of proceedings. In England, it can arise whenever arrest is made under a warrant, because, as mentioned in the last chapter, magistrates in England are authorized to fix bail at the time they issue such a warrant.[1] The amount so fixed is endorsed on the warrant, and the police, without further judicial action, can themselves attend to the taking of bail. The practice of setting bail at the warrant stage is unusual in the United States and indeed contrary to the modern trend, which is to impose other than monetary conditions on release and to carefully investigate the background of the accused as a preliminary to deciding what should be done with him pending trial.

Furthermore, the English police have authority to admit to bail any person arrested without a warrant if they do not regard his case as a serious one;[2] and if he cannot be brought before a magistrate within twenty-four hours, they are required to grant bail. They do not, however, take cash from the accused. The English bail system generally extracts from the accused (and his sureties, if any) no more than a promise to forfeit a sum of money if and when he does not appear. It is this sort of promise, or 'recognizance', which the police demand when they admit a person to bail.

There are examples in some American states of police power to admit to bail, but these differ significantly from the English system, extending only to very trivial matters, mainly traffic offences. Bail is given in the form of cash, and not in order to ensure the defendant's appearance in court, but as a disguised means of fining him. The cash bail is fixed in the same amount as the maximum fine for the offence involved; it is forfeited on non-appearance, and the matter is taken no further.

The problem of bail can also arise after conviction and before sentencing, or after sentencing while the case is on appeal. After conviction the defendant is in a radically different position from that which he occupied before. He usually has a much weaker case for bail. His conviction removes the presumption of innocence, and adds to the possibility that he may try to escape. Furthermore, the easy grant of bail might be an inducement to him to engage in dilatory and frivolous appeals. In England it is assumed that bail after conviction should be granted rarely, and then on much more stringent terms than are usual before conviction. In the United States practice in this

---

[1] Devlin (1960), p. 71.
[2] Magistrates Court Act, 1952, 15 & 16 Geo. VI and 1 Eliz. II, c. 55, § 93.

regard varies greatly. In some states the practice is close to that in England, but in others, bail pending sentence or pending appeal is granted with comparative ease and on terms not much different from those required before conviction. The difference is partly due to different attitudes towards appeals. In the United States the point has almost been reached where it is thought no one is definitely guilty unless he has had at least one appeal. In England, on the other hand, the strong presumption is that conviction at trial establishes guilt.

THE PRELIMINARY EXAMINATION

English and American practice differ sharply as to the necessity of having preliminary examinations in cases which are to be tried in higher courts rather than by the magistrates themselves. In England a preliminary examination (sometimes called a 'committal proceeding' or a 'preliminary investigation' or a 'preliminary inquiry') is held in virtually every such case, whereas in the United States there are many cases where no examination is held because alternative methods of bringing cases to trial are available.

In many American states, the grand jury still functions. A prosecution may be begun before that body and the accused committed for trial without his ever having been before a magistrates' court. In England, the grand jury has disappeared.

In some American states an 'information' by a district attorney is given the same effect as an indictment by a grand jury, and the defendant may be brought to trial upon the basis of this accusation alone, without any preliminary hearing having been held. In England, the only rough equivalent in the case of a misdemeanour is the filing of an information by the Attorney-General, and in the case of a felony the filing of an 'indictment' by permission of a judge of the High Court. The former procedure is hardly ever used, and the latter procedure is used only in exceptional situations, such as where the accused is apprehended after his companions in crime have already been committed for trial, or where a preliminary hearing has already been held but a formal order for commitment has not been entered because of the illness of the magistrate.

In the United States the coroner's inquest may take the place of a preliminary hearing in a homicide case. In England such inquest is almost invariably followed by a preliminary examination of the usual type.

Waiver

Finally, in the United States the accused may waive the preliminary examination where he is entitled to have one.[1] This is done often and for a variety of reasons. One is the fact that a great majority of defendants plead guilty anyway; and for them the preliminary hearing serves no purpose other than to prevent the prompt disposition of their cases.[2] Another reason is that many defendants appear in the magistrates' court without counsel and are ignorant of any values which the preliminary hearing might have for them.[3] While the magistrate informs them of their right to a preliminary hearing and of their right to counsel, they seldom have either the knowledge or the money to avail themselves of these rights. Except in a few communities, it is uncommon to appoint counsel for indigents at this stage of the proceedings. Even defendants who are represented by counsel sometimes feel it is tactically advantageous for them to waive a preliminary hearing. They may expect the prosecutor to repay their co-operation by using his discretion to reduce the charge, or they may feel that, in any event, there is little to be gained from a preliminary hearing, because of the fact that in the United States the prosecution is not required to produce all of its evidence but only enough to make out a prima-facie case,[4] thus sharply curtailing the value of the hearing as a discovery device for the defendant. The net result is that the preliminary hearing is waived in a large proportion of all cases in the United States. There are some states where the prosecution as well as the defence must consent to a waiver of the preliminary examination, but such consent is usually forthcoming. The only time when it is not likely to be given is when the prosecution is anxious to get on record the testimony of witnesses who may change their stories by the time of trial, or when the prosecution seeks to compel answers from uncooperative witnesses. These goals, however, can often be better realized in grand jury proceedings in states where the grand jury is still active.

In England the preliminary examination cannot be waived by

---

[1] See Miller & Dawson, 'Non-Use of the Preliminary Examination: A Study of Current Practices', 1964 *Wis. L. Rev.* 252.

[2] If a defendant at his initial appearance before a magistrate indicates his intention to plead guilty, this may be taken as an implied waiver of a preliminary examination. Miller & Dawson, op. cit., pp. 255–60.

[3] Ibid., p. 264.

[4] See Note, 'Preliminary Hearing—An Interest Analysis', 51 *Iowa L. Rev.* 164, 167 (1965).

either the prosecution or the accused. Partly this is because the only basis for drafting a formal accusation (anomalously called an 'indictment' in England) is the evidence produced at the preliminary examination, and partly it is because of the fact that the defendant gains a real advantage from the preliminary examination. As we shall see in more detail in a later section, the English preliminary hearing amounts to a virtually full disclosure of the prosecution's case.

Function

When a preliminary examination is held in the United States, its basic function is the same as in England: to provide an early and independent check on the initial decision of the police or the district attorney to prosecute. This is a far cry from the original purpose of the preliminary examination in sixteenth-century England. Then it was an investigative tool by which justices of the peace might examine a suspect to see what evidence they could extract from and against him and to preserve it for trial. Only by slow degrees, as the functions of a magistrate became differentiated from those of a policeman, did the examination become a device for protecting an accused against unfounded accusations. Now the accused is entitled to be released from custody if the prosecution's evidence is insufficient.

In both countries the prosecution is required to produce enough evidence to make out a prima facie case, i.e. evidence sufficient, without anything said by the accused or his witnesses, to support a jury verdict of guilty. In England the prosecutor presents all the evidence then available to him which he thinks it is likely he will call on trial. In the United States the general rule of prosecutors is to produce only so much evidence as will ensure that the accused is bound over. In simple cases the difference is not likely to be great, but in cases of some complexity it is. This difference is important for its effect on discovery, which we shall consider later in this chapter.

In both countries, once the prosecution has made its case, the accused is given the opportunity of making a statement and of calling witnesses, but only after he has been warned that he is under no obligation to do either and that what he says may be used at trial. In neither country is it usual for the accused to put in any defence at a preliminary examination. In England, he is seldom legally represented at this stage, and unless he is, he will usually not avail himself of the opportunity to cross-examine prosecution witnesses to extract material useful at the trial. Sometimes legal aid is granted at this stage of proceedings, in which case the solicitor will very likely cross-examine the prosecution's witnesses. But even lawyers consider it wasted effort, and tactically unwise, to offer a defence (as distinguished from cross-examination) at this point unless it is so strong as to compel the accused's discharge. In the United States, as in England, the accused may have a lawyer at the preliminary hearing if he can afford one. In the majority of states an indigent still has no right to have a lawyer appointed for him at this stage, although more and more states are coming to provide free legal aid from the time of 'first appearance' onwards.

A significant contrast between preliminary hearings in the two countries concerns the effect of a finding by the magistrate that the prosecution's evidence is sufficient to hold the accused. In England at this point the accused is 'bound over' for trial in a higher court. In the United States he is 'bound over' for action by the grand jury or by the district attorney. Where the grand jury is used, it makes its own assessment of the evidence and decides whether or not to indict the defendant. Where the grand jury is not used, the district attorney has virtually complete discretion as to whether he will file an information or not. In subsequent sections of this chapter, we shall consider in further detail the role of the grand jury and the district attorney in drawing up accusations.

Reducing the Testimony to Writing

As to the mechanics of conducting preliminary examinations, the requirement in England is that the evidence of each witness be reduced to the form of a deposition, read over to or by him, and signed by him at the conclusion of his testimony. In some courts the clerk writes out the evidence in longhand, but in others silent typewriters are used or tape recordings made of the clerk's dictation for immediate transcription. Whatever method is used, an incidental effect is to enhance the dignity of the proceedings because of the necessity of having a reasonably quiet and orderly court room. Sometimes effective cross-examination is frustrated because of the delays while the answers are being taken down, but an experienced clerk develops great facility in condensing into narrative form the substance of what a witness says, eliminating irrelevancies, and so producing with reasonable speed a document which the parties and witnesses are usually willing to accept. The drawback is that any transcript short of a verbatim record of questions and answers (never attempted) may mislead or contain omissions, the significance of which becomes apparent only later.

The depositions so produced are used for a variety of purposes. They provide the material on which the indictment is based. They enable the trial judge to have a preview of a case before the trial starts. They help the prosecution by reducing the chance of witnesses altering their testimony. They are useful to the defence in revealing the prosecution's case and so indicating to the defence solicitor what lines of inquiry ought to be pursued, and helping to brief the barrister who handles the defence at the trial. Either side may use them to impeach a witness by showing prior inconsistent statements.

Depositions are also used in England to perpetuate testimony. If a witness dies or becomes otherwise unavailable for trial, his deposition may be offered in evidence. This is not altogether satisfactory because of the fact that the accused, often unrepresented by counsel at this stage, will ordinarily not have conducted a very effective cross-examination; and even lawyers in England tend to be restrained in cross-examining at the preliminary hearing, for the same reason that they generally refrain from putting in a defence at that point—to avoid giving away the defence case to the prosecution. Sometimes both sides agree to dispense with the presence of a witness at the trial if there is no dispute as to what he said at the preliminary hearing, in which case his deposition is admitted into evidence.

In the United States practice varies with regard to the manner of recording and using the preliminary examination. A few states require that in all cases the evidence be transcribed, while others require no record at all or else provide that a record need be made only if the prosecution or the defence requests it. Where a record is made a stenographic report of the full hearing is favoured, prepared by a court-employed stenographer or stenotypist. Where a written record is made available to both sides (this is not always the case), it can be used in much the same manner as in England except for the fact that the testimony of a prosecution witness cannot ordinarily be used at the trial, except for purposes of impeachment, without the consent of the accused. In other words, the preliminary examination cannot ordinarily be used to perpetuate prosecution testimony. This is explained chiefly by the constitutional requirement that the accused is entitled to be confronted by his accusers, which is ordinarily interpreted to mean that the confrontation must take place at the trial, not at any preliminary proceeding—at least not unless the accused was then represented by counsel.[1]

In the United States the quality of the preliminary hearing varies greatly with the quality of the magistracy. In some areas it is conducted, as it usually is in England, with relative decorum. But the situation is sometimes very bad in rural areas where justices of the peace are inexperienced or incompetent and is at its worst in some large cities where magistrates' courts are of poor quality. In such courts it is not unusual to find a noisy, crowded courtroom with policemen, defendants, bondsmen, and lawyers milling together in great disorder. In such an atmosphere, the unrepresented defendant is prone to succumb to pressure to waive the preliminary hearing or to get it over quickly.

Dismissal of Charges

In light of these conditions, it may be surprising that in such courts about half of the felony cases brought are dismissed at preliminary hearings. [2] This has been interpreted to mean that the police make too many unjustified arrests on felony charges, or that magistrates release suspects too freely. But it has also been suggested, with some truth, that many of these discharges do not result from magisterial decisions at all, but rather from decisions by the district attorney not to proceed further—at least not with felony charges when the accused agree to plead guilty to misdemeanours.

We have thus far been speaking as if the preliminary hearing were a judicial proceeding before a 'court'. In some respects it is not such a proceeding. In England and some American jurisdictions the preliminary examination is in theory held before the magistrate as an individual. In England this carries the consequence that preliminary inquiry can proceed before a single justice of the peace—although this does not often happen in practice—while the trial of a case always requires at least two lay justices. Another consequence is that the magistrate may exclude the public during the preliminary exami-

---

[1] In *Pointer* v. *Texas*, 380 U.S. 400 (1965), the chief witness for the state testified at the preliminary hearing. He was not cross-examined by the unrepresented indigent defendant. At the trial, the state introduced a transcript of the witness's testimony after showing that he had left the jurisdiction and would not return. The Supreme Court reversed the conviction, holding that the confrontation clause of the Sixth Amendment applied to the states, and the unrepresented defendant had been denied confrontation.

[2] Tappan, p. 332 (1960); Trebach, p. 62.

nation. Ordinarily the hearing is open to the public in both countries, but the holding of the preliminary examination *in camera* is one solution which has been suggested for a problem much discussed in England—namely the possible prejudice to the accused which results from publication in newspapers of the evidence given at this stage by the prosecution. It is, however, a suggestion which was rejected by a committee appointed to consider the matter,[1] which proposed instead that the press should be allowed to report virtually nothing other than the name of the accused and the charge until the ultimate trial was over.[2] Finally, because the preliminary examination in both countries is not a trial, a complaint dismissed by the magistrate may be subsequently reinstated without twice putting the accused in jeopardy. This practice is barred by statute in some American states, but is permitted in others and in England.

THE GRAND JURY

England abolished the grand jury in 1933. No American state has yet taken this step, although some states have constitutional provisions which allow their legislatures to take it. But while all states retain the grand jury in theory, only about half use it as a regular and indispensable adjunct of criminal prosecutions. In about twenty states prosecutors are granted the option in all cases of proceeding by information in lieu of grand jury indictment. There are some occasions in which prosecutors prefer to use the grand jury even where the law permits them to do otherwise, but on the whole where the prosecutor has the option to bypass it he usually does so. In California, for example, where the alternative is allowed, informations are used in ninety-seven per cent. of all felony cases.[3]

In over twenty states there is a constitutional provision which guarantees the right to grand jury indictment; and in about half a dozen other states statute law requires it. There are differences, however, as regards the categories of crime to which the right applies. At one extreme, South Carolina requires indictment for any crime where the punishment exceeds a fine of $100 or imprisonment for thirty days. At the other extreme, Florida requires it only in capital cases, and four other states only in cases punishable by death or life imprisonment.

---

[1] *Report of the Departmental Committee, Proceedings before Examining Justices*, Cmnd. 479 (1958).

[2] For a further discussion of this problem, see ch. 8.

[3] Comment, 'Some Aspects of the California Grand Jury System', 8 *Stan. L. Rev.* 631, 644 (1956).

The most common provision is that grand jury indictment is required in all felony cases, with an information by the district attorney being the ordinary method of accusation for misdemeanours.[1] In the federal courts, grand juries are required by the Fifth Amendment for 'capital, or otherwise infamous' crimes. This provision applies only to the federal government and the Supreme Court has held that the states do not violate the Fourteenth Amendment if they prosecute the same kinds of crimes without indictment.[2]

In the federal courts and in a number of states the defendant may, with consent of the district attorney, waive his right to grand jury indictment, just as he may waive the preliminary hearing.[3] If he does, the case may be prosecuted by information. In other states, including New York, the grand jury cannot be waived.

The members of a grand jury are laymen, selected by lot from tax or voting rolls, or, in some states, by local officials who exercise discretion in their selection. Generally, there are from twelve to twenty-three members, as was formerly the case in England, although there are states where there may be as few as five members. In rural areas grand juries sit infrequently; but in large urban areas there may be several grand juries sitting simultaneously in continuous session, with members serving for a term of a month or more.

Secrecy

Grand jury sessions are universally supposed to be secret. The jurors are generally required to take an oath of secrecy, which in some states is supported by criminal sanctions for disclosure. Witnesses before a grand jury are not generally sworn to secrecy, although such an oath is required by a few courts. In most cases there is probably no occasion for a juror or witness to violate his oath, but a problem arises in a few sensational investigations in which the newspapers take an interest. It is not unknown for the result of the jury's poll to appear in the press. In such situations it has been held that the informer may be subject to contempt proceedings (which are rarely instituted), but that an indictment is not affected by his disclosures since the rule of secrecy is intended to benefit the prosecution, not the accused.

Grand jury proceedings in the United States, however, are always properly attended by the district attorney or his deputy, in many

---

[1] For a general discussion, see Orfield (1947), pp. 142–4.
[2] *Hurtado* v. *California*, 110 U.S. 516 (1884).
[3] Orfield (1947), pp. 212–14.

states by a court stenographer, and sometimes by a bailiff or court clerk. The presence of the public prosecutor is not considered an exception to the rule of secrecy, for he is deemed to be an integral part of the machinery of the American grand jury and usually has a duty, as well as a privilege, to attend its sessions, chiefly to conduct the examination of witnesses. This practice has historical roots in the old English procedure in which the grand jury could invite the solicitor for the complaining party to attend its sessions while witnesses were examined.[1]

The minutes of the grand jury are ordinarily kept secret from private persons, including the defendant. They are, however, often made available to law enforcement agencies and are customarily in the possession of the prosecution at the time of trial. A few states allow the defendant a grand jury transcript, but elsewhere, requests by an accused for a pre-trial inspection of the minutes are consistently refused. Some states, including New York, require the court to inspect the minutes *in camera* upon a motion of the defendant to quash the indictment because of the insufficiency of the evidence before the grand jury.

Basis of Inquiry

Unlike the magistrate at a preliminary examination, the grand jury does not need a formal charge in order to conduct an inquiry into criminal conduct. It has power to inquire into any offence which has been called to its attention by the judge in his charge, or which has been brought to its attention by the public prosecutor, or which is within the personal knowledge of one of its members, or which is disclosed in the course of its investigations. The power of the grand jury to undertake an inquiry into criminal conduct on its own motion is rarely exercised, although not altogether quiescent. The usual practice is for a grand jury to investigate under the direction of the district attorney. There is a sharp conflict of authority as to whether the grand jurors may act on the allegations of a private informer, the prevailing view being that they may, although practically they hardly ever do so.

The close connexion of the district attorney with the grand jury's work has, in the opinion of some persons, turned the grand jury into 'the prosecutor's puppet'. This view has been sharply contested, mainly by public prosecutors. The secrecy of the proceedings makes it difficult to know just what goes on, but objectively it is known that

[1] Stephen, p. 274.

grand juries sometimes 'ignore' (dismiss) indictments (this happens in roughly ten per cent. of the cases in New York) and reduce many charges from felonies to misdemeanours. On the other hand, it is not inconceivable that the finding of a 'no bill' often results from a hint or suggestion by the district attorney, particularly in the routine case where the grand jurors do not have the time to develop real familiarity with the facts. Even in the case of a sustained investigation there is a tendency for the district attorney to direct the operations of the grand jury.

The American grand jury is not entirely concerned with the investigation of crime. In most states, it is also empowered to inquire into certain enumerated aspects of county government, such as the condition and management of prisons, the county treasury, poor-houses, and the courts. In a few states, notably California, the list is quite extensive, covering virtually the whole of local government. Concern with such matters continues even in some states where the grand jury is no longer used in ordinary criminal matters.

In about twenty states the grand jury is empowered by statute to inquire into public corruption and misconduct in office by public officials. In a few states, notably Michigan, a judge of a superior court may act as a 'one man grand jury' for the purpose of conduct-ing such an investigation. However, depending partly on statutory language and partly on judicial attitudes, it is held in some states that grand juries are limited in such investigations to instances where there is reason to believe that criminal misconduct will be discovered; and that there is no general power to proceed with an inquiry simply on the chance or speculation that a crime may be unveiled. Even where a grand jury has properly exercised its general power to investigate, the weight of authority is that it has no power to issue a 'report' criticizing the conduct of public or private persons unless it furnishes the basis for an indictment against them.[1] Upon proper motion by an individual named therein, such a report may be ex-punged, and there are cases in which libel actions have been allowed on the ground that such a report was extrajudicial and unprivileged. On the other hand, there are a few states (e.g. California, Florida, New Jersey) where such reports are allowed and made frequently. New York was long considered the leading exponent of the position

[1] See Kuh, 'The Grand Jury "Presentment": Foul Blow or Fair Play?', 55 *Colum. L. Rev.* 1103 (1955); Note, 'The Grand Jury as an Investigatory Body', 74 *Harv. L. Rev.* 590 (1961).

that there was no power to issue them, but the New York cases were not clear and a few New York grand juries continued to make such reports until 1961. At that time the Court of Appeals ruled that the practice was unlawful. However in 1964 the state legislature by statute restored the power in large part.[1]

The Value of the Grand Jury

Grand juries are often criticized as cumbersome, expensive, and time-consuming, and the claim is made that most of their functions can be performed just as effectively and with greater fairness to the accused by preliminary examinations. It was mainly for such reasons that England abolished grand juries in 1933. The contrary arguments are as follows: First, the grand jury provides a forum in which baseless accusations can be examined and rejected without exposing the accused to unfavourable publicity. Second, the grand jury's broad power to inquire into allegations of misconduct or corruption makes it a useful and impartial tool for maintaining the purity of public administration. In England this function may be adequately performed by Royal Commissions and Tribunals of Inquiry, but in the United States the alternatives, such as investigation by legislative committees, seem to be less satisfactory. Third, and most important to prosecutors, the grand jury is a vehicle for securing sworn testimony in secret from uncooperative witnesses. This can be particularly useful in cases involving organized crime and large-scale commercial fraud. Without the grand jury the police and the prosecutor cannot compel testimony in advance of trial. The unofficial pressures which they can exert are apt to have little effect on professional criminals working in disciplined gangs or on white collar criminals acting under expert legal advice. In 1964 there was an example of a large-scale fraud in England involving the bribery of professional football players which escaped police detection but was uncovered by a newspaper which induced a participant (for a substantial fee) to tell his story. That is the sort of situation in which a grand jury inquiry might have enabled official investigators to make progress.

PROSECUTOR'S DISCRETION

In both England and the United States the police exercise a wide discretion with regard to offenders against whom they will proceed.

[1] *N.Y. Code Crim. Proc.*, § 253 (*a*).

In the United States a similar discretion is exercised by the district attorney throughout the pre-trial stages of a case and sometimes even during trial. In England there is no comparable discretion. No prosecutor in England can of his own motion drop the proceedings once he has started them, and the Attorney-General's power to enter a *nolle prosequi* is very rarely exercised. One reason may be that the English police are more careful than those in the United States about the cases they take to court; another may be that the availability of summary trial before the magistrates in the great majority of cases in England makes it unnecessary to resort to non-judicial methods of easing the calendars of the superior trial courts. The main explanation, however, seems to lie in the fact that England has no professional prosecutors. Since counsel for the prosecution are briefed on a case by case basis by the solicitor for the local police, or by the Attorney-General, they are not committed to obtaining a conviction either for the offence charged or for any lesser included offence. Unlike many American prosecutors, they have no compunction about going to trial with a case they may lose.

The American district attorney exercises enormous power over the course of criminal proceedings.[1] Before a preliminary hearing or grand jury proceeding, he has virtually complete discretion not to accuse; and no one is likely to challenge his estimate that the evidence is insufficient to warrant going further. In the grand jury room, he effectively controls the proceedings, for although it is possible for a grand jury to act in defiance of the district attorney, it hardly ever does so. In states where an information usually follows a preliminary hearing when the defendant is bound over, the prosecutor may refuse to file one. A number of states require that he must then file in writing the reason for failing to proceed with an information, but these reasons are usually accepted without question. After filing an indictment or information, the district attorney enjoys the common-law power of the English Attorney-General to enter a *nolle prosequi*, and often does so. A number of states try to control this power by requiring that the consent of the trial court must be obtained, but courts usually grant such consent as a matter of course. It is generally felt that the American advocate should somehow be committed to

---

[1] See, e.g., Kaplan, 'The Prosecutorial Discretion—A Comment', 60 *Nw. U. L. Rev.* 174 (1965); Nedrud, 'The Role of the Prosecutor in Criminal Procedure'; 32 *U. Kan. City L. Rev.* 142 (1964); Note, 'Prosecutors Discretion', 103 *U. Pa. L. Rev.* 1057 (1955).

his cause, and that it is useless to compel a prosecutor to go to trial with a case which he would rather drop. There may be legitimate reasons for his declining to prosecute—especially since the screening of cases by the police and the magistrates in the United States is sometimes perfunctory. At any rate, throughout the United States, many criminal cases are terminated by the prosecution, and formal methods for reviewing the prosecution's discretion in terminating them are largely non-existent.

The Negotiated Plea

A frequent occasion for the exercise of the prosecutor's discretion is in connexion with the 'negotiated' guilty plea. This sort of plea is not unknown in England, where it happens once in a while that the prosecution may ask the court for permission to withdraw one or more charges if the defendant indicates that he will plead guilty to the others.[1] In the United States this practice is a predominant feature of criminal procedure. There are a few prosecutors who refuse to engage in such negotiations, but in most localities a very large number of guilty pleas are entered as a result of bargains struck by defendants and the district attorney. Usually the accused agrees to plead guilty on the prosecution's agreement to reduce the charge from a felony to a misdemeanor; and often he does so on the prosecutor's promise to recommend a lenient sentence, a recommendation which prosecuting counsel has no power to make in England, and which the courts in the United States are not bound to accept. This whole process is subject to abuse.[2] On the other hand, a prosecutor may have legitimate reasons for bargaining with the defendant—reasons which relate to the strength of the prosecution's case and the expense and uncertainty of a contested jury trial. Furthermore, in light of the general severity of American penal statutes, the bargained plea is a useful device for insuring that a defendant will be punished while avoiding at the same time the risk of an unduly harsh penalty allowed by the legislature.[3]

[1] Fitzgerald, p. 158.

[2] A recent federal District Court decision has pointed up the constitutional difficulties inherent in plea bargaining—at least where the court itself participates. *Elksnis* v. *New York* (S.D.N.Y. 13 June 1966) in *N.Y. Times*, 14 June 1966, p. 1, col. 7.

[3] See Ohlin & Remington, 'Sentencing Structure: Its Effect upon Systems for the Administration of Criminal Justice', 23 *Law & Contemp. Prob.* 495 (1958); Note, 'Statutory Structures for Sentencing Felons to Prison', 69 *Colum. L. Rev.* 1134 (1960).

Granting Immunity from Prosecution

A distinct species of prosecution bargaining is a grant of immunity from prosecution to a witness in order to compel his testimony. In both the United States and England a witness enjoys the common-law privilege against self-incrimination. In the United States this privilege is enshrined in the Fifth Amendment and now by virtue of the Fourteenth Amendment applies to the states as well as to the federal government. In England it is possible to remove the privilege by tendering to the witness a pardon under the Great Seal in respect of all offences for which he might be prosecuted by reason of his evidence. This is cumbersome and rarely used, but no need is thought to exist for an alternative procedure in ordinary criminal cases. In the United States a pardon can be used in the same way (although the witness can retain his privilege by rejecting the pardon) but the usual basis for granting immunity is statutory.

The statutes differ in their provisions, but they are of two main varieties. One type provides that the witness must answer incriminating questions as a matter of course with reference to investigations into specific types of crime, but that he shall not be prosecuted in consequence of his answers. The other empowers the prosecutor to offer immunity to a recalcitrant witness in his discretion, although sometimes with the approval of the trial judge or grand jury members. A reason why such statutes have been thought necessary in the United States but not in England is that they counteract the effects of the doctrine of implied waiver of privilege developed by American courts. Under this doctrine, if a witness answers without objection the early questions in a series concerning a particular transaction, he may lose his privilege for the whole series. The result is to make witnesses over-cautious about saying anything. Refusal to testify occurs, and is often upheld, at what to English observers seems an absurdly early stage of the inquiry. In England a judge allows the claim of privilege only when there is substantial danger of prosecution.[1]

The American prosecutor has to be careful about deciding when to offer immunity. Owing to the early stage at which the privilege may be asserted, he cannot be sure as to the extent of the 'immunity bath' he will confer.

The American federal system used to raise a difficulty in the granting of immunity because of the idea that a state could not grant

[1] Williams, 'The Privilege against Self-Incrimination—England', 51 *J. Crim. L., C. & P.S.* 166 (1960).

immunity from prosecution by other states or by the federal government. However, the Supreme Court has now held that a necessary corollary of the Fifth Amendment is that immunity once granted binds all other agencies, federal and state.[1]

METHODS OF ACCUSATION

The methods of accusation commonly employed in England and the United States have been touched upon earlier at several points,[2] but a brief summary may be useful here.

In England a magistrates' court can try a case simply by stating to the accused the substance of the charge against him, even though his appearance in court has been secured on the basis of an 'information' or 'complaint'. 'Information' in this context refers to the statement which accompanies a request for issuance of a summons or warrant of arrest. The information used to support a warrant must be in writing. That used to support a summons need not be, but then the accused has the language of the summons as a written indication of the charge against him. 'Complaint' refers to the charge made against the accused who is arrested without a warrant. It does not have to be reduced to writing, but English police practice is to give the accused a written copy of the charge upon his being charged.

A preliminary inquiry requires a written statement of the charge. In substance, this statement is no different from that used in summary proceedings. It consists of a short summary, often in one or two lines, of the nature of the offence charged. When, after the preliminary hearing, the accused is committed for trial, the initial charges are discarded. The depositions and a copy of any statement made by the accused are used by the clerk of the court of trial to prepare a 'bill of indictment'. The clerk's signature on the indictment is all that is needed to bring the accused to trial. The term 'indictment' in this context is a carry-over from the days of the grand jury in England; logically, it should have been abolished along with the grand jury, but this was not done.

In the United States a complaint signed by a policeman or private party may sometimes be used to commence a prosecution in a lower court. This is often the case with regard to petty offences such as traffic violations. Otherwise, a case must be begun by either presentment,

---

[1] *Murphy* v. *Waterfront Comm'n*, 378 U.S. 52 (1963); see Sobel, 'The Privilege against Self-Incrimination "Federalized" ', 31 *Brook. L. Rev.* 1, 44–47 (1964).

[2] See generally Devlin (1960), pp. 101–6, 109–11; Kenny, pp. 576–84; Orfield (1947), pp. 194–265: Puttkammer, pp. 125–43.

indictment, or information. A presentment, which is recognized in some but not all states, is an accusation returned by a grand jury on its own initiative. This is a rare occurrence, and when it happens the prosecution usually steps in to draft the instrument. An indictment is an accusation returned by a grand jury on the basis of evidence laid before it by a district attorney. An information is an accusation signed and filed by a district attorney on his own authority. The drafting of indictments and informations is nearly always done in the prosecutor's office. As indicated earlier, the trend in the United States has been towards use of the information instead of the indictment. There are a few states which require leave of the trial court before an information can be filed. Most do not, although many require that a preliminary examination be held before an information is filed in any felony case; and some provide for preliminary examination in any case where an information is used. However, it is generally held that an accused can waive his right to the preliminary examination and permit an information to be filed against him without it.

About the only thing he cannot waive at this stage is his right to the accusation itself.[1] Under the common law charges were kept concealed from the accused until the last minute. It was considered that the accused was adequately put on notice of the charge if the indictment was read to him at the opening of trial. Today, in both England and the United States, an accused can generally get a copy of the indictment or information as soon as it has been filed. Besides allowing better preparation by the defence, this makes possible a pre-trial determination of important questions as to the sufficiency of the pleadings and the admissibility of evidence. The consequence is a saving of time and money on trial if a motion or preliminary hearing results in quashing the indictment or in the exclusion of evidence without which the prosecution cannot hope to succeed. This development has gained great impetus in the United States from the rapid spread of exclusionary doctrines and promises to gain more from the growing receptivity of judges to pre-trial claims by defendants for discovery of the prosecution's evidence.

DISCOVERY

The English Pattern

In England the system of preliminary inquiry has been transformed into a very extensive discovery process. A convention has been estab-

---

[1] Orfield (1947), pp. 204–8.

lished that the prosecution must introduce not only so much evidence as will support committal, but all the material evidence then at its disposal.[1] Furthermore, if the prosecution wishes to use at the trial evidence which it obtains later, it must, in advance of trial, serve on the defence a notice setting out in the form of statements by witnesses the gist of the additional evidence it proposes to adduce. In this way the defence gets to know virtually the whole of the prosecution's case. These conventions are faithfully observed and enforced. While the judges do not usually hold evidence inadmissible when the prosecution has failed to give proper notice, they give the defence an adjournment if it is taken by surprise.

Neither of these conventions has become established in the United States. Furthermore, in many states the prosecutor can avoid a preliminary hearing altogether by presenting his case to a grand jury or proceeding forthwith to file an information.

English discovery is not based entirely on the preliminary examination. Another important element is the tradition that the prosecuting counsel does not go all out for conviction, but is willing to share with the defence any information in his possession which may help the accused. This convention applies theoretically in the United States, where, indeed, it is a rule of law to the extent that the prosecutor's suppression at trial of evidence favourable to the accused constitutes a denial of due process of law.[2] But courts do not grant relief

---

[1] The development in England of the preliminary hearing as a discovery vehicle is traced in Traynor, 'Ground Lost and Found in Criminal Discovery in England', 39 *N.Y.U. L. Rev.* No. 749 (1964); see also Louisell, 'Criminal Discovery: Dilemma Real or Apparent?', 49 *Calif. L. Rev.* 56, 64–67 (1961).

[2] The suppression cases evolved from Supreme Court holdings that a prosecutor's knowing use of false or perjured testimony violated due process. Note, 'The Prosecutor's Constitutional Duty to Reveal Evidence to the Defendant', 74 *Yale L.J.* 136–40 (1964). Early suppression cases found a violation where the prosecutor intentionally suppressed exculpatory evidence. Note, 'The Duty of the Prosecutor to Disclose Exculpatory Evidence', 60 *Colum. L. Rev.* 858 (1960). More recently the federal courts have found a violation where the evidence, although it would not exonerate the defendant, was potentially useful to him in constructing his defence. *Brady* v. *Maryland*, 373 U.S. 83 (1963) (evidence useful in attempt to avoid capital punishment); *Ashley* v. *Texas*, 319 F. 2d 80 (5th Cir. 1963) (evidence of professional opinion that defendant was insane, although insanity was not used at trial). Further, the prosecutor no longer has to intentionally suppress evidence to violate due process. *United States* v. *Consolidated Laundries Corp.*, 291 F. 2d 562 (2d Cir. 1961) (negligent suppression of documents resulting from misplacement of file by someone in government's employ), 62 *Colum. L. Rev.* 562 (1962). For a discussion of the most recent cases, see Note, 'The Prosecutor's Constitutional Duty to Reveal Evidence to the Defendant', 74 *Yale L.J.* 136 (1964). See also Everett, 'Discovery in Criminal Cases—In Search of a Standard', 1964 *Duke*

unless the defendant was prejudiced, and conventions are not observed as scrupulously in the United States as they are in England. The English are generally accustomed to follow informal canons of conduct; and the position of prosecuting counsel as independent members of the bar, engaging in the work of defence as well, aids in the observance of such rules. As a result, a number of rules have emerged in addition to those mentioned above concerning disclosure to counsel for an accused of material in the hands of the prosecution. Some of these rules have been reinforced by opinions of the Court of Criminal Appeal, but they depend mainly for their effectiveness on the tightly-knit character of the English Bar. The most important of these rules are as follows:

1. If a person who may help the accused and who has not been called at the preliminary examination has been interviewed by the police or by the prosecution, his name, but not a copy of his statement, must be supplied to the defence.[1] If he is to be called to testify, the substance of his evidence must also be supplied to the defence.[2]

2. If a prosecution witness has made a statement to the police which contains material favourable to the accused, a copy of that statement is ordinarily supplied to the defence.[3]

3. If at the trial a prosecution witness gives testimony that conflicts with a statement he has previously given to the police, either the statement or the inconsistent portion of it is ordinarily supplied to the defence.[4]

4. If a prosecution witness has a previous criminal conviction which affects his credibility, that fact must be communicated to the defence.[5]

L.J. 477, 511–17; Note, 'Discovery and Disclosure: Dual Aspects of the Prosecutor's Role in Criminal Procedure', 34 *Geo. Wash. L. Rev.* 92, 101–4 (1964); Comment, 39 *N.Y.U. L. Rev.* 565 (1964), 77 *Harv. L. Rev.* 1528 (1964). An important distinction between the suppression and discovery cases is that the former are founded on due process while state and federal courts have uniformly found no constitutional foundation to claims for discovery. Louisell, op. cit., p. 90 n. 159. In California the appellate courts have developed plenary forms of criminal discovery upon the foundation of the supervisory power of the courts. See Traynor, 'Ground Lost and Found in Criminal Discovery', 39 *N.Y.U. L. Rev.* 228, 245 (1964).

[1] *R.* v. *Bryant* (1946), 31 Crim. App. R. 146 (C.C.A.).
[2] Ex parte *Downes* [1954], 1 Q.B. 1, 6 (1953).
[3] Traynor, op. cit., pp. 765–6.
[4] Ibid.
[5] See *R.* v. *Collister* (1955), 39 Crim. App. R. 100, 104–5 (C.C.A.).

5. If the accused has a previous criminal conviction, that fact must be supplied to his counsel.[1]
6. If the accused has made a written statement to the police which has not been put in at the preliminary examination, a copy of this statement must be supplied to the defence.[2]
7. If the accused while in custody has been examined by a prison doctor with regard to his mental responsibility, a copy of any report made by that doctor must be supplied to the defence.[3]
8. If a scientific laboratory examination has been conducted in the case, the results of that examination must be supplied to the defence on request. If the results are clearly favourable to the accused, they must be supplied without request.[4]
9. If there are documents in the case which the police have seized from the accused or obtained from other sources, they may be examined by the defence upon request. Whenever these documents may help the accused, the defence is notified and given facilities for inspecting them without having made a request.[5]

The American Pattern

In the United States it is difficult to portray accurately the extent of discovery. Partly this is because formal rules on the subject vary widely from state to state, and partly it is because much information is disclosed to the defence only as a matter of grace or only in connexion with procedures designed for purposes other than discovery.

Formal rules, whether embodied in statute, court rule, or decisional law, or a combination of these, differ markedly from state to state both as to the information which can be reached and as to the procedure by which discovery is accomplished. Considering the United States as a whole, one can find isolated rules granting the right to discover almost any item of information which could be desired by the defence. But in any given jurisdiction one is likely to find alongside of a liberal rule granting broad discovery of certain kinds of information or in certain situations, another rule severely restricting discovery of other kinds of information or in other situations. What is lacking in all jurisdictions is a comprehensive set of rules, based on an appreciation of the defence's legitimate discovery needs weighed against

---

[1] Practice Note, 39 Crim. App. R. 20 (1955).
[2] Traynor, op. cit., p. 362.
[3] *R.* v. *Casey* (1947), 32 Crim. App. R. 91 (C.C.A.).
[4] Traynor, op. cit., p. 861.   [5] Ibid., pp. 761–3.

the legitimate needs of the government to protect information and witnesses, and set in a regularized and feasible procedural framework that minimizes abuse and makes discovery equally available to all defendants.

Much of the discovery currently available results from procedures and practices that operate outside formal discovery rules. This informal discovery is of two types.

First, many prosecutors voluntarily make available evidence and information to defence counsel in whom they have special confidence.[1] Sometimes this is done in return for stipulations of fact but sometimes simply out of a sense of fairness. The practice operates outside the orbit of judicial supervision and is of such low visibility that there is no way to accurately gauge the volume of the information exchanged thereby.

Second, the defence derives much information from pre-trial procedures which in theory have nothing to do with discovery. Such are the preliminary hearing to determine probable cause, and hearings on motions to quash or suppress unlawfully obtained evidence, including confessions.[2] All require pre-trial determinations which involve some of the same evidence and witnesses to be used at the trial proper, thus providing the defence with a preview of parts of the prosecution's case. At best, however, the information provided is spotty and incomplete rather than comprehensive.

There is strong resistance by many American prosecutors to the establishment of discovery as an explicit right of the defence. The principal reason given is the possibility of corrupt action by the accused to weaken or destroy the prosecution's case, as by terrorizing witnesses, suborning perjury, or forging documents. In the estimate of many prosecutors and some judges, there are American defence attorneys who are not beyond assisting their clients in such endeavours. In consequence, devices which would assure discovery as a matter of course are not favoured in most jurisdictions. In the greater part of the United States, pre-trial discovery is 'not only inadequate, but riddled with arbitrary rules'.[3] In the eyes of English observers this is

---

[1] The prosecutor's acquaintance with and confidence in defence counsel is a significant factor in fostering informal discovery practices. Discovery in Federal Criminal Cases, 33 F.R.D. 47, 116, 120 (1963); see Comment, 'Five Years under *State* v. *Thompson*—Criminal Pre-trial Discovery in Washington', 39 *Wash. L. Rev.* 853, 867 (1964).

[2] See, e.g., *People* v. *Huntley*, 15 N.Y. 2d 72, 204 N.E. 2d 179, 255, N.Y.S. 2d 838 (1965).   [3] Traynor, op. cit., p. 235.

one of the most serious criticisms to be made of criminal justice in the United States. It seems barbarous to them that a defendant should be forced to trial ignorant of the case he has to meet—and anomalous in view of the very broad discovery allowed in civil cases in the United States.

Prosecutors tend to minimize the discovery features of the preliminary examination by disclosing as little as possible at that stage or, when they can, by going directly to a grand jury, whose minutes are shrouded in secrecy. Although there are grounds for quashing a conviction if it can be shown that the prosecutor withheld evidence helpful to the defence at trial, this idea has not been translated into a rule governing pre-trial disclosures, or one which covers material not clearly exculpatory. In many but not all states, the names of witnesses before the grand jury are required to be endorsed on the indictment; but if the prosecution calls a witness whose name is not on the list, he will almost invariably be permitted to testify.[1]

Witnesses' statements in the prosecutor's file are not, as a rule, freely available to the defence. In the federal courts an act of Congress confirms this point.[2] This statute arose as the sequel to *Jencks* v. *United States*[3] in which the Supreme Court held that in a federal prosecution the defence counsel was entitled to obtain for use in cross-examination any statement given by a witness to the government which touched on his testimony at trial. The decision was criticized as opening investigatory files to every spy and gangster in the country, and it was misinterpreted by some lower federal courts to require that the defence be allowed pre-trial discovery of the prosecution's entire file. The statute was passed to make it clear that the prosecution was not required to disclose any statement unless the witness had taken the stand and testified. In some states similar rules have evolved, permitting limited discovery of statements of prosecution witnesses.[4]

---

[1] See Goldstein, 'The State and the Accused: Balance of Advantage in Criminal Procedure', 69 *Yale L. J.* 1149, 1185 (1960).

[2] 18 U.S.C., § 3500(*a*) (1958).

[3] 353 U.S. 657 (1957).

[4] It has been held that the *Jencks* case did not announce a constitutional principle, and state courts generally have declined to follow it. For example, *State* v. *Aubuchon*, 381 S.W. 2d 807 (Mo. 1964). However, the decision did influence the New York Court of Appeals to hold that before cross examination of a witness the defence may inspect his prior statement even where the court sees no variance between the statement and his direct testimony. *People* v. *Rosario*, 9 N.Y. 2d 286, 173 N.E. 2d 881, 213 N.Y.S. 2d 448 (1961).

In the federal courts an accused has not generally been allowed to inspect even a copy of his own statement or confession in the prosecution's hands. Some states have likewise denied him the right, but a few by statute have provided that the defence must be supplied with the statement if it is to be used in evidence, and others have left the matter to the discretion of the trial judge. In such jurisdictions an abuse of discretion may be found if discovery is denied.[1]

As to allowing the defence to obtain scientific laboratory reports, there are few cases in point, and they go both ways. Perhaps this reflects a tendency of prosecutors to allow the defence to inspect such reports without court compulsion, since they represent the type of evidence least susceptible to tampering by the accused.[2]

It is generally assumed that trial courts possess discretion to allow the defence an inspection of documents and tangible evidence in the hands of the prosecution, but many courts have denied such discovery.[3] The federal courts[4] and those of a few states are governed by a rule which provides that the defence may obtain before trial documents and tangible objects which were obtained from or belong to the accused or which were obtained from others by seizure or process, but even this has been restrictively interpreted.[5] A proposed amendment to the Federal Rules is now under consideration which would allow pre-trial inspection by the defence of virtually all material, except statements of witnesses, in the hands of federal prosecutors, including both statements of the accused and scientific reports.

From the foregoing discussion it is clear that while most American states allow relatively little discovery explicitly and as of right, there are some in which the accused's rights to discovery are quite extensive —albeit on a piecemeal basis, without a comprehensive or articulate pattern. There is great variation from state to state, but it is clear that criminal discovery is not unknown in the United States, as is sometimes carelessly asserted. In California, which has gone further in permitting discovery than any other state, a defendant has a right to disclosure of virtually all facts known to the prosecution.[6] This is true in minor cases as well as the more serious ones, since discovery is not tied to the preliminary examination but exists independently of it, operating in response to motions.

---

[1] Note, 'Developments in the Law—Discovery', 74 *Harv. L. Rev.* 940, 1053–4 (1961).   [2] Ibid., p. 1061.

[3] Comment, 'Pre-Trial Disclosure in Criminal Discovery', 60 *Yale L.J.* 626, 627–8 (1951).   [4] Fed. R. Crim. P. 16.

[5] Traynor, op. cit., p. 234.   [6] Ibid., pp. 243–5.

Adequacy of Discovery in the Two Nations

In broad terms, English discovery is superior to what is found in most of the United States. However, as against what is permitted to the defence in California, the English system of discovery has a number of drawbacks.

First, the English system allows of relatively little discovery in summary trials held in magistrates' courts. The only information that the defence gets in such cases is whatever is contained in the summons or charge plus copies of any written statements by a co-defendant, and, sometimes, on request, a copy of the written statement of the accused. In general, it never gets statements of witnesses or information about an oral statement of the accused, although some police forces, notably that in London, will on request and unofficially acquaint the defending solicitor with their case. But most defendants are unrepresented. The situation is even worse in the lower courts of most states of the United States, but the jurisdiction of these courts is ordinarily restrained within narrow limits; the cases they hear are reasonably well suited to a quick and informal hearing with a minimum of pre-trial preparation. In the English magistrates' courts the limitation on discovery is far more serious because, as we have seen, their trial jurisdiction has been steadily enlarged to include 97 per cent. of all cases tried in England.

Second, in England the defence takes a risk in interviewing witnesses for the prosecution. The English attitude is that such interviews are liable to result in witness-tampering and should be avoided. Most solicitors try to avoid them, and so are likely to remain ignorant of any information which cannot be had by discovery from the prosecution. In the United States interviewing witnesses, with or without discovery, is considered essential to the proper preparation of a defence. In California the defence has an explicitly recognized right to do so, and may obtain an order that the prosecution refrain from interfering with that right.

Third, to Americans the English system seems to rely too heavily on professional courtesy and the discretion of prosecuting counsel. The danger is not so much in the granting of special favours for selected defence counsel, for the nature of the English legal profession is such that favours are generally distributed equally. The significant criticism is rather that so many of the English canons of discovery depend on the prosecution's deciding that certain material may be useful to the defence. It is open to doubt whether prosecuting counsel is always the best person to make this decision. Defence counsel, given access to information in the hands of the prosecution as a matter of right, might well find evidence useful to his client which the prosecutor overlooked because his business was not primarily to seek every possible advantage for the accused.

In both countries there is some concern over the lack of reciprocity in criminal discovery procedures,[1] which may become more important as the scope of discovery in favour of the defence is extended. In the United States, there have been attempts to make the defence give notice of its intention to rely on one or the other of two defences: alibi and insanity. Fourteen states require such notice in the case of an alibi defence, and seventeen require it in the case of a defence of insanity.[2] Some writers in both countries have argued that in all matters the defence as well as the prosecution should be prevented from practising trial by ambush. The California Supreme Court has held that in certain circumstances the prosecution is entitled to pretrial discovery against an accused who raises an affirmative defence.[3] The possibilities of discovery in favour of the prosecution are, however, somewhat limited in the United States by the constitutional guarantee against self-incrimination. English tradition imposes a similar limitation. Perhaps equally important in preserving lack of reciprocity in discovery will be the humane tradition of both countries to give the defendant a 'break', reinforced by the feeling that fairness in criminal justice cannot be determined by purely logical considerations.

[1] Devlin (1960), pp. 63–64; Traynor, op. cit., pp. 756–7; Traynor, op. cit., pp. 246–50.
[2] 75 *Harv. L. Rev.* 838 (1963).
[3] *Jones* v. *Superior Court* 58 Cal. 2d 56, 372 P. 2d 919, 22 Cal. Reptr. 879 (1962).

8

THE TRIAL

BOTH in the United States and England a more summary procedure is provided for minor cases than is used for cases of greater gravity. We shall start with the way in which the choice is made between the two modes of trial, then describe briefly the summary procedure, and then devote the bulk of the chapter to the trial of the more serious cases.

CHOICE OF COURT AND MODE OF TRIAL

In England the most serious offences can be tried only by Assize or Quarter Sessions courts, and the least serious offences, like traffic infractions, can be tried only in magistrates' courts. Between the two extremes is a wide range of offences which can be tried in either type of court, depending upon the desires of the accused and the discretion of the magistrates. All cases start in the magistrates' court, but some continue there only through the preliminary hearing, whereas others are heard and finally determined there. It is in that court also that a decision is made as to the mode of trial and the appropriate tribunal.

If the accused, having been advised of his rights, demands trial by jury for one of the medium-grade offences, as he is privileged to do, his case will automatically be removed from the magistrates' court and sent to Quarter Sessions for trial. The magistrates have no power to empanel a jury. In most cases the accused is willing to waive his right to trial by jury in the hope of receiving a lighter sentence, and concluding the proceedings quickly. When this happens, the magistrates must decide whether they should handle the case themselves or refer it to a higher court.

They have no difficulty with this problem if the maximum penalty for the offence is less than the maximum sentence they are empowered to impose—generally speaking, imprisonment for six months and a fine of £100 for a single offence. The case will remain in the magistrates' court. If, however, the maximum penalty for the offence is beyond the sentencing power of the magistrates, they must consider whether, in the event of conviction, a heavier sentence is likely to be necessary. At the outset of proceedings they are likely to know virtually nothing about the circumstances of the offence and the character of the accused, and their knowledge will continue to be inadequate until all the evidence has been heard and the previous record of the accused has been revealed. Nevertheless, they must make an initial and possibly tentative choice before that information is fully available. Because of the general nature of the charge, the magistrates may conclude that the case is one that they should not handle themselves, in which case they conduct the preliminary hearing only; and if they find probable cause to hold the accused, they send the case on to a Quarter Sessions or Assize court for trial. If they reach the opposite conclusion, they hear all of the evidence—that offered by the defence as well as the prosecution—and decide whether the accused is innocent or guilty. If they find him guilty, they proceed to consider personal data about him, including his record of previous convictions, if any, in anticipation of imposing sentence. It would be improper to receive this information before guilt or innocence had been determined. If, in the light of all this knowledge, they are still of the opinion that they can administer proper punishment, they pronounce sentence, thus concluding the case except for any appeal that the defendant might take. If, on the other hand, they now see the case in a more serious light and conclude that a stiffer sentence is warranted than is within their power to impose, they suspend further proceedings and transfer the case to Quarter Sessions. That court, without reconsidering the question of guilt or innocence, will then impose sentence. This happens relatively infrequently, for, as noted earlier, the vast majority of all criminal cases in England are finally disposed of in magistrates' courts.

In the United States no equivalent flexibility exists as to where a case will be tried or by what procedure. The jurisdiction of courts and the procedure followed in each is ordinarily fixed rigidly by statute, and a particular case falls either within or without the competence of a particular court. Hence there is ordinarily no occasion for the exercise of discretion by anyone as to where or by what procedure a given case shall be tried. In some situations, however, two or more courts have concurrent jurisdiction over the same case. Where this is so, the choice between them is either pre-determined by generally accepted tradition in the community or is made by the police officer or district attorney in charge of the prosecution. The defendant has no option, and neither has any judicial officer.[1] Also it is possible, prior to indict-

[1] An exception to this pattern which approaches English practice occurs in

ment, for a felony charge to be reduced by the district attorney with the consent of the court to a misdemeanour charge. This has the effect of allowing the case to be tried in a lower court than had originally been intended. To this very limited extent American procedure approaches the English procedure just described.

SUMMARY TRIAL

Cases tried in the magistrates' courts of England are heard by a panel of justices of the peace, usually, but not invariably, three or five in number. As noted earlier, these are men and women of standing in the community, appointed to office by the Lord Chancellor, and serving part time and without compensation. Usually they are not legally trained themselves, but they have the assistance of a lawyer-clerk to give them such advice as they desire on questions of substantive law, procedure, and evidence. The usual rules apply, just as in the superior courts. The magistrates sit without a jury, themselves determining guilt or innocence and imposing sentence. Many cases are conducted without the help of lawyers, and those lawyers who appear are more likely to be representing the defence than the prosecution (the police, it will be remembered, normally prosecute) and more likely to be solicitors than barristers. They, as well as the magistrates and the clerk, wear ordinary clothes, not wigs and robes. The atmosphere is informal, without the pomp and ceremony that characterizes proceedings in the superior courts of England, but also without the bustle and confusion that characterizes many minor courts in the United States. Courtrooms are usually unpretentious but adequate.

In London and a few other cities the lay justices of the peace are supplemented, though not replaced, by stipendiary magistrates. These full-time, legally trained, professional judges sit alone to try the same kinds of cases which in other places are heard by panels of justices.

In the United States the minor courts are less uniform than in England. In relation to population there are fewer justices of the peace and more professional judges, these being found in all large cities and most small cities as well. Today justices of the peace are

---

connexion with certain offences committed by juveniles. If the court where such a case is originally brought is a juvenile court, it may retain the case for final disposition or transfer it to an ordinary criminal court. Similarly if the original tribunal is an ordinary criminal court, it has the option of retaining the case for disposition or transferring it to a juvenile court.

seldom found outside rural areas. The character of American minor courts—both the justice of the peace type and the professional magistrate type—varies enormously from state to state and from community to community. Some are part time, others are full time; some are elected, others are appointed; some are legally trained, others are not; some wear robes and sit in court-rooms of dignity, while others wear overalls and hold court in barns, filling-stations, stores, and kitchens.

A few qualified generalizations, however, may be ventured. First, minor courts in America are almost always presided over by a single judge, panels of two, three, or more judges being very rare. Second, the cases which they hear and determine (as distinguished from those in which they only conduct preliminary hearings) are almost always minor in nature, for their jurisdiction, unlike that of the English magistrates, is not expansible to cover cases of serious crime. Third, many proceedings before them are conducted without the help of lawyers, although lawyers can and sometimes do appear—district attorneys as well as defence lawyers. Fourth, they rarely if ever have the assistance of legally qualified clerks. Finally, while theoretically juries can be empanelled in some of the minor courts, they very seldom are.

TRIALS IN THE SUPERIOR COURTS

Externals—Dress and Physical Facilities

To the spectator there is a vast difference between an English and an American trial. In England the barristers are robed and wigged, as is also the judge. If he is a High Court judge he wears a red robe and is known as 'the Red Judge'. There is punctilious attention to decorum, barristers addressing the judge as 'My Lord' and bowing to him when entering or leaving the court-room. This is done not only by the barristers who are engaged in a case but also by those who come into the court-room as observers. Such ceremony, however, is characteristic only of the Assize courts and the Court of Criminal Appeal. In the Courts of Quarter Sessions, which hear many more cases, the general style is less ceremonious. While barristers always wear robes, as do recorders presiding in courts of Borough Quarter Sessions, the chairman of a County Quarter Sessions court may or may not wear a robe, as he pleases. In the United States no wigs at all are used, and counsel do not wear robes. In some courts the judges wear robes; in others they sit in ordinary business suits. They are addressed as 'Your Honour'.

A striking contrast is also found in court-room architecture. In England the defendant traditionally sits in the dock in the centre of the court-room, flanked by prison officers on either side, and isolated from his lawyer and others in the court-room by the walls of the enclosure, which are sometimes surmounted by iron spikes. It is almost as if he were in a cage. He reaches the dock from a trapdoor in the floor of the court-room, and, when there is an adjournment, as for lunch, he climbs back through the trapdoor to a jail below. This is generally true even if he has been out on bail until the time of the trial. At the commencement of trial, bail is revoked, so as to make absolutely sure of his presence and avoid his mingling with jurors and witnesses during recess. It should be noted, however, that in magistrates' courts and in a few cases in the higher courts, the accused is not put in the dock, but allowed to sit near his counsel. Some judges and lawyers in England deplore the existence of the dock. Furthermore, bail is sometimes allowed during trial.

In most parts of the United States the dock has disappeared, and the accused sits at the counsel table with his lawyer.[1] If he has been out on bail until trial, it usually continues, and he comes and goes from the court-room like any other free person. In short, during trial, he is treated like an ordinary innocent citizen—which he is in the eyes of the law. The English institution of the dock seems at odds with the presumption of innocence.

The position of the witness is also different in the two countries. In England he stands in a box constructed in such a way that only the upper half of his body can be seen. In the United States he sits, his body in full view.

English court-rooms generally provide for a higher, throne-like setting of the judicial bench than is customary in the United States, so that the judge dominates the scene. The English bench is also usually closer to the public seats than is the case in the United States, less space being preserved 'within the bar' for counsel, witnesses, jury, and court officials. Thus the American judge is given a horizontal aloofness from the public, whereas the English judge is given a vertical

[1] Some traces of the dock remain in a few of the original eastern states. Even in most of these, however, the dock has fallen into disuse, being employed rarely except in Boston where the defendant sits in a dock located some four feet behind defence counsel. The Law Society, *The Use of the Dock in Criminal Courts*, Memorandum by the Council of the Law Society, Appendix II, pp. 8–10 (undated).

aloofness. One of the factors making for a large area within the bar in American court-rooms is the desire to provide counsel with what might be called 'prowling space'. In English court-rooms, there is usually a fixed, long table in front of and parallel with the judicial bench at which counsel sit facing the judge. Barristers, when speaking, rise at the table and stay there in the one position, turning towards witness and jury as occasion arises, but leaving the bar table only for some practical necessity such as pointing out a passage in a document to a witness. In the United States counsel on the two sides are usually provided with separate small tables at a considerable distance from the bench, and while they can and do address the court from those tables, they frequently leave them and approach close to the witness stand when examining and cross-examining, and stand by the jury box while addressing the jury. Many of them employ a highly peripatetic style of oratory. The American lawyer sometimes even turns his back on the bench in the course of his perambulations, which no English counsel would dream of doing. The difference contributes to the tendency of American counsel to dominate the proceedings, rather than the judge as in England.

A feature detracting from the dignity of many American as compared with English courts is the demeanour and conduct of court officials—clerks, guards, police officers, etc. In England these officials are circumspect, unobtrusive, and disciplined in their bearing, as befits their role. They add to the dignity of the occasion, where their American counterparts often detract from it. American clerks and court attendants sometimes seem anxious to give the public an impression that the solemnities of the law have nothing to do with them. They are often dressed in slovenly fashion, and when not actively occupied, they tend to adopt lounging attitudes.

In both countries insufficient attention has been paid to court-room acoustics, so that spectators often find it impossible to hear what is being said, and even jury, counsel, and judge may have difficulty; but in both microphones and public address systems are beginning to be used in some courts to overcome these difficulties. Acoustics have a bearing upon the right to a public trial. In both nations there is constant pressure from news media to insure that judicial proceedings are open to public scrutiny, as two recent incidents illustrate. In England a man was held in contempt of court and sent to jail by proceedings in chambers because the judge thought that the facts of the case, involving the morals of a minor, ought not to be ventilated publicly.

After an outcry by the press, judicial discretion to conduct proceedings *in camera* was limited. In the United States the much publicized trial of Billy Sol Estes was televised against the protest of the defendant. Television cameras are banned in most court-rooms and condemned by American Bar Association Canon of Ethics Number 35, but the matter is left to local judicial option in Colorado and Texas. The latter was where the Estes case was tried. The case finally reached the Supreme Court of the United States, where a brief *amicus curiae* was filed on behalf of the American Bar Association arguing (as did the defendant himself) that televising the trial against the consent of the accused was a deprivation of due process of law. The court upheld the contention.[1] The incidents just related involve elements going far beyond simple audibility in the court-room, but they cause one to wonder whether the concept of a public trial in its most elementary and universally approved form is being adequately implemented in either nation.

PUBLICITY BEFORE TRIAL

An English trial is likely to be freer of an atmosphere charged with prejudice than an American trial. That is because English news media are rigidly controlled as to what they can publish about pending cases. In general, they cannot comment upon a defendant's guilt or innocence, describe his deeds or disclose his previous criminal record. Those who violate these rules do so at the peril of being held in contempt of court and subjected to heavy fines or imprisonment. The only exception to these prohibitions—and it is a very important one—is that which allows full reporting of what goes on in open court, including what transpires at the preliminary hearing. Since the prosecution puts on substantially all of its evidence at that stage, and since the defence rarely discloses its case then, the result of publication may be to poison the minds of potential jurors against the defendant, and sometimes on the basis of statements not afterwards admitted in evidence. This is particularly serious in view of the fact that in England cases are reached for trial quickly and there is no machinery for inquiring of prospective jurors on *voir dire* examination how they may have been affected by pre-trial publicity. Proposals are presently pending in England to curtail or eliminate the publicizing of committal proceedings. They have aroused sharp controversy. The principal

---

[1] *Estes v. Texas*, 380 U.S. 926 (1965).

arguments in favour of the present system and against any limitation of publicity may be summarized as follows:

(1) publicity given to preliminary hearings tends to make the magistrates less perfunctory than they otherwise might be;

(2) it tends to make witnesses more responsible in their testimony because of the realization that their statements may be published;

(3) not infrequently it induces persons who have knowledge to contribute about a case under consideration to come forward as witnesses;

(4) it substitutes in the public mind a sober account of sworn testimony for gossip and rumour;

(5) publicity can be avoided in the few cases where it might be harmful by the simple expedient of conducting the preliminary hearing *in camera*; and

(6) there is no proof that pre-trial publicity is generally harmful to the rights of accused persons.[1]

In the United States trial by newspaper, radio, and television has been all too common. News media have been accustomed to publish confident statements that an accused is guilty, deride his defence, give details of his past criminal record and demand that he be heavily punished, and in so doing have relied on hearsay evidence or allegedly confidential sources of information. Until recently little was done to stem the flow of such publicity or to counteract its effect. Use of the contempt power along the lines of English precedent is thought to be prohibited by the constitutional guarantee of freedom of the press as presently interpreted by the Supreme Court of the United States. Hence only indirect assaults on the problem are made. One traditional avenue of attack is through the *voir dire* examination of prospective jurors, questioning them as to how they may have been affected by publicity and challenging for cause those who have become too biased to serve.[2] This is not always sufficient to prevent injustice because the prospective jurors themselves may be unable or unwilling to reveal the depth of their prejudice. Sometimes the entire community may be so influenced that it becomes impossible to find

[1] See letter from David Napley to *The Times* (London), 26 Jan. 1965.

[2] See Goldfarb, 'Public Information, Criminal Trials and the Cause Celebre', 36 *N.Y.U. L. Rev.* 810, 819–20 (1961).

twelve persons who are unaffected. If so, the only solution may be to change the venue of trial to another community where the publicity has not penetrated, or to grant a continuance until the newspaper reports have been forgotten and tempers have cooled.[1] However, neither of these solutions is helpful in a truly notorious case like the trial of Jack Ruby or Alger Hiss.

A relatively new and promising approach to the problem is to try to shut off the sources of information about pending cases. In 1954 District Attorney Frank S. Hogan of New York inaugurated a policy against anyone in his office disclosing to reporters alleged confessions made by persons awaiting trial. He was sharply criticized for imposing a 'press gag', a 'news blackout', and an 'iron curtain of censorship', but he persisted in the policy[2] and thereby set what may ultimately become a general pattern. In 1964 the Supreme Court of New Jersey instructed prosecutors and defence counsel of that state not to hold press conferences where guilt or innocence is asserted or evidence is discussed. As officers of the Court, they are presumably subject to contempt proceedings or other disciplinary sanctions for disobedience. Also included within the scope of the Supreme Court's instructions not to supply information to the press were detectives and police officers. Since they are not officers of court, they are not directly under judicial control, but they are subject to some authority which could issue instructions and back them up with appropriate sanctions. The Court said that statements by such persons 'are an improper interference with the administration of criminal justice and constitute conduct unbecoming a police officer. As such they warrant discipline at the hands of the proper authorities.'[3] The Attorney-General of the United States has recently issued instructions to the FBI, local United States district attorneys, and other law enforcement officials under the jurisdiction of the Department of Justice as to what they may and may not disclose to the press.

Very recently the Supreme Court of the United States added the sanction of its all-powerful voice to this approach. It held that an accused was deprived of due process of law guaranteed by the federal constitution if his trial was dominated by unfair publicity permitted or encouraged by judge, prosecutor, or law enforcement officer.[4]

---

[1] Ibid., pp. 818–19. See Orfield (1947), pp. 366–73.
[2] Letter to the Editor of the *N.Y. Times* by Frank S. Hogan, 16 Apr. 1964.
[3] *State* v. *Van Duyne*, 43 N.J. 369, 204 A 2d 841 (1964).
[4] *Sheppard* v. *Maxwell*, 86 S. Ct. 1507 (1966).

THE ROLES OF JUDGE AND COUNSEL

In England the trial judge is the central and dominant figure in the administration of criminal justice. He has wide discretionary powers not only over the conduct of proceedings but also over the admission of evidence and in summarizing and commenting upon the evidence. Because the right of appeal is very limited, everyone assumes that what he does will probably be decisive and that the judgment entered by him will be final. In the United States, on the other hand, the tradition is equally strong that the discretionary power of a judge in a criminal case should be as limited as possible and subject to appellate review. The prevailing idea is that every accused should have the right to at least one appeal. Consequently, underlying all the proceedings in an American trial is the knowledge that they are not final but subject to review. This tends to shift control from the trial court to the appellate court.

The second dominant figure in an English trial is the defence counsel. The barrister who prosecutes is inhibited by tradition from vigorously seeking a conviction, for the philosophy that the government can neither win nor lose a criminal case, being as concerned to see an innocent man go free as to see a guilty man convicted, is taken very seriously in England. (It is also taken seriously by some prosecutors in the United States, but others only pay it lip service.) The English prosecutor is also, by the discovery rules, debarred from the possibility of surprise. This leaves the advantages of surprise and vigour to the defence counsel. He decides what theory of defence to pursue, what witnesses to call, what evidence to adduce, what strategy to follow, and what arguments to make. He must leave to the accused himself the decision as to whether to plead guilty or not guilty and as to whether to take the witness stand, but otherwise the defence counsel has virtually complete control. He can 'go for the jugular', concentrating upon the strong points of defence and disregarding the weak, doubtful points. He can forego what he considers unimportant objections and futile arguments. In following such an approach, he is supported by his brothers at the bar and by the bench, for the legal profession in England is small and cohesive.

The American defence counsel is less favourably situated. He is not protected against surprise because his client is entitled to little discovery of the prosecution's evidence. He is not insulated from vigorous prosecution, for that is the American tradition. Worse still, control of the case is not firmly in his hands, but uneasily shared with the appellate courts and with the accused himself and his jailhouse advisers, some of whom are self-taught legal experts. He is haunted by the ever-present possibility that he will later—upon appeal or in some post-conviction collateral attack—be accused of incompetence or negligence in waiving rights of the accused. An unsuccessful defendant is prone to make such charges, believing that a better lawyer could hardly have failed to secure an acquittal. Hence, in trying a case, the defence counsel is forced to worry about protecting himself as well as the defendant, for if he deliberately fails to raise a certain objection or pursue a certain line of argument, he may some day discover that he was wrong in the hindsight of a judge who later considers the case. This discourages a jugular approach and encourages instead a diffuse and sometimes ineffective defence in which the potentially strong points are submerged in a welter of trivial objections and half-hearted arguments.

The net effect of American practices as compared to English practices is to shift ultimate power from the trial court to the jury and appellate court, and to denigrate the position of defence counsel, while exalting the role of the prosecutor and the accused himself. A counterbalancing factor, tending to inhibit the prosecutor, has already been noted: the fact that his conduct during trial is subject to greater appellate scrutiny and reprimand than defence counsel's.

BRINGING A CASE ON FOR TRIAL

In England a case is reached for trial more quickly than is customary in the United States. The average time between arrest and the commencement of trial is not much more than a month. If more than two months elapse, the delay is considered excessive. In the United States, on the other hand, many cases are delayed far longer. No national statistics are available, but an insight into the situation can be gained from statistics in two American jurisdictions which enjoy generally high esteem. In New Jersey, as of February 1965, 25 per cent. of all active indictments were more than one year old. In Maryland in 1963–4, an average of over three months elapsed between the date of indictment and the date of trial. The indictment stage, it should be noted, almost always follows by some considerable period the stage of arrest.

One reason for England's greater speed in bringing cases to trial is the fact that the criminal dockets are under tight judicial control. With a split legal profession and cases prepared by solicitors but conducted in court by barristers, an adjournment is rarely granted even because a conflicting engagement prevents a barrister from handling a case that he was scheduled to handle. Because the case has been prepared by a solicitor, another barrister can be quickly instructed and brought in at the last moment to conduct the case. Such a procedure would be violently resisted in the United States, however much it might speed the calendars. Most American judges would be extremely reluctant to force a defendant to trial without the lawyer of his choice being fully ready, or to force the prosecution to trial before it felt it was ready.

Another reason why a trial is reached more quickly in England is the fact that defence counsel needs relatively little time to prepare his case. During the preliminary hearing he is accorded a full preview of all of the prosecution's evidence. This renders largely unnecessary the extensive interviewing of potential witnesses which is necessary in the United States by reason of the lack of pre-trial discovery there.

Another factor that slows criminal justice in the United States is the extensive pre-trial manœuvring that takes place before trial. A succession of separate motions, entailing separate hearings, can be made by the defence. Furthermore, in many courts the arraignment takes place not at the beginning of trial but at a separate hearing in advance. An interval, ranging from three or four days to three or four months, elapses between arraignment and trial. It is used for the purpose of scheduling sentencing in cases where there are pleas of guilty, and in contested cases for fixing trial times to suit the convenience of counsel, and for the hearing of motions raising objections to the indictment, seeking to quash evidence or the like. At the end of that period, when the defendant is brought in for trial, he is again asked how he pleads, and the plea then entered supersedes the earlier plea. In England, on the other hand, the normal expectation is that the trial will proceed forthwith upon completion of the arraignment. The convenience of counsel is not a matter of concern, and preliminary motions which are so prominent a feature of American practice are unusual.

Not only is there more delay in the United States than in England in reaching cases for trial. There is also more delay in disposing of them. Protracted criminal cases are commonplace. For example, a mail fraud case tried in the Federal Court for the Southern District of New York lasted from 27 February 1962 to 7 February 1963—almost a year. Another trial in the same court lasted seven months. Still another resulted in a mistrial after about five months. Indeed, in the period from 1 July 1959 to 30 June 1962, one-sixth of the total of 500 criminal cases tried in that court lasted five days or more. Eight of the protracted cases lasted for thirty days or more. Such cases are by no means confined to the federal courts. Recent protracted cases in the state courts of notorious memory are the Finch murder trial in California and the Sheppard murder case in Ohio. In England, by way of contrast, protracted cases are rare. The trial of James Hanratty at Bedford Assizes in 1962 is the longest murder trial on record. It lasted twenty-one trial days.[1]

Among the reasons for this difference, some of which are discussed elsewhere in this book, may be mentioned: the American tendency to multiply offences and join many defendants, especially in conspiracy charges; excessive objections to evidence in the United States; methods of selecting American juries; and the ethical standards and professional skills of American judges and lawyers.

THE RIGHT TO TRIAL BY JURY

In both nations the accused in a serious criminal case has a right to trial by jury. The right can be waived in many cases in either nation, but the manner of waiver is quite different. In England it takes the form of the accused consenting to have his case tried summarily by magistrates. If he insists upon his right to a trial by jury, the case goes to a different court—Assize Court, Central Criminal Court, Quarter Sessions Court, etc.—there to be tried before a different judge and in different surroundings. In the most serious cases, like murder, waiver of jury trial is impossible.

In the United States, where the jurisdiction of the criminal courts is fixed more rigidly, the accused is ordinarily allowed to waive trial by jury in any type of case. If he does, he is tried in the same court and by the same judge who would preside at a jury trial. The extent of jury waiver varies from one community to another, in some places reaching very substantial proportions. In Baltimore, Maryland, for example, waiver is very common. In normal felony cases tried there, the judge sits alone and without a jury; in capital cases he usually

---

[1] Blom-Cooper, p. 240. The famous trial of eleven defendants involved in the $7 million 'great mail train robbery' at Aylesbury lasted 48 days, a record. *N.Y. Times*, 27 Mar., 1964, p. 6.

requests one or two of his colleagues to sit with him, since no judge likes to take the responsibility of imposing capital punishment without the concurrence of at least one of his fellow judges.

SELECTION OF THE JURY

Methods of selecting juries in the two countries are markedly different. In England very little attention is paid to the matter except to see that the statutory qualifications for jury service are met. These are presently that a person be a qualified elector between the ages of 21 and 60, and either the head of a household or a property owner.[1] Women as such are not excluded, but since it is normally the husband who is head of the household, relatively few women are eligible for jury service. The same is true of young adults living with their parents, and persons living in hotels, rooming houses, etc. Other more significant factors such as intelligence, physical and mental capacity, good moral character and the like, are not made qualifications for jury service. Paradoxically, however, they are indirectly made a ground for excuse from jury duty, for peers, members of Parliament, judges, clergymen, and many others are given the right to claim exemption from jury duty. The net result, according to Lord Devlin, is that the English jury is 'predominantly male, middle-aged, middle-minded and middle class'.

Apart from requiring voting registrars to see that the statutory qualifications are met, the English system of selecting a jury involves virtually no screening of those who may be called upon to serve. The challenge to the array has fallen into disuse, so that the method of making up the list of qualified jurors is never challenged in the course of a lawsuit.

More important, there is no *voir dire* examination during which prospective jurors can be questioned by counsel in an effort to determine their fitness to serve. If a prima facie case has been made out for a challenge for cause, in theory the juror in question can be examined on *voir dire*, but in fact challenges for cause have been all but forgotten, chiefly because there is no effective machinery for discovering any basis for their exercise. Peremptory challenges are available,[2] but even these are seldom used. On the few occasions when a peremptory

---

[1] See Devlin (1956), pp. 17–27; Jackson, pp. 274–80.

[2] The prosecution may ask a prospective juror to 'stand aside' until the others in the panel have been called. He is then in fact not empanelled. In name this is not a peremptory challenge but in substance it is.

challenge is used, it is likely to be exercised upon the basis of a hunch rather than knowledge, as where a tall, broad-shouldered man of mature years is challenged by the defence on the theory that he might be an ex-policeman. While either side is entitled to inspect the list of prospective jurors, giving their names, addresses, and occupations, this is rarely done. In general, the practice of both sides is to accept without question the first twelve people who step into the jury box. It sometimes happens, therefore, that men serve on juries who are ignorant of the English language, or who are ex-convicts.

In April 1965 a departmental committee on jury service, appointed by the Home Office, rendered a report recommending a number of substantial reforms in the English system of choosing a jury. While the committee did not recommend the institution of the *voir dire* examination, it did recommend a system of screening prospective jurors in advance of the time that a case is called for trial, and a more rational set of qualifications, exemptions, and exclusions.[1]

American methods of selecting a jury are far more elaborate than the English method just described. Although there are variations from state to state in the qualifications for and exemptions from jury duty and in the mechanics of selection, a composite pattern can be discovered. In general, any person is eligible for jury duty who is a citizen and a resident of the judicial district where he is called upon to serve unless he has been convicted of a serious crime, or is unable to read, write, speak, and understand the English language, or is incapable by reason of mental or physical infirmity of rendering efficient jury service.[2] No state may systematically and intentionally exclude from jury service, upon the basis of race, colour, creed, or other unreasonable discrimination, persons who are qualified intellectually, physically, and morally to serve.[3]

In some communities the technique of making up a list of qualified jurors is haphazard, with the clerk of the court merely naming persons whom he happens to know and consider eligible. In others, it is much more careful and systematic, superintended by specially appointed jury commissioners and carried out by extensive administrative machinery involving such techniques as questionnaires and personal interviews. Whatever the method, if there is any claimed abuse in the

[1] Departmental Committee on Jury Service, *Report*, Cmnd. 2627, pp. 115–19 (1965).
[2] Fellman, p. 96. See, e.g., 28 U.S.C. § 1861.
[3] *Swain* v. *Alabama*, 380 U.S. 202 (1965). *Norris* v. *Alabama*, 294 U.S. 587 (1935). See Fellman, pp. 99–105.

statutory or administrative exclusion of a racial, religious, economic, or social group, it can be reached by a challenge to the array.[1]

In addition to prescribing the qualifications for jury service, most states also provide 'exemptions' which allow persons otherwise qualified to serve on juries to escape that duty. These are persons whose normal work, it is felt, should not be interrupted for jury service (like firemen) or persons who are seldom accepted by lawyers (like other lawyers) or persons who, having performed special community tasks, are rewarded by freedom from jury service (like members of the National Guard). The list in any state is likely to be a rather peculiar one, covering a motley congregation of people. Unfortunately, many persons possessing the best brains of the land are relieved by law of the necessity of lending aid to the courts in their search for justice.[2] Roughly the same situation, however, prevails in England, as we have seen.

The central feature of the jury selection process in the United States, totally missing in England, is the *voir dire* examination. This is a questioning of prospective jurors to determine their fitness to serve, either generally or in the specific case on trial. The purpose is to lay the foundation for challenges, both for cause and peremptory. As a preliminary to the questioning, the jurors are told something about the case—who the parties are, what kind of a case it is, who the lawyers are, what issues of fact will have to be resolved, etc. Lawyers tend to make this statement and the questions that follow an occasion for indoctrinating the jury to their point of view, sometimes interjecting bits of legally irrelevant information, such as the fact that the defendant has a good war record. This is one of the things that gives the *voir dire* examination its bad name. The other is the excessive amount of time consumed by the lawyers in their questioning, sometimes running to days or weeks.

Because of these abuses some jurisdictions have allowed the judge strictly to control the *voir dire* or have placed the examination in the hands of the judge himself.[3] He then conducts the questioning himself, although he receives and considers requests by lawyers as to lines of inquiry that ought to be pursued. When the questioning of jurors is handled by the judge, the amount of time taken is generally very small, normally not more than a half hour to an hour.

[1] See Orfield (1947), p. 403.
[2] Ibid., pp. 399–401; Knox, 'Jury Selection', 22 *N.Y.U. L.Q. Rev.* 433 (1947).
[3] See, e.g., Fed. R. Crim. P. 24(*a*). Cf. Orfield (1947), pp. 401–2.

Some of the prospective jurors who are qualified in general for jury service may be unfit for service in the particular case on trial, for they may be related to one of the parties or financially interested in the outcome, or they may have formed, as a result of publicity, a fixed opinion as to the merits of the case. If so, they can be challenged for cause and not allowed to serve. Furthermore, there is the possibility that some of the people summoned for jury duty may not in fact meet the statutory qualifications, being incapable, for example, of understanding the English language. They should not be allowed to serve either. After challenges for cause have been exercised and passed upon, peremptory challenges are made by both the prosecution and the defence. These are challenges which require no reason to be assigned for their use, thus in effect giving the lawyers a right of choice among presumptively qualified jurors.

ORIENTATION OF THE JURY

In England jurors are given virtually no help in understanding their functions until the end of the case. There is no *voir dire* examination wherein they might learn something about the case they are to hear, and they are given no oral or written explanation of the nature of the proceedings in which they are about to participate, or as to the general duties they will be called upon to perform. While some of them may know a good deal about trials and about the role of jurors, others may be badly in need of guidance.

In the United States, in addition to the *voir dire* examination and opening statements by both sides at the outset, help in orienting the jurors to the general nature of their work comes from the court itself. It often takes the form of a handbook distributed to jurors at the outset of their service, giving them the basic terminology they are about to encounter, an explanation of the respective roles of jury, judge, and counsel, a statement as to the importance of their participation, etc. Jury handbooks are very common in the United States.[1] Sometimes orientation takes the form of a short speech by the judge in addition to or in place of the handbook.[2]

The English Departmental Committee on Jury Service mentioned earlier has recommended for England an adaptation of the American idea of a jury handbook.

[1] See *United States* v. *Gordon*, 253 Fed. 2d 177 (7th Cir. 1958).
[2] 'Prettyman, 'Jury Instructions—First or Last?' 46 *A.B.A.J.* 1066 (1960).

OPENING STATEMENTS

After a jury has been sworn, the next step in both nations is for counsel for the prosecution to give the jurors an outline of the proof about to come, so that they will be able intelligently to appraise particular pieces of evidence as they are produced. In England, however, counsel for the defence is not heard at this time. He makes a speech only after all the prosecution's evidence is in, and as a preliminary to putting his own evidence.[1]

In the United States a different practice is followed. Immediately after the prosecution has opened, defence counsel is privileged to make his opening speech, giving the jury a preview of the defence evidence.[2] In some jurisdictions, he may postpone the speech until after all of the prosecution's evidence is in—in other words, to the same point in the trial where English defence counsel is first allowed to speak. The advantage of the American system is that judge and jury are advised as soon as possible that there is a defence, and its nature. Thereby the impact of the prosecutor's speech is lessened and the proceedings are made more intelligible, for the jurors are given a frame of reference for the evidence about to be received from both sides.

EVIDENCE

Some of the principal contrasts between the English and American rules on evidence have already been discussed, particularly the treatment of illegally obtained evidence and the 'fruit of the poisoned tree' doctrine. A few other significant contrasts are worthy of mention here.

One of them concerns the position of the accused as a witness in his own behalf. Both nations recognize the privilege against self-incrimination, but they implement it in quite different ways. In England, the accused is under substantial pressure to testify. If he does not, his failure to do so may be commented upon by the judge. The prosecutor may not comment, but the judge may suggest to the jury that it draw an adverse inference from the defendant's failure to explain away the evidence against him.[3] Until very recently, a similar rule prevailed in a few of the states of the United States, including California, which had an explicit provision in its constitution allow-

[1] Jackson, p. 134. For a critical view of this practice see Kennedy, *The Trial of Stephen Ward* (1964).
[2] See, e.g., *N.Y. Code Crim. P.*, § 388. Orfield (1947), pp. 428–30.
[3] Criminal Evidence Act, 1898, 61 & 62 Vict., c. 36. Williams, pp. 58–63.

ing such comment. Most States, however, followed a contrary rule. In 1965 the Supreme Court of the United States held it to be a violation of the due process clause of the Fourteenth Amendment to allow either the judge or the prosecutor to comment on the accused's failure to take the stand.[1] As a result, the type of pressure that exists in England for the accused to testify is outlawed throughout the United States. That, however, does not prevent the jury from drawing the inference without any outside suggestion.

Another rule in the United States actively discourages some defendants from taking the stand. The prosecution is allowed to cross-examine the accused about his previous convictions merely because he has taken the stand.[2] This is on the theory that they have a bearing on his credibility even though they are not admissible on the question of guilt or innocence. The result is to face the accused who has a previous record with a fearful dilemma. If he remains silent, the jury may infer guilt from that fact; but if he testifies he will be revealed to the jury as a bad man who probably committed the crime with which he is now charged. In England, when the accused takes the stand to testify in his own behalf, he cannot by reason of that alone be cross-examined as to previous convictions. They become admissible only if evidence of them is necessary to prove the crime charged, or if the defence offers evidence of the accused's good character, or if it attacks the character of a prosecution witness or that of a joint defendant, and then subject to the discretion of the judge.[3]

The combination of the rule which allows proof of previous convictions when the accused takes the stand with the rule which prohibits comment if he fails to take the stand results in American juries frequently being deprived of what is likely to be the most vital evidence in the case, the defendant's testimony—evidence which in all probability would be received as a matter of course in England.

Despite the broad scope of the American privilege against self-incrimination,[4] it does not prohibit anything beyond 'testimonial' or 'communicative' compulsion. In other words, fingerprints, blood samples, and like evidence can be taken from him without his consent.[5]

[1] *Griffin* v. *California*, 380 U.S. 609 (1965).
[2] McCormick, § 43. See Comment, 'Procedural Protections of the Criminal Defendant—A Reevaluation', 78 *Harv. L. Rev.* 426, 440–2 (1964).
[3] Criminal Evidence Act, 1898, 61 & 62 Vict., c. 36, § 1(*f*). See Wigmore, *Evidence*, vol. 1, § 194(*a*) (3rd ed. 1940); Williams, pp. 181–91.
[4] See *Miranda* v. *Arizona* and discussion in Chapter 6.
[5] *Schmerber* v. *California*, 34 U.S.L. Week 4586 (U.S., 21 June 1966).

Another contrast between English and American rules of evidence concerns statements made by the accused when first charged with having committed a crime. In the United States, if he makes an admission, that can be received in evidence as an exception to the hearsay rule, but if he makes a denial, that cannot be received because it does not fall within the logic of the admissions exception or any other recognized exception to the hearsay rule.[1] England, with greater fairness and less logic, admits either an admission or a denial by the accused.[2]

Objections to Evidence

A contrast in practice more than in formal rules concerns the making of objections. In England it is rare for counsel on either side to object to evidence offered by the other side. In the United States objections tend to be incessant and vociferous. Some of the reasons for the contrast have already been suggested: in England the philosophy of prosecution is different than in the United States, and there are no professional prosecutors whose political careers and fortunes depend upon securing convictions; defence counsel in England have greater control over their cases so that they can concentrate on essential, vital points, disregarding the others without fear that they will be accused of incompetence or negligence in waiving the rights of their clients by failing to object.

There are additional reasons worthy of mention. One is the fact that defence counsel in the United States, normally being deprived of any pre-trial discovery, and so being ignorant of the prosecution's evidence, tend to object out of a sheer fear of the unknown, whereas English defence counsel, knowing in advance what is coming, do not have to bother. Another is the fact that both judges and counsel in England are probably more familiar with the law than their American counterparts. There is more specialization on the English bench and at the bar. There are fewer reports to read and there is more opportunity to be familiar with the latest relevant decisions. Another is the fact that English barristers frequently agree between themselves before trial as to what evidence is and is not admissible. If they cannot agree, they at least define the issue between them and then pause for a judicial ruling at the appropriate stage of trial in the absence of the jury. Another is the fact that in American courts the trial judges are more circumscribed by statutes and rules of various kinds than are the

---

[1] See McCormick, § 275 (1954).   [2] Williams, pp. 178–81.

English judges. Fewer questions are left to their discretion. Appellate courts, confronted with violations of rules, are less inclined to overlook such violations than if they were reviewing the exercise of trial court discretion.

More important still, the general rule in the United States, contrary to that which prevails in England, is that no error can be considered on appeal unless it has been objected to at the trial court level.[1] Since an objection is ordinarily waived by not being asserted during the trial, and since no serious penalty is incurred by making an objection which is overruled, there is a strong temptation to err on the side of making an objection if there is even a slight chance of its being sustained either initially or upon appeal. Exceptions to adverse rulings, however, are no longer necessary, having been eliminated by the modern rules of procedure in most states.[2] None the less, proceedings are sometimes both enlivened and impeded by old-fashioned lawyers who, indignant at adverse rulings, are able to relieve their sense of outrage by 'excepting' in tones which leave no room for doubt as to their feelings or their intention to seek reversal on appeal.

The frequent American objections tend to be dealt with by the judges rapidly and firmly, and further argument is unusual. In England, on the relatively rare occasions when objections are interjected, they are apt to lead to considerable argument, and the jury frequently has to retire while this goes on. In the United States, even where there is some substantial argument on points so arising, it is often conducted without the need for the jury retiring, because counsel approach the judicial bench and a muttered discussion ensues. The effect unfortunately is to exclude the public and the press from the discussion. This practice, added to the inadequate acoustics mentioned earlier, detracts from the meaningfulness of a public trial.

MOTIONS

When the prosecution rests, and again at the conclusion of all the evidence, defence counsel in the United States is allowed to make a motion for a directed verdict of acquittal, and the court is required to grant it if the evidence is such that reasonable men could not find the accused guilty.[3] In England substantially the same effect is achieved

---

[1] *Sturm* v. *Chicago & N.W. Ry Co.*, 157 F. 2d 407 (8th Cir. 1946); cf. *State* v. *Garcia*, 19 N.M. 414, 143 P. 1012 (1914). See, e.g., *Fed. R. Crim. P.* 30. Orfield (1939), p. 93. [2] Vanderbilt, pp. 332–4.
[3] See, e.g., *Fed. R. Crim. P.* 29; Orfield (1947), p. 435.

upon a 'submission' by defence counsel that there is 'no case to answer' by the judge instructing the jury to bring in a verdict of acquittal. The English practice requires the jury actually to reach such a verdict, and in the unlikely event that the jurors should stubbornly refuse, the only way the matter could be set right would be by appeal to the Court of Criminal Appeal.[1] In many states of the United States no formal action is required by the jury, for the judge's ruling itself has the effect of a verdict of acquittal. The difference seems to be more a matter of form than of substance.

In neither nation can the judge direct a verdict of guilty. In England, however, the judge can tell the jury plainly that it ought to convict on the evidence, so long as he also tells them that they are entitled to find differently.[2] In the United States, even in jurisdictions where judicial comment on the evidence is not prohibited, any statement urging conviction is likely to result in reversal on the ground that it infringes on the jury's function, however much the statement may be wrapped up in directions to the jury that they are entitled to acquit.[3]

SUMMATIONS

Contrary to the practice in England, the federal courts, and most American state courts, there are a few states in the United States where the closing arguments of counsel follow rather than precede the instructions of the judge.[4] The theory is that counsel ought to know how the judge instructs the jury on the law before he argues the application of that law to the facts. Most states solve this difficulty by requiring the judge to advise counsel in advance of their arguments what instructions will be given. That problem being solved, the conclusion is that the last word spoken to the jurors before they retire to deliberate on their verdict ought to come from a neutral source, speaking dispassionately, rather than from partisan sources, speaking fervently.[5]

A substantial contrast between the two countries concerns the order of closing arguments. In many parts of the United States the district attorney speaks first, then the defence counsel, and finally the district attorney speaks again in rebuttal.[6] In theory, the advantage

---

[1] Devlin (1956), p. 78.   [2] Ibid., p. 84.

[3] *United States* v. *Woods*, 252 F. 2d 334 (C.A. 2d, 1958); see Orfield (1947), p. 457.   [4] Vanderbilt, pp. 233–4.

[5] Ibid., and also cf. *Fed. R. Crim. P.* 30.   [6] Orfield (1947), p. 447.

here given the prosecution balances the disadvantage of having to carry the burden of proof. This, however, is not a universal pattern, for there are many variations from state to state. In some, the defence counsel speaks first and the prosecution last, each side being limited to one speech. In England, as a result of legislation passed in 1964, the prosecutor always speaks first and defence counsel always has the right to the last word.[1] This helps to give greater force to the presumption of innocence and the requirement of proof beyond a reasonable doubt than do some of the American patterns.

Finally, there is a contrast in the style of oral argument in England and the United States. Because of the differing philosophies of prosecution, far more vigorous speeches, demanding convictions and sometimes heavy sentence as well,[2] are made in the United States than in England. Even the defence speeches in England are likely to be analytical and intellectual rather than fervent emotional appeals, as they often are in the United States. Partly this is because of the general style of the English bar, partly because of the split profession in England with the consequent lack of identification between barrister and client, and partly because today's jurors approach their task more analytically than emotionally. Neither counsel in England is allowed to say anything at all to the jury about sentence. That is regarded as completely out of bounds.

INSTRUCTIONS

The judge's instructions to the jury may play an important part in the verdict, but whether they do so or not, they are likely to be of great importance on appeal. In both countries the most common single ground of appeal is objection to something said by the trial judge in his charge.

The differences between the two countries in the preparation, contents, and function of the judge's charge are striking. In England judges can invite counsel to indicate whether there is some particular point they think should be included or emphasized in the summing up, and counsel can and occasionally do, during or at the close of a summing up, raise with the judge objections to its contents. Such happenings are on the increase, but in the great majority of cases the

---

[1] Criminal Procedure (Right of Reply) Act, 1964. Public General Acts 1964, p. 400. This was recommended by the *Fourth Report of the Criminal Law Revision Committee*, Cmnd. 2148 (1963).

[2] See Annot., 120 A.L.R. 502 (1939); Annot., 95 A.L.R. 566 (1935).

judge prepares and delivers his summation without either assistance or criticism from counsel. Indeed, counsel do not always stay to hear a summing up. Failure to object to the judge's charge is never fatal on appeal, though such failure may help to show that the error complained of was immaterial. In the United States it is provided by rule in most jurisdictions that the defence waives its right to complain on appeal about what the judge says unless it requests contrary instructions or objects to those given by the judge.[1] Consequently, in many jurisdictions, the judge's charge is more the result of what counsel do than of any initiative on the part of the judge.

English judges often jot down notes to guide them in their summing up, but then speak freely from the notes, extemporizing the exact form of the address. In shorter cases they may speak wholly without notes. The virtuoso performances of English trial judges when summing up have attracted the admiration and envy of most American observers. The admiration is the greater because the English summing up habitually extends to a discussion of the facts of the case, with a temperate indication by the judge of any opinions he holds on credibilities and probabilities. He is required to warn the jury that it alone has the responsibility for deciding the facts, but he is not prevented from expressing an opinion—even a strong opinion—on those facts.[2] Clearly the power is subject to abuse, and there have been times when English judges were arbitrary and oppressive. Today, however, the practice seems to yield general satisfaction to the profession and the public.

In the United States many states have statutory or constitutional provisions requiring that the judge's charge be in writing.[3] These did not originate as a means of restricting judicial influence, but were meant to ensure that there should be a reliable record of the summing up for purposes of appellate control. The requirement has continued into an era when a charge can be delivered orally and taken down by the court stenographer just as effectively for appellate court purposes as if first reduced to writing and then read aloud to the jury. It is now nothing more than a cause of delay and an obstruction to spontaneity of expression. Even in jurisdictions which do not compel written instructions, the judges habitually write them out and read them as written.

---

[1] See, e.g., Fed. R. Crim. P. 30.
[2] Devlin (1956), p. 118.
[3] Orfield (1947), pp. 448, 452.

A majority of states also provide by statute or constitution that a judge may not comment on the evidence.[1] This prohibition originated in the nineteenth century when the policy of popular decision was at its strongest—the same movement, associated with Jacksonian democracy, which caused the widespread adoption of short-term elective judiciaries. It was feared that juries would be overawed by judicial opinion as to the facts if judicial comment were allowed. In a few states the matter went even further: juries were given the final decision on questions of law as well as questions of fact. Today this excess has all but disappeared and the jury is supposed to take the law from the judge.[2] The distrust of judicial influence on juries has remained a powerful influence, however, so that even in the federal system and in states where the judges are not prohibited from commenting on the facts, they do so rarely and in the most circumspect terms. In many jurisdictions the charge contains no reference to the facts at all; it is confined to a statement of the abstract rules of law relevant to the decision of the particular case. The American summing up tends to become a ritualistic performance which carefully abstains not only from influencing the jurors, as intended, but also from giving them any effective assistance. Appellate courts have approved various forms of words and disapproved others; trial judges have worked sedulously to produce formulae, and have carefully recorded those which have been found beyond successful appellate challenge, or which at least have not in fact been challenged. From these activities have emerged published collections of instructions for all occasions called 'pattern', or 'standardized', or 'boilerplate' instructions,[3] or where such are unavailable there are unpublished collections in the private files of individual judges, courts, and law offices. Constructing a charge becomes a mechanical exercise in the putting-together of such formulae, requiring skill in the wielding of scissors and paste pot. The principal thought of the judge seems to be to avoid laying a basis for appeal, not to help the jury. It is possible that the enviable concentration of English trial judges on helping the jury owes something to the relative paucity of appeals in that country, and to the fact that trial judges sit on the Court of Criminal Appeal and consider the sufficiency of the directions to the jury in a practical way, with a knowledge of the conditions under which trials are conducted.

---

[1] Ibid. [2] Ibid., p. 470.
[3] Pinola, 'Standard Jury Instructions', 58 *Dickinson L. Rev.* 354 (1954); Note, 'Standard Jury Instructions', 98 *U. Pa. L. Rev.* 223 (1949).

VERDICT

The basic common-law rule, still generally operative in both England and the United States, requires a unanimous verdict of twelve jurors.[1] Hence, if illness or other emergency necessitates the withdrawal of a juror, the trial ordinarily comes to an end and proceedings have to be recommenced. The same result follows the inability of a jury to agree. Some provision has been made, however, to deal with the problem of a juror becoming physically incapacitated during trial. In England the Criminal Justice Act[2] allowed the trial to continue so long as there remained at least ten jurors, provided that both prosecution and defence agreed. A further change recently enacted allows a verdict by nine jurors, without the necessity of consent by counsel. In the United States the Federal Rules and the rules or statutes of many states also permit trial by a jury of fewer than twelve, often without specifying a mimimum number, if both sides consent.[3] The federal and many state provisions also specify another solution for incapacity of a juror, namely, the swearing in of alternate jurors who sit with the first twelve chosen, and replace any casualties among the latter as they occur. This provision, which has no English parallel, is becoming increasingly popular in the United States, especially when it is anticipated that a trial will extend over a long period of time. It has the advantage that its use is not dependent on agreement of the parties, but can be directed by the judge.

In a few states majority verdicts of nine or ten out of twelve jurors are allowed in certain cases.[4] In a few states also there are certain cases in which juries of less than twelve can be used, regardless of whether either or both sides consent.[5]

In both countries the jury can return a special verdict, either on its own motion or at the suggestion of the parties or the judge, but in neither country can it be compelled to do so. Hence, notwithstanding the urging of the judge and both parties, it can insist on returning a general verdict of guilty or not guilty. In practice, special verdicts are exceedingly rare in both nations.

---

[1] See Devlin (1956), pp. 48–57; Orfield (1947), pp. 481–3.
[2] 48 Criminal Justice Act, 1925, 15 & 16 Geo. V, c. 86, § 15.
[3] See Fed. R. Crim. P. 23(*b*). Fellman, p. 87; Orfield (1947), pp. 396–7.
[4] Fellman, pp. 88–89; Orfield (1947), pp. 482–3.
[5] Ibid.

RETRIALS

In the United States, when there has been a conviction which the judge feels is unfair, he can order a new trial. This is not so in England.[1] The trial judge has no such power, and neither does any higher court. If an appeal is taken, the Court of Criminal Appeal can reverse the conviction, but the effect of this is to free the defendant, not to retry him, as will be explained more fully in the chapter on appeals.

In both countries a verdict of acquittal is final. Common to both nations is a policy against allowing successive prosecutions for substantially the same set of incriminating circumstances. There are technical differences between the American conception of 'double jeopardy' and the British conception of *autrefois acquit* and *autrefois convict*, but the general thrust of both is the same. Both doctrines leave open the possibility of abuse, as where a second prosecution is brought arising out of the same facts as a previous one, but for an offence not then charged.

In the United States there is a further difficulty arising out of federalism. The Supreme Court of the United States has held that an earlier state trial is no defence to a federal charge based on the same facts, and vice versa.[2] This ruling is now of diminishing importance. In 1959 the Attorney-General of the United States issued a directive to United States district attorneys instructing them not to prosecute where there had been state proceedings arising out of the same facts, and not to assist state proceedings after a federal prosecution upon the same facts. Similarly, many states have statutory provisions which forbid state prosecutions after federal prosecutions when the accused was put in jeopardy. Since the doctrine of the Supreme Court is the subject of widespread criticism,[3] it may well be that the idea of a single act constituting an offence against two sovereignties is on the way to oblivion.

[1] See Devlin (1956), pp. 75–78. New trials are further discussed in Chapter 10 below.

[2] *Bartkus* v. *Illinois*, 359 U.S. 121 (1959).

[3] See Pontikes, 'Dual Sovereignty and Double Jeopardy: A Critique of *Bartkus* v. *Illinois* and *Abbate* v. *United States*', 14 *W. Res. L. Rev.* 700 (1963); cf. also 'Double Jeopardy Where Both City and State Prosecute for the Same Act', 38 *Wash. L. Rev.* 819 (1963).

9

SENTENCING

FOR the great majority of defendants, who plead guilty, in both England and the United States, sentencing is the only critically important stage in the proceedings. For the minority who are convicted after a trial, it is still of immense importance. In both countries the court normally affords the defendant a hearing on sentence at which he may be represented by counsel, ordinarily provided free of charge for the indigent defendant, especially if he was provided with representation at the trial. Yet in contrast to the strict rules which govern the trial up to the point of conviction, the sentencing decision in both England and America is left very largely to the discretion of the trial court. There are some qualifications to this statement: in England, appellate review of sentencing provides some control over the discretion of trial judges; and in the United States, some of their discretion has been transferred to administrative agencies. Nevertheless, within the limits of punishment specified by statute for a particular offence, the trial judge has an almost free hand in deciding what the sentence should be, not being bound to consult anything beyond his own preference in the matter. The breadth of his discretion is complicated by the fact that in neither country is there agreement as to the purposes of punishment or as to how these purposes can be realized.

We have already discussed in Chapter 5 the forms of treatment available to courts in dealing with juvenile and young offenders. Apart from these, and apart from provisions for the hospitalization of mentally disordered offenders, the chief sentences in both countries are death, imprisonment, probation, and monetary fines.[1] Other forms of punishment, while not unknown, are very rare. Corporal punishment was abolished as a sentence in England in 1948, and is obsolete in all of the United States except Delaware, where whipping may be, but rarely is, ordered. In both England and the United States, however, whipping is used once in a while as a measure of

---

[1] For a general discussion see Fitzgerald, pp. 195–275; Home Office, *The Sentence of the Court* (1964); Jackson, pp. 204–28; Rubin *et al.*; Tappan, pp. 421–75.

prison discipline.[1] Sterilization or castration of mentally defective sex offenders is not recognized as a penal measure in either country, although there are a few American states which permit it as a supposedly eugenic measure, and there are a few American judges who have used castration as an extra-legal sentence by offering probation to sex offenders who are willing to submit themselves to it.[2]

CAPITAL PUNISHMENT

In England, where the death penalty was once very common, it is now, as a result of recent legislation, confined to treason, certain forms of piracy, and arson of royal ships and dockyards.[3] In a case of treason death is a mandatory sentence, although the accused may be reprieved and imprisoned. In the United States there are an increasing number of states in which the death penalty has been entirely or almost entirely abolished, or where it is virtually never used. On the other hand, some states still retain it, not only for murder but for such offences as kidnapping, rape, armed robbery, burglary, arson, and train wrecking; and a few have recently made the sale of narcotic drugs a capital crime. In almost all states, however, the mandatory use of the death penalty has disappeared.

IMPRISONMENT

If an offender's sentence involves detention, his time must be served in one of the institutions discussed in Chapter 5. In the case of a juvenile or young offender, it is often the court which chooses the type of institution to which he shall be committed. In the case of an adult, the court ordinarily does nothing more than impose a sentence of imprisonment, and then the decision as to whether the convicted man shall go to one facility or another is up to the prison authorities. In this respect, the range of sentencing alternatives open to a court in dealing with adults is in both countries more narrow than it is in dealing with younger persons.

American prison terms are in general longer than those imposed in England.[4] This may reflect differences in the amount and kind of

[1] Rolph (1961), p. 116; Tappan, p. 703.   [2] Tappan, pp. 425–6.
[3] Murder (Abolition of Death Penalty) Act, 1965; *N.Y. Times*, 29 Oct. 1965, p. 18, cc. 3 and 4. The Act expires in 1970, unless before that time Parliament makes it permanent. Should the Act expire, capital punishment for certain types of murder would be reinstated.
[4] See Sobeloff, 'The Sentence of the Court: Should There Be Appellate Review?' 41 *A.B.A.J.* 13, 15 (1955).

crime in the two countries, and differences in public and official reaction to the growing rate of crime, or it may be explained by the fact
that American legislatures and courts sometimes deliberately set
penalties high in order to compensate for the chance that a prisoner
may be granted too early a release by the parole authorities.

England and all but a few of the American states have special provisions for incarceration of habitual criminals. The American
statutes, which have been widely criticized because of their severity,[1]
generally permit or require a court to increase the term of an ordinary
sentence upon an offender's third or fourth conviction for a felony.
In some states an increased term must be imposed; in others the court
must sentence the offender to the maximum number of years provided
by law for the offence committed; in others a life sentence is permitted; and in still others it is mandatory.[2]

English methods of dealing with persistent offenders, while comparatively mild, are a source of dissatisfaction to the penal authorities. They are (a) corrective training, and (b) preventive detention,
both of which require that the offender be convicted of an offence
punishable by two years' imprisonment or more.

Corrective training is an anomalous type of punishment for an
habitual offender because it is the same treatment that is given as a
reward to a prisoner who is not an habitual offender. It can be imposed for a period of two to four years on an offender over 21 who
since the age of 17 has twice before been convicted of an offence
punishable by two years in prison. The object is to educate him in
some vocation and so minimize the likelihood that he will become a

---

[1] Rubin *et al.*, pp. 392–403; Tappan, pp. 471–5. Although recidivism statutes
are presumably intended to control organized crime, their main force is felt most
by the relatively trivial offender rather than the desperado. The result is prison
sentences which are longer than either public protection or individual rehabilitation requires. This is an important factor in America's comparatively high ratio
of prisoners confined to the civilian population. See Rubin *et al.*, pp. 398, 400–2.
At the beginning of 1964 this ratio was 115 per 100,000 population. Federal Bureau
of Prisons, *National Prisoner Statistics: Prisoners in State and Federal Institutions*,
1963, p. 1. This figure is about two and a half times greater than the comparative
English figure. Sobeloff, op. cit., p. 15.

[2] Even where an habitual criminal statute is mandatory in terms, it may be
rendered discretionary in practice by a prosecutor who fails to apprise the court
of prior convictions. The prosecutor can bargain for a plea of guilty to a lesser
offence; the criminal with a prior record will generally acquiesce rather than run
the risk of a much longer sentence under a recidivism statute. Tappan, pp. 472–3.
Rubin *et al.*, p. 397, states that 'the characteristic of enforcement of these rigid
recidivism laws is not mandatoriness, but avoidance; and, because they are rigid,
the avoidance occurs in legal shadows'.

professional criminal. A sentence to corrective training differs from imprisonment in one of the English regional training prisons only in the sense that the corrective trainee is undergoing training by virtue of his sentence by the court, whereas the ordinary prisoner is selected for such training by the prison authorities. A judicial sentence to corrective training limits the discretion of prison authorities, and, because facilities for such training are limited, deprives them of the power to give such training as a reward to deserving prisoners. For this reason, both major political parties are in favour of its abolition.

Preventive detention in England can be ordered for an offender over 30 who since the age of 17 has been convicted three times before of offences punishable by two years' imprisonment or more, and who has on at least two occasions actually been sentenced to a penal institution.[1] A sentence of preventive detention may be from five to fourteen years' duration, but in practice today it is for a minimum of seven years.[2] Its object is to protect the public from the depredations of confirmed criminals. However, in 1963, a Home Office Advisory Council found preventive detention to be ill suited to its purpose because of the fact that 'nuisances' rather than dangerous criminals were the persons usually so sentenced, and recommended its abolition.[3] This recommendation, like the proposal to abolish the sentence to corrective training, is presently under consideration.

PROBATION AND SUSPENDED SENTENCES

In the United States probation (discussed in Chapter 5) and the suspended sentence are almost inseparable. Indeed, many courts take the

[1] It is not the general practice of the English courts to impose preventive detention when the offender has only the minimum of three convictions or when he has committed an offence of a different type. In 1956 over half of those sentenced to preventive detention had six or more qualifying convictions. Taking into account non-qualifying convictions as well, over two-thirds had twenty or more previous convictions. Home Office, *Preventive Detention*, pp. 5–6 (1963).

[2] In *R. v. Sedgwick* (1950), 34 *Crim. App. R.* 156, the Court of Criminal Appeal stated that, except for the elderly or the sick, seven years ought to be the minimum sentence of preventive detention. This suggestion has been followed: in 1961 about 85 per cent. of the 218 persons sentenced to preventive detention received seven or eight year sentences. See Home Office, *Preventive Detention*, p. 8 (1963).

[3] Ibid., pp. 23, 29. Witnesses stated that 'nuisances' rather than the dangerous criminals were the persons usually sentenced to preventive detention. As a result of a psychiatric survey, it was concluded that 'the majority of preventive detainees are of the passive-inadequate type, feckless and ineffective in every sphere, who regard the commission of crime as a means of escaping immediate difficulties rather than a part of a deliberately anti-social way of life'. Ibid., p. 8.

position that they have no power to suspend a sentence unless they simultaneously order probation.[1] However, there are statutes in a minority of states[2] which authorize use of the suspended sentence as a distinct punishment. A suspended sentence may take either of two forms. In one, a sentence to imprisonment is imposed but its execution is suspended, usually on condition that the defendant refrain from committing another offence. If he fails to live up to his obligation and the court revokes the suspension, the prison sentence originally fixed is carried into execution. In the second form, the imposition of sentence itself is suspended, again subject to the defendant's keeping within the law. If the defendant misbehaves, the court for the first time imposes a sentence of imprisonment for the original offence, taking into account the defendant's subsequent misconduct. In some states the law provides that if a court suspends sentence and the suspension is not revoked, no criminal conviction results to deprive the defendant of his civil rights or to be used against him in subsequent proceedings.[3]

England does not use the term 'suspended sentence', but has three practices which resemble it. One is absolute discharge, in which no sanction is imposed against the offender, and all that happens is that the conviction is noted in his record—for possible future consideration if he should get into trouble again. The second device is conditional discharge, which is in effect suspension of the imposition of sentence for twelve months or less, on condition that the defendant refrain from committing another criminal offence during that period. The third device is 'binding over': the offender is required to enter into a recognizance, with or without sureties, to be of good behaviour for a specified period. If he violates the conditions of his release, the sum stated in the recognizance is forfeited and the offender is brought back for sentence. Binding over differs from conditional discharge in that it requires a recognizance; it can be for longer than twelve months; it allows imposition of sentence not merely on commission of another criminal offence, but for any misbehaviour; and it permits the court to add special conditions, such as non-residence or residence within a specified area, which could not be imposed in conditional discharge. Binding over is also used in magistrates' courts without an offence having been committed to prevent prospective breaches of the peace.

[1] Rubin et al., p. 157.   [2] Tappan, pp. 422–3.
[3] Cf. ibid; Rubin et al., ch. 17.

MONETARY FINES

A fine is the most commonly used penalty in both countries.[1] In England statutes specify the fines for a great number of minor offences, but not for most misdemeanours and felonies, as to which there is a general power in the courts to impose whatever fines they choose. Practically all magistrates' courts' fines for summary offences are subject to a statutory maximum for the individual offence but a general maximum fine of £25 applies to a few offences, based upon old statutes, for which no particular maximum is prescribed. For an indictable offence, £100 is the maximum fine a magistrates' court may impose. There is a general prohibition in Magna Carta and the 1689 Bill of Rights against 'excessive fines'. In the United States fines are fixed by statute, and ordinarily provided as an alternative or supplemental punishment, even with regard to the most serious offences. The Eighth Amendment to the federal constitution, which now applies to the states by virtue of the Fourteenth Amendment, provides that 'excessive fines shall not be imposed nor cruel and unusual punishments inflicted', but it is generally held that a fine is not excessive if within the maximum fixed by the legislature.[2]

SENTENCING RESPONSIBILITY

In both England and the United States sentencing is ordinarily done in the same court which tried the offender or before which he pleaded guilty. However, as indicated earlier, in England, if the

[1] In 1962, of those found guilty of non-indictable offences in England, about 98 per cent. were fined. For those convicted of indictable offences, the figure was about 34 per cent. Home Office, *The Sentence of the Court*, p. 2 (1964).

Statistical data on utilization of fines in the fifty states is incomplete. It has been estimated that fines constitute 75 per cent. of all sentences in the United States, being used more frequently for lesser offences. However, in the federal trial courts there appears to be a decreasing use of the fine as a sole method of punishment. See Rubin *et al.*, pp. 239–44. For 1964 only about 9 per cent. of the sentences imposed by the federal district courts consisted solely of fines. Director of the Administrative Office of the United States Courts, *Annual Report*, p. 259 (1964).

[2] Rubin *et al.*, pp. 248–9. In *United States* v. *United Mine Workers of America*, 330 U.S. 258 (1946), the Supreme Court held that a $3,500,000 fine imposed upon the union for contempt of court was excessive. (The governing statute did not limit the amount of fine that could be imposed for criminal contempt in actions brought by the United States.) However, the Court did sustain $700,000 of the penalty and conditioned remission of the remainder upon compliance with the court order. This action, said the Court, was 'required in order to emphasize the gravity of the offence' since the union's conduct constituted 'a serious threat to orderly constitutional government, and to the economic and social welfare of the nation'. 330 U.S., pp. 305–6.

magistrates try a fairly serious offence themselves and then find that the accused has a particularly bad record, they may commit him to Quarter Sessions for sentence. This enables Quarter Sessions to impose any sentence that might have been given had the offender been tried before it originally; the limits governing magistrates' court sentences no longer apply. Furthermore, lay justices of the peace take turns serving in the magistrates' courts, and it sometimes happens that after conviction and before sentence a probation officer's report is called for, which is not ready until another set of justices is sitting on the bench. In that case the new justices impose sentence after they first inquire into the circumstances of the case.[1] Similar arrangements exist in Quarter Sessions and Assize courts, which also experience a changing composition.

In the United States sentencing is almost always done in the court where the trial was conducted or the plea of guilty received. American courts generally sit continuously with a permanent membership, so that the trial judge is nearly always available for sentence.

In the English magistrates' courts, and in County Quarter Sessions, the responsibility for sentencing devolves on the whole panel of justices. In the other English courts, as well as everywhere in the United States in so far as sentencing is a judicial task, it is the responsibility of a single judge. In a small minority of American states the jury is empowered to determine sentence as well as guilt or innocence in all cases tried before it.[2] This is a relic of the nineteenth-century movement in the United States to reduce the authority of judges. In most American states which retain capital punishment, the jury is also empowered to decide whether life imprisonment shall be imposed instead. With these exceptions, sentencing is the judge's responsibility.

In England trial courts exercise broad discretion in sentencing, but they are subject to some limitations and controls. They must, of course, act within the range of legal penalties provided by statute; but mandatory penalties are provided only for treason (carrying the death sentence) and murder (carrying life imprisonment). The First Offenders Act of 1958 provides that a magistrates' court may not sentence a first offender to imprisonment unless it enters in writing its opinion that no other method of dealing with him is appropriate;

[1] Jackson, p. 220.

[2] Rubin *et al.*, pp. 122–4. The ability of a jury to fix a light penalty may lead to compromise verdicts of guilty when otherwise there might be an acquittal or a hung jury. See Comment, 'Consideration of Punishment by Juries', 17 *U. Chi. L. Rev.* 400 (1950).

and other statutory provisions require a court to decide that a particular form of treatment is appropriate to a young offender or an habitual offender; but these are guides rather than limitations on discretion.

A genuine limitation is found in the power of the Court of Criminal Appeal to review sentence. In some of its judgments that Court has laid down principles which the lower courts are expected to follow with regard to particular types of offences and offenders. Further, the power of courts to determine the fate of offenders is affected by the power of the executive branch of the government (exercised by the Home Secretary) to deal with sentences. The Royal Prerogative of Mercy can be used in exceptional cases to grant a free pardon where innocence has been established by new evidence, or to remit part of a sentence on compassionate grounds. There is also a system by which a prisoner serving a sentence of life imprisonment may be released 'on licence' on specified conditions, subject to recall for the rest of his life. (This and the system described earlier of releasing juveniles early are the only close English counterparts to the American system of parole.) Finally, a prisoner may be released under the Prison Rules after serving two-thirds of his sentence unless he has forfeited some part of the period of remission for misconduct in prison. For the ordinary adult prisoner serving a sentence of less than life imprisonment, there is no such thing as early release at the discretion of an administrative board.

Similar limitations on judicial sentencing powers exist in the United States—mandatory penalties, good-time remission and, in a handful of states, appellate review. The most important qualifications of judicial authority in America, however, are ones which do not exist in England, namely: sentencing by the jury, already mentioned, and a general system of parole, coupled with indeterminate sentences.

As explained in Chapter 5, parole is the conditional release of a prisoner before the expiration of his term of imprisonment, leaving him at large but under supervision for the remainder of the period of the original sentence. Whether a prisoner shall be released on parole is within the discretion of an administrative agency usually known as a 'Parole Board'.

The parole system does not generally operate with regard to sentences of less than a year, which are usually served in local jails, and which therefore tend to be of fixed duration;[1] but it is available in

[1] Rubin *et al.*, p. 489.

all jurisdictions for offenders sentenced to over one year's imprisonment. The net result is a general system of indefinite terms for such offenders, with the date of release being determined by the judgment of the parole authorities.

American sentences are not entirely indeterminate, for in every state some maximum term is imposed, and in some states a minimum term as well. The effect of the lower limit is generally to make a prisoner ineligible for parole until the minimum period has been served.[1] There are many differences among the states as to how and by whom maximum and minimum sentences are set, and frequently there are different provisions for different situations within a single state. However, five patterns can be discerned:[2]

1. In the first, both the maximum and minimum terms of imprisonment within statutory limits are fixed by the judge.
2. In the second, a judge is required to impose the maximum term of imprisonment permitted by law, but is allowed himself to fix the minimum term.
3. In the third, the judge himself sets both the maximum and minimum terms, but he is not allowed to fix the minimum at more than a certain fraction of the maximum. This assures a reasonable period of parole eligibility before the prisoner's sentence has entirely expired.
4. In the fourth type, only the maximum term of imprisonment is fixed by the judge, while the minimum is determined by the law governing parole. The sentence is for a fixed term of years, subject to the prisoner being paroled after a certain portion of his sentence has been served.
5. In the fifth type, the court is required to impose both the maximum and the minimum term if any provided by statute for the offence. The effect is to vest virtually complete control over the length of imprisonment in the parole authorities, for once the court has committed the offender to prison they take over full responsibility. This pattern of sentencing, which is found in California and Washington, is based upon the theory that sentencing ought to be taken out of judicial hands altogether and vested in a separate sentencing body—a theory which has had more impact in the United States than in England, but which every-

---

[1] Rubin *et al.*, p. 550.

[2] Note, 'Statutory Structures for Sentencing Felons to Prison', 60 *Colum. L. Rev.* 1134 (1960).

where seems to have passed the peak of its influence. Indeed, current thought in the United States seems to be directed toward bringing into the sentencing functioning a greater measure of fair judicial procedure.

Some of the limitations on judicial sentencing power just discussed have as their purpose the promotion of a uniform and coherent sentencing policy throughout the jurisdiction. Others are predicated on the notion that nothing in the education or experience of judges equips them to determine the treatment criminals should receive. The problem of how judges can be better trained for the task of sentencing is one to which much attention has been paid in recent years in both countries,[1] especially as evidence has accumulated of enormous disparities in sentences meted out by different judges in roughly equal situations.[2] The problem can be partially solved by providing judges with adequate information about the backgrounds of offenders who are before them for sentence. We shall discuss this in a later section. Another partial solution to the problem lies in keeping the judges aware of accumulated knowledge with regard to the law and practice of sentencing.

SENTENCING INSTITUTES

In 1958 federal courts in the United States were authorized by statute to convene periodical 'sentencing institutes' in order to formulate 'sentencing principles and criteria which will assist in promoting the equitable administration of the criminal laws of the United States'. In 1959, under this Act, the first national sentencing institute was held in the form of a seminar attended by federal judges from all over the country. Subsequent institutes have been held at least once in each federal circuit; and in 1964 a second national institute was held for newly appointed federal judges to familiarize them with the problems of sentencing. At these meetings the judges had an opportunity to discuss sentencing problems among themselves and with probation,

[1] For a comparative study of sentencing alternatives and recent developments in England, Canada, and the United States (federal courts), see Parker, 'The Education of the Sentencing Judge', 14 *Int. and Comp. L.Q.* 206 (1965).

[2] For one convicted of interstate transportation of a stolen car in 1955, it would have made a great deal of difference which federal court imposed sentence. From one of the district court judges in Illinois, the defendant would have received, on the average, a sentence of about nine months. Had he appeared before one of the district court judges in Oklahoma, he could have expected a sentence of about four and a quarter years. See Tappan, p. 443.

prison, and parole administrators. They also had an opportunity to engage in workshops where actual case histories were examined and the participants talked over the sentences they would have imposed in those cases and the reasons for them. As an aid to the conducting of these conferences, and as a tool for actual sentencing, a *Deskbook* was prepared, furnishing a guide to the law and experience of the federal courts in correctional matters.[1]

A related development is the growing use of a 'sentencing council' in federal trial courts, as pioneered by the federal court for the Eastern District of Michigan. It involves the several judges of a multi-judge court sitting down with a colleague who has to impose sentence in an actual case and discussing with him his ideas as to appropriate disposition. This provides a pooling of wisdom (not unlike that found in English magistrates' and Quarter Sessions courts) but responsibility for the ultimate sentence remains that of the sentencing judge alone.[2]

Sentencing institutes in the United States are not limited to the federal system. They are becoming a feature of the many professional meetings of state trial judges which are being held throughout the country. They are even included in programmes such as that conducted by the State of New York for the mandatory training of lay justices of the peace.[3]

In England, in 1961, the Streatfeild Committee reported on its review of 'present arrangements . . . for providing the courts with information necessary to enable them to select the most appropriate treatment for offenders'.[4] It strongly urged that judges keep themselves informed on penological matters, and recommended that a guidebook for sentencing be prepared. This was done by the Home Office, and *The Sentence of the Court—A Handbook for Courts on the Treatment of Offenders* was published in 1964. It is an excellent, compact volume. In September 1963 the Lord Chief Justice, possibly influenced by the American experience just described, convened a one-day conference of Queen's Bench Judges, Recorders, and Chairmen of Quarter Sessions to discuss sentencing policy. Another such meeting was held in 1964, and in January 1965 a meeting of some 100 criminal judges was held, both to hear lectures and to take part in workshop sessions designed to promote uniformity of sentencing.

[1] See Institute of Judicial Administration, *Judicial Education in the United States* (1965), ch. VIII.
[2] Ibid.   [3] Ibid.
[4] *Interdepartmental Committee on the Business of the Criminal Courts, Report,* Cmnd. 1289, p. 1 (1960).

This is expected to be the prelude to similar nationwide meetings and a series of regional and local meetings to be held throughout England. Considerable attention has also been given to the training of lay magistrates. The Lord Chancellor has appointed a special advisory council to deal with this problem.

PRE-SENTENCE INVESTIGATIONS AND REPORTS

If a sentence is to be appropriate to the needs of an offender, the judge imposing it should have adequate information about the offender's personality and background.[1] Such information is not necessarily, or even usually, developed in the course of a criminal trial; and it certainly does not come by itself when the accused pleads guilty.

In the American federal courts a procedure is now available whereby a convicted defendant can be committed to prison for two or three months of study and observation, culminating in a report to the court. He is then returned to court for sentencing, with the hope that the sentence will rest on a firmer foundation of fact than is ordinarily possible. The same kind of procedure is available in England in certain cases. There the prison authorities routinely prepare reports in all cases as to their observations of an accused person while he is held in pre-trial custody. Such reports are required by statute as a prerequisite to a sentence of corrective training or preventive detention (in the case of an habitual offender). The usefulness of these reports is sometimes limited by inadequate opportunities for close observation where the accused has been at liberty on bail or where he has been in custody only a short time before conviction. In these cases the court may remand the accused after conviction so that a report may be prepared and considered before the imposing of sentence.

Such a procedure is exceptional in both countries. More commonly a court has available to it only a pre-sentence report by a probation officer, and even this is a relatively recent innovation in both countries. Traditionally, the courts had to rely on their observation of the accused during trial, informal statements by the police and the prosecution, affidavits and testimony of defence witnesses, statements of defence counsel, and possibly an interview with the accused himself

---

[1] For a general discussion of pre-sentence investigation see Jackson, pp. 220–8; Rubin *et al.*, pp. 73–108; Note, 'Employment of Social Investigation Reports in Criminal and Juvenile Proceedings', 58 *Colum. L. Rev.* 702 (1958).

at the time of sentence. In some American states a procedure developed by which the accused could be required to be sworn as a witness after conviction to submit to questioning concerning his personal history; and this procedure is still frequently used in some places, notably New York, despite the recent availability of probation reports.

In England the courts rely heavily on statements prepared by the police. At the time of arrest the police begin to gather personal information about the accused which, upon conviction, is given to the court in the form of a brief pre-sentence report. It is a less elaborate type of report than a probation officer would prepare, but certainly better than no report at all. Some American courts rely on similar sources of information when no probation officer's report is available.

With the growth of probation services, it has come to be accepted in both countries that the best sentencing practice requires the judge to be guided by what is called in the United States a 'pre-sentence' report, and in England a 'social inquiry' report, prepared by an experienced social worker, preferably a probation officer. Such a report is based on interviews with the accused, his family, neighbours, friends, and employers. It collects and analyses the data thus obtained in a summary form usable by the sentencing court. Some American states require the use of pre-sentence reports as a matter of course in serious cases; some require them wherever probation is granted or sentence suspended. Even when they are not required, courts have assumed the power to order them to be made. On the other hand, the absence of funds and the necessary organization has sometimes made it impossible to obtain them, especially for use in the lower courts. The quality of pre-sentence reports in the United States varies from place to place, depending on the quality of the local probation service. In England a centralized service assures a uniform and generally high standard.

American procedure has readily conformed to the use of pre-sentence reports largely because most American courts have a permanent membership and are in continuous session, so that sentencing can be adjourned for the several weeks that it takes a probation officer to make his inquiries. American judges are not reluctant to postpone sentencing for this purpose.

One obstacle to the use of probation reports in the higher courts of England was the fact that Assize or Quarter Sessions sat only for limited periods, and their composition changed from session to session as different judges went on circuit or different justices took their turn on the bench. This obstacle has now been circumvented by permitting sentence to be imposed by any convenient court. Another circumstance inhibiting more extensive use of reports in England is the strong judicial preference for expedition in the criminal process. It has long been customary for sentences to be announced immediately after conviction but this is impossible if probation officers are to obtain their information after conviction. The influential Streatfeild Committee took the position that with first and young offenders, for whom reports are most needed, the social inquiry should be made before conviction provided the accused did not object.[1] There are difficulties in preparing a report to be used in the sentencing of someone who has not yet been convicted, but given the strong English preference for speedy disposition, it seems to be the only feasible course.

In any event, reliance on social inquiry reports has been steadily increasing in England. It is most marked in the lower courts, where it tends to be lacking in the United States. This is partly because the justices of the peace play an important role in control of the probation services, and partly because magistrates' courts, sitting continuously, can easily postpone sentencing until the reports are prepared.

Many American probation officers, and some English ones, would like to prevent pre-sentence reports from being communicated to the accused. They fear that their best sources of information will dry up if their identity is disclosed to the accused, and they anticipate strained relations with the man whose probation they may have to supervise if he can read what they say about him to the court. This view has become the dominant one in American practice.[2] A small

---

[1] Interdepartmental Committee on the Business of the Criminal Courts, op. cit., pp. 100–1. The Committee felt that if sentencing did not follow immediately upon conviction, there would be an unnecessary waste of time 'in recapturing the atmosphere of the case'. Furthermore, it was thought that the public impact of the sentence would be reduced if it were made known at a date later than the finding of guilt. Ibid., p. 88.

[2] Tappan, p. 557. Criticism of non-disclosure is often based on the quality of the pre-sentence report. The information supplied may be distorted and inadequate; one critic has said that many of these reports are filled with 'emotionally toned value judgments' and 'prejudicial epithets'. Ibid., p. 558.

The Model Penal Code adopts a compromise solution which requires neither disclosure of sources nor delivery of the report. Under the proposal, the court would advise the defence of the factual content and the conclusions of the pre-sentence report. The defence would then have an opportunity to controvert it. Model Penal Code, § 7.07 (5) (Tent. Draft No. 2, 1954). See also Rubin et al., pp. 87–101.

number of states require that the pre-sentence report be shown to the accused, but in most others the judge has discretion to permit or deny disclosure. He generally denies full disclosure, although he is likely to orally disclose so much of the contents of the report as he feels should be open to factual rebuttal, such as the list of prior convictions. Disclosure to counsel is regarded as tantamount to disclosure directly to the accused himself, who under American tradition could and probably would demand to see any document given to his lawyer.

In England the contrary view has prevailed on the ground that fairness requires that the accused know the information on which his sentence is based and be given an opportunity to refute inaccurate statements. Accordingly, it is provided by statute that the report must be shown 'to the offender or to his counsel or solicitor' if the offender is over 17, or if he is under 17, to his parent or guardian. Whenever possible the report is handed to counsel, which under the English tradition governing the relations between lawyer and client means that the report will not necessarily reach the accused himself, or at least not in verbatim form, if counsel thinks that would be harmful.

The danger of disclosure is further alleviated by the fact that English probation officers put in their reports only what they feel is sufficient for the court to come to a proper judgment, not necessarily all the information which will be useful in case work supervision.

10

APPEALS AND POST-CONVICTION REMEDIES

SUBSTANTIAL differences exist between the United States and England with respect to the right of review in criminal cases, and the manner in which such review is conducted.

APPEALS BY THE PROSECUTION

In both nations the right of the prosecution to appeal is extremely limited. In England the only situation which permits such an appeal in the first instance is where a question of law is decided adversely to the prosecution in a magistrates' court. Then the case may go up to a Divisional Court of the Queen's Bench Division on a 'case stated'. This means that the magistrates, through their clerk and with the assistance of the parties, prepare a document which formulates the issue of law to be decided by the appellate tribunal in the light of the charge made, the evidence adduced, and the action taken below. If, on the basis of this document and oral argument, the Divisional Court reverses the decision below, it sends the case back to the magistrates' court with directions to convict the defendant or to rehear the case.[1] Any other acquittal is beyond appellate review. If a jury in an Assize court or a Quarter Sessions court finds the accused not guilty, that is the end of the case, regardless of any errors of fact or law that may have been committed. Indeed, the prosecution in England is not even allowed to appeal from rulings before trial upon questions of law dealing with such matters as the sufficiency of indictments.[2]

Much the same situation prevails in the United States. In the federal courts and the courts of all except three states, there can be no appellate reversal of a judgment of acquittal. In the three states (Connecticut, Vermont, and Wisconsin) which depart from the usual pattern, the prosecution is allowed to appeal from an acquittal, but only upon

[1] Karlen (1963), p. 132.
[2] However, the prosecution may apply to the Divisional Court for appropriate orders of *certiorari*, prohibition, and *mandamus* with respect to jurisdictional questions. The discussion in the text concerns only appeals on the merits. See Jackson, pp. 40–43, 113–14.

the basis of errors committed by the trial judge in his rulings upon evidence, instructions to the jury, and the like; no appeal is allowed on the claim that the jury erroneously acquitted the accused.[1] Even in these three states appeals by the prosecution are rarely taken. In some additional jurisdictions in the United States, the prosecution is allowed to appeal from pre-trial rulings upon questions of law;[2] or from acquittals for the sole purpose of clarifying the law, and without hope of reversal.[3] Again, such appeals by the prosecution are seldom taken.

In both nations, if the defendant takes the first appeal, the prosecution may seek further review without violating the concept of double jeopardy.[4] But, as we shall see later, such second appeals are very rare in England.

Since appeals by the prosecution are so unusual, the discussion which follows is confined to the review of a judgment of conviction at the request of the defendant.

APPEALS BY THE DEFENDANT

Minor Cases

In both nations men who have been convicted without trial by jury in inferior courts presided over by laymen have a right of appeal to other courts where they receive a trial *de novo*. In England a man who has been convicted in a magistrates' court takes such an appeal to a Quarter Sessions court, which hears the case without a jury.[5] An appeal involving only questions of law may also go up at the option of the defendant by way of a 'case stated' to a Divisional Court of the Queen's Bench Division.[6] The procedure is the same as that described earlier with respect to appeals by the prosecution on questions of law. In the United States a man who has been convicted by a justice of the peace may have his case retried, before a jury if he so desires, in a trial court presided over by a professional judge. If, however, the case was heard initially by a professional judge (as is often the case in metropolitan centres), then there is usually no retrial, but an ordinary appeal based upon the record of trial in the court below.[7] The main difference between the two nations with respect to these minor cases

---

[1] Cf. *Palko* v. *Connecticut*, 302 U.S. 319 (1937); also Karlen (1964), pp. 87–88.

[2] e.g. *N.Y. Code Crim. Proc.*, § 518. See generally Comment, 'State Appeal in Criminal Cases', 32 *Tenn. L. Rev.* 449 (1965); Note, 42 *N.C.L. Rev.* 887 (1964).

[3] Orfield (1939), pp. 59, 61–68.   [4] Ibid., pp. 58, 68.

[5] Jackson, p. 113; Karlen (1963), p. 131.

[6] Karlen (1963), pp. 131–2.   [7] Mayers, p. 145.

is that in England an appeal lies against sentence as well as against conviction, whereas in the United States, as will appear more fully hereafter, no appeal is ordinarily allowed against a sentence which is within the jurisdictional limits of the court imposing it, and within the upper and lower boundaries fixed by statute for the offence involved.

More Serious Cases

With respect to more serious cases—those ordinarily tried by jury before professional judges—the practices of the two nations differ markedly. The American philosophy is that the accused in such a case is entitled to at least one appeal as a matter of right. This does not mean that appellate review occurs automatically, but only that the defendant can initiate an appeal without securing permission from any court. While such a right is not guaranteed either by the state or federal constitutions, it is so firmly established in practice that it has come to be regarded by the profession and the public as virtually inalienable. Furthermore, the defendant, if indigent, is entitled to be given the assistance of counsel without expense to himself,[1] and to be provided free of charge with any papers necessary to the effective taking of the appeal (such as a transcript of the trial record).[2]

In England a different philosophy prevails with respect to convictions in courts presided over by professional judges. There an appeal as of right lies only on questions of law as, for example, an improper charge on the burden of proof, or the interpretation of a statute. Relatively few such appeals are taken. Very likely this is because the criminal law of England is more simple, stable, well understood, and accepted by the legal profession and by the public generally than is the law of the United States. Having no federal system, England is not plagued by the problems engendered by double sovereignty. Having no written constitution and accepting the doctrine of parliamentary supremacy, English judges and lawyers proceed on the assumption that they are bound by precedent and that if the law is to be changed, that must be done by Parliament rather than by the courts. Those who conduct trials are in general both competent and experienced, leaving relatively few errors in their wake. The population of the nation is homogeneous and little beset by the type of racial, religious, and ideological struggles that complicate law enforcement in the

[1] *Douglas* v. *California*, 372 U.S. 353 (1963).
[2] *Griffin* v. *Illinois*, 351 U.S. 12 (1956).

United States. Finally, law in England is assigned a more modest role than in the United States, seldom being used as an instrument for effectuating major social changes. In consequence, all concerned tend to operate on the assumption that a case is properly conducted at the trial level in accordance with rules which are not in dispute. Whatever the reasons, relatively few criminal cases are appealed as of right in England on the basis of claimed errors of law only.

Leave to Appeal in England

If the accused wishes to question the sufficiency of the evidence to sustain his conviction or to raise a question of mixed law and fact, he must obtain leave to appeal either from the trial court or the Court of Criminal Appeal.[1] If he wishes to challenge the propriety of a sentence, he must obtain leave from the Court of Criminal Appeal.[2] In seeking such leave, he ordinarily does not have the effective assistance of counsel. If he is an indigent, who has been granted legal aid during trial, he may theoretically be entitled to advice as to whether and how to take his appeal. But he may not want advice from the same solicitor who acted during the trial, or he may not know that he is entitled to it, or the time (ten days) may be too short to seek and get such advice, or, lacking a transcript, there may be no adequate foundation for such advice. Sometimes the only help the accused gets at this stage is the printed advice concerning his rights which appears on cards posted in gaols, and such informal counsel as may be offered by fellow prisoners or police and prison officials. Sometimes trial counsel advises the prisoner informally about an appeal, but most applications for leave to appeal are prepared by the prisoners themselves, not infrequently in handwritten form. Several significant changes in the procedure have been recommended recently by an Interdepartmental Committee on the Court of Criminal Appeal.[3] If accepted, the time limit for applying for leave to appeal would be extended from ten to twenty-eight days, and defending counsel would be given the duty at the conclusion of the trial of providing the accused with a brief written statement of any possible grounds of appeal.

The most common ground of appeal is some alleged inaccuracy in the judge's summing up of the facts or his failure to put adequately to the jury the whole of the case for the defence. When an application reaches the court, the registrar of the court prepares a record of proceedings for consideration of the judges both on the question of

[1] Karlen (1963), p. 109.   [2] Ibid.   [3] Cmnd. 2755, pp. 70–74.

granting leave to appeal, and in the event that leave is granted, on the merits. In most cases little more than the accusation, the transcript of character evidence, and, in cases where there was a trial, the charge of the judge are included in the papers prepared by the registrar.[1] In capital cases a full transcript of the evidence is also included, but this is not considered necessary for the less serious cases. In most applications for leave to appeal against sentence only, and in some of the other applications, the papers are sent to one of the judges assigned to the Court of Criminal Appeal, who considers them and makes an individual decision on the application. If he decides to grant leave, the case is scheduled for hearing on the merits before the court. If he denies leave, that fact is communicated to the prisoner, who then may either drop any further attempt to secure review or ask that his application be reviewed by a full panel of the court. About half the prisoners do not pursue their application beyond its denial by a single judge, chiefly because the time they spend in gaol awaiting further action may be ordered not to count against sentence. In the remaining half, the prisoner persists. In these cases and in those which were not initially referred to a single judge, each judge of the panel (normally three in number) receives a set of the papers, together with a memorandum summarizing the case prepared by the registrar of the court. If any one of the judges is desirous of granting leave to appeal, the case is taken up for plenary consideration and oral arguments are heard. However, the majority of applications are denied. In recent years only about 16 to 18 per cent. of the applications for leave have been granted, so that roughly four-fifths of the attempted appeals have not even received plenary consideration.

Successive Appeals

As the foregoing discussion makes clear, few English cases are reviewed on appeal even once. There are far fewer that receive more than one appellate scrutiny. The House of Lords has power to hear criminal appeals, but only in those exceptional cases where the Court of Criminal Appeal or the Divisional Court certifies that a point of law of general public importance is involved in the decision, and where, in addition, either that court or the House of Lords grants leave to appeal.[2] These conditions are met in only a few cases a year,

---

[1] See below, p. 223.
[2] Karlen (1963), p. 118. See Administration of Justice Act, 1960, 8 & 9 Eliz. II, c. 65. See also Jackson, pp. 118–19.

and consequently as a practical matter, appellate review seldom goes beyond the Court of Criminal Appeal or the Divisional Court of the Queen's Bench Division.

In both nations, if an appeal is initiated by the defendant, further review at the behest of the government is possible.

In the United States successive stages of appeal are much more frequent than in England. Many states have not only a supreme court but also an intermediate appellate court.[1] Cases go from the trial court to the intermediate appellate court as a matter of right, as explained above, and then are subject to further review in the state supreme court, ordinarily not as a matter of right but in the discretion of that court. Similarly, in the federal court system, cases go as a matter of right from the district trial courts to the United States Courts of Appeal, and then are subject to further review by the Supreme Court of the United States, ordinarily not as a matter of right but as a matter of that Court's discretion.[2] Finally, because the United States has a federal system of government in which the federal constitution and laws are supreme, cases heard in the state courts are subject to further review in the Supreme Court of the United States with respect to the federal questions involved, such as those pertaining to the validity, under the federal constitution, of state statutes, practices, or procedures. Again, review is not ordinarily a matter of right, but is discretionary with the Supreme Court.

Discretionary Review in the United States

Wherever discretionary review exists in the United States, there is some procedure for screening the cases to be accepted for review not dissimilar to the English procedure for screening applications for leave to appeal.[3] In some courts of the United States, however, all of the judges are required to participate in the choice of cases which will be accorded plenary consideration. Thus the *certiorari* procedure of the Supreme Court of the United States does not involve any delegation of authority to a single judge, or even to a committee of judges, to decide whether appeals should be allowed. Every case is considered by every justice, and every justice votes on each application. If four

[1] Karlen (1964), pp. 6–7.

[2] For a description of federal appellate review see Karlen (1963), pp. 42–43, 57–62.

[3] In New York, the Court of Appeal takes cases on leave granted by a judge of that court or a judge of the intermediate appellate court.

of them wish to take a case for review, the case goes up; and if less than four vote to accept the case, *certiorari* is denied, and there is no review of the case on the merits. Less than 10 per cent. of the petitions for *certiorari* are granted, with the result that over 90 per cent. of the applications are disposed of by a refusal of the court to entertain jurisdiction[1]—a statistical result similar to that reached by the English Court of Criminal Appeal in passing upon applications for *initial* appellate review of cases tried in that country.

Not only are the opportunities for appellate review in criminal cases greater in the United States than in England. They are, in fact, far more frequently availed of. In a single populous state, like New York or California, more criminal appeals are heard in the course of a year than are heard in all of England. It is almost a matter of course for an American defendant, either operating on his own independent means or, if indigent, through the assistance of court-appointed counsel, to exhaust all possibilities of appellate review, carrying his case as high as the appellate system allows, and then finally resorting to collateral challenge of his conviction (in a manner to be described) with the possibility of still further appeal.

APPELLATE TRIBUNALS

In England appellate review of criminal cases is almost invariably done by judges who devote the great bulk of their time to handling trials in the first instance. This is true of the lowest level of appeal, where a minor case goes from magistrates' court to the Court of Quarter Sessions, a tribunal whose principal activity is the exercise of original rather than appellate jurisdiction. It is also true of the Court of Criminal Appeal which is concerned with appeals from serious cases which have been tried by juries and professional judges.[2] This court has no personnel of its own, its members being drawn from the trial judges who compose the Queen's Bench Division of the High Court. The only member of the Court of Criminal Appeal sitting regularly is the Lord Chief Justice, who, as administrative head of the Queen's Bench Division, also designates the other judges who will sit to hear appeals. Assignments are rotated frequently so as to allow every judge to hear criminal appeals once or twice a year. The court

---

[1] During the 1963 term, the Supreme Court disposed of 2,002 petitions for *certiorari*. *Certiorari* was granted in 176, or 8·8 per cent. of the cases. 'The Supreme Court, 1963 Term', 78 *Harv. L. Rev.* 143, 180 (1964).

[2] Karlen (1963), pp. 106–7, 130–2.

ordinarily sits in panels of three, but the number of judges is subject to being increased at the discretion of the Lord Chief Justice for especially important or difficult cases to five. The judges who make up the Divisional Court of the Queen's Bench Division, hearing appeals on questions of law from the magistrates' courts, is composed of precisely the same personnel made up in the same way.

The men who compose the Court of Criminal Appeal, when acting in their capacity as trial judges, handle civil as well as criminal cases. When acting in their capacity as appellate judges, however, they are restricted to hearing criminal appeals. Civil appeals are handled by an entirely distinct tribunal, namely the Court of Appeal. Both the Court of Appeal and the Court of Criminal Appeal are specialized tribunals, composed of different judges, and operating according to different procedures. The House of Lords, on the other hand, possesses both civil and criminal jurisdiction, but since as a practical matter it hears very few criminal cases, its primary character is that of a civil appellate court. The Lord Chief Justice is empowered to sit in the Court of Appeal and the House of Lords as well as the Court of Criminal Appeal, but he rarely does so.

The Interdepartmental Committee on the Court of Criminal Appeal mentioned earlier has recently recommended a merger of that court with the Court of Appeal. Under this proposal the resulting tribunal would have a civil and a criminal division, with the latter absorbing all of the jurisdiction of the present Court of Criminal Appeal. The Criminal Division would sit in two panels for most of the year and, for part of the year, in three. The first would be concerned principally with hearing appeals and would consist of the Lord Chief Justice (presiding), a Lord Justice of Appeal and a Queen's Bench judge. The other two panels would be concerned principally with passing upon applications for leave to appeal, and each would consist of a Lord Justice of Appeal (presiding) and two Queen's Bench judges. If there were a division of opinion in any panel, the case would be reheard before a five-judge court consisting of the Lord Chief Justice, two Lords Justices of Appeal, and two Queen's Bench judges. The Lords Justices of Appeal assigned to such work would spend a few weeks each year trying criminal cases at the trial level.[1]

In the United States judges are not as fluidly interchangeable between appellate and trial courts as in England.[2] Those who are

---

[1] Cmnd. 2755, pp. 21–23.   [2] Karlen (1963), pp. 146–7; Mayers, pp. 374–5.

appointed or elected to appellate courts, generally speaking, do nothing but appellate work, and in this respect they are more specialized than their English counterparts. In another respect, however, they are less specialized, for an American appellate court typically handles both civil and criminal appeals in substantial volume. For example, the Supreme Court of the United States, unlike the House of Lords, handles many criminal appeals as well as many civil appeals. The same is true of most state supreme courts and the United States courts of appeal. The only states which have different courts for hearing criminal appeals from those which hear civil appeals are Texas and Oklahoma.[1]

COLLATERAL ATTACK

An English defendant who has exhausted or neglected the avenues of appeal within his system described in the preceding sections of this chapter has reached the end of the judicial road. If there has been a miscarriage of justice in his case, all he can hope for is executive clemency from the Home Secretary. This is given as a matter of grace rather than right, and it may or may not involve reconsideration of the case by judges. If the Home Secretary in exercising the Crown's prerogative of mercy wishes the help of judges, he may refer the whole case to the Court of Criminal Appeal, whereupon it will be treated for all purposes as if it were there on appeal; or he may refer a particular problem to the Court for its opinion, or he may handle the case or problem himself, relying on his own resources or upon whatever advice and assistance he deems proper. Under no circumstances is a prisoner entitled as of right to have his case reconsidered in a court of original jurisdiction.

An American defendant, on the other hand, who has exhausted the avenues of appeal within his system described in the preceding section of this chapter, still has open to him not only the same general type of executive clemency as is found in England, but additional judicial remedies, and these not as a matter of grace but as a matter of right in certain situations. It is anomalous in view of current English practices that these remedies take the form of ancient writs of habeas corpus and *coram nóbis*, now stretched almost out of recognition from their original shape, or statutory substitutes for them. The old writs have been revived and expanded partly out of the desire

[1] Ibid.

to escape from the rigid time limits and procedural restrictions of traditional appeals, partly because sentences of extreme severity seem to call forth extreme counter-measures of caution (sentences in the United States tend to be far heavier than in England and without the corrective of appellate review as to their propriety), and partly because of the feeling that rights guaranteed by the federal constitution are of greater importance than rights given by statute or common law and so deserve special consideration.

Habeas corpus was originally used to inquire into the legality of detaining a person without legal process or as a result of his conviction by a tribunal lacking jurisdiction. Today in the federal courts and in the courts of some of the states, it can be used to inquire into the legality of his detention after conviction by a tribunal admittedly possessing jurisdiction in the traditional sense. The theory is that a man in custody has a continuing right to challenge the legality of his confinement. If he has been deprived of rights guaranteed him by the United States Constitution, his imprisonment is rendered improper. This is so even if the court is unaware of the existence of the right— even if the right is later declared by the Supreme Court of the United States and given retroactive effect.[1]

Coram nobis was originally used to vacate a judgment previously rendered because of defects not appearing on the face of the record and so not reachable by ordinary processes of trial and review. It can still be used for that purpose; and today in those states which have not expanded the remedy of habeas corpus to cover generally violations of constitutional rights, *coram nobis* has been expanded to that job, or a statutory substitute has been created.[2]

Both *coram nobis* and habeas corpus are historically remedies which were sought in trial, rather than appellate, courts. In their expanded form, they are still sought in trial courts, resulting sometimes in a situation where a single trial judge must reconsider a case which has already been reviewed and approved in a multi-judge appellate court. Furthermore, the collateral proceeding may start a new round of appeals as complex and time-consuming as the original round. Compounding these difficulties is the fact that there are no time limits on the seeking of these writs and no prohibitions against successive re-applications.

Finally, if a man who has been convicted in a state court cannot

---

[1] Note, 'State Post-Conviction Remedies and Federal Habeas Corpus', 40 *N.Y.U. L. Rev.* 154, 155–9 (1965).   [2] Ibid., pp. 159–61.

secure the redress to which he considers himself entitled in the appellate or trial courts of his own state, he may seek habeas corpus in a federal court. The usual concomitants of collateral attack are present: the possibility of long delays, successive applications, reconsideration by a trial court of a case already reviewed on appeal, and the inauguration of a fresh round of appeals.[1]

It is the existence of these collateral avenues of attack rather than normal appellate procedures which explains the extreme delays which have occurred in some American criminal cases of great notoriety, like the Caryl Chessman case, in which a dozen years elapsed between the imposition of the death penalty and its execution.[2] In England, by way of contrast, when the death penalty is imposed (this may be exceedingly rare in the future as a result of the legislation noted in the preceding chapter) it is normally carried out, reversed, or commuted within six weeks. The idea of a man being confined to gaol for a long period of time awaiting execution is so abhorrent to the English mind that if such a delay occurred, the death sentence would in all probability be commuted to life imprisonment.

THE SCOPE OF REVIEW

Although the right of appeal in England is more limited than in the United States, the scope of appellate review is broader. That is because sentences as well as convictions are subject to review. The Court of Criminal Appeal has power not only to consider whether a sentence is within the limits specified by the legislature in creating the offence and within the jurisdiction of the court imposing it, but also whether it is fair and proper.[3] The Court possesses power to substitute for the sentence originally imposed either a lesser or a greater sentence, and while it does not lightly interfere with the discretion of trial judges, it has used its power to correct what it considers undesirable trends in sentencing in the lower courts, and to prevent marked disparities in sentences for comparable offences and circumstances. The power to increase sentence has been exercised rarely, but often enough to discourage some appeals. Today, if the Court is contemplating an increase in sentence, it is likely on its own motion to appoint counsel under the legal aid scheme for the prosecution of

---

[1] Karlen (1963), pp. 40–41, 158.
[2] Where the state has imposed the death penalty, the interval in recent years between sentence and execution varies from eight months to five years. Appellate Delay, *Report*, p. 6.　　　　　　　　[3] Karlen (1963), p. 111.

the appeal. This tends to be regarded as a hint that the prisoner would be well advised to withdraw his appeal. On the whole, the Court's power to increase sentence appears unduly harsh to prisoners and seems to have accomplished little if any good. The Interdepartmental Committee on the Court of Criminal Appeal mentioned earlier has recommended that the power be abolished.[1]

The accused may appeal against conviction alone, in which case the Court of Criminal Appeal cannot deal with his sentence, or against sentence alone, in which case the conviction stands; or against both, in which case both sentence and conviction are open to review.

In the United States the power of appellate courts to deal with sentence is more limited than in England. The only question open to most of them is the legality of the sentence: is it within the statutory limits? Is it within the jurisdiction of the court imposing it? As for sentences which are within legal limits, most American appellate courts act upon the premise that they have no power to either increase or decrease them. This seems paradoxical in view of the power of American appellate courts to review questions relating to damages in civil actions.[2] In a minority of states, however, the English practice is followed to the extent of vesting power in the appellate courts to direct substitution of a lower sentence than that originally imposed. This is the situation in seven states. There are two others—Massachusetts and Connecticut—where there is power to increase as well as to decrease sentence. In the remaining forty-one states and in the federal court system, review of sentences is limited to the question of their legality. It does not extend to questions of their propriety if within legal limits.

One consequence of the lack of American appellate review of sentencing is that sentencing institutes are being developed as described in Chapter 9. Another consequence is that American judges may sometimes be tempted to invalidate a conviction when their real objection is not to the conviction but to the sentence imposed.

POWER OF THE REVIEWING COURT

While the English Court of Criminal Appeal has broad power to see that an appropriate sentence is given, it is circumscribed in the way in which it can deal with convictions where some error has been committed below. It must choose between reversing and freeing the

[1] Cmnd. 2755, pp. 45–47, 72.
[2] Mayers, p. 130. See Mueller, 'Penology on Appeal: Appellate Review of Legal But Excessive Sentences', 15 *Vand. L. Rev.* 671 (1962).

defendant or affirming his conviction. It does not have power to order a new trial which would be free of the error that vitiated the first trial.[1] Depending upon the circumstances, sometimes that would be the appropriate course of action, but the English court does not have that alternative. The basis for distinguishing between the two available alternatives is, translated into American terms, whether the error is 'harmless' or 'prejudicial'. It is considered harmless if the Court believes that a jury would have come to the same conclusion even if the error had not occurred, and in such case, the judgment is affirmed. The Court reaches this result, however, only after reviewing all the evidence or acting with the concurrence of counsel for the prisoner; but even so, it is guessing as to what a jury would do rather than actually finding out by test. Furthermore, the lack of power in the Court of Criminal Appeal to order a new trial creates a temptation to the judges to label an error as harmless whenever they are convinced that the defendant is vicious and guilty. That temptation is being successfully resisted at the present time according to qualified observers, although it was not always so in the past and may not always be so in the future.

The principal reason for not giving the Court of Criminal Appeal power to grant a new trial is the idea that it is unfair to subject a man to trial twice, bolstered perhaps by the idea that trial judges should be kept under pressure to do their work correctly the first time, with no hope of a second chance. Many attempts have been made to change the rule and to give the Court of Criminal Appeal power to order a new trial, but they have not yet been successful. In 1964 a partial advance toward the goal was made in Parliament's grant of permission to the Court of Criminal Appeal to order a new trial on the ground of newly discovered evidence.[2] It is still, however, without power to order a new trial on the ground of error.

Appellate courts in the United States possess the power which is lacking in England. They are not limited to affirmance or reversal, but can grant a new trial whenever that appears to be appropriate in the circumstances of the case.[3] If a purely technical, minor error has occurred, not affecting the substantial rights of the accused, it is labelled harmless and disregarded, and the judgment of conviction is affirmed. If an error has been committed of such a nature that it

---

[1] Karlen (1963), p. 110.
[2] See Cmnd. 2755, pp. 30–31.
[3] Mayers, pp. 132–3.

cannot be cured—if, for example, the accused has been tried on an indictment which fails to charge any offence known to the law—the conviction must be quashed and the accused released. But if an error has been committed which is prejudicial to the substantial rights of the accused but still of such a nature that it might be avoided upon a second trial, the solution is to grant a new trial. This is the most common consequence of a successful appeal. The tendency, indeed, is to stretch the concept of prejudicial error, and find prejudice in error which probably had little or no effect upon the result below. Especially is this true when the error is one affecting the accused's constitutional rights. No matter how clear his guilt, any ruling which denies him a constitutional right will almost inevitably be declared prejudicial and made the occasion for granting a new trial.[1] Many appellate decisions grant new trials not because of any fear that an improper result has been reached, but because of the desire of the appellate judges to discipline trial judges, lawyers, and police officials, reminding them sharply of what they are expected to do and refrain from doing. In short, the tendency in the United States is exactly the reverse of that in England: to upset convictions rather than to save them.

REHEARINGS

Just as there is no possibility of a new trial in England except for newly discovered evidence, so also there is no possibility of a re-hearing of an appeal once decided, except in so far as a case once heard may be referred again to the Court of Criminal Appeal by the Home Secretary.[2] The only recourse ordinarily is the remote chance of further review in a higher tribunal.

In the United States, on the other hand, rehearings are not un-common. They are applied for frequently, and occasionally granted, sometimes resulting in the court reversing a position it has just taken. The petition for rehearing is but one more opportunity among many already noted for a court to avoid error. Doubtless it consumes time and judicial energy, but American courts are willing to pay the price, albeit reluctantly, in their anxiety to avoid penalizing an innocent man.

PAPERS ON APPEAL

One of the major contrasts between American and English practice is in the documents submitted to the appellate court.

---

[1] See Chapter 6 above.   [2] Karlen (1963), p. 116.

In England even the record on appeal is an abbreviated affair, consisting mainly of the trial judge's charge to the jury—if the case was contested—supplemented by the formal accusation, the plea, the verdict, the evidence as to the accused's previous record and character, the speech, if any, in mitigation of sentence, the sentence, any observations by the judge, and any 'submissions by counsel' (contentions) as to the admissiblity of evidence.[1] If the defendant pleaded guilty so that the appeal is on sentence alone, there is no charge to the jury, and the appellate court is deprived of the help of the trial judge's summary of the case. If the appeal is based upon the insufficiency of the evidence to sustain the conviction, the other documents are supplemented by a transcript of so much of the evidence as the registrar of the Court of Criminal Appeal or the judges granting leave to appeal consider necessary for intelligent consideration of the problem. It is not the general practice, except in capital cases, for all the evidence to be obtained for the perusal of the appellate court.

More startling to American eyes than the brevity of the record is the complete absence of written arguments of the type that are called 'briefs' in the United States.[2] These are simply unknown to English practice.

In the United States, on the other hand, the brief is the central feature of an appeal. It is a full-dress argument in writing, sometimes running fifty or more printed or mimeographed pages in length. It states the facts, outlines the claimed errors in the proceedings below, and cites and discusses the authorities claimed to justify a reversal or affirmance. The appellant serves his brief on the other side well in advance of the time for argument and then the respondent serves his answering brief on the appellant, again well in advance of oral argument. Sometimes the appellant serves a reply brief.[3]

Supplementing the briefs in American practice is the record on appeal, which ordinarily contains all or a substantial part of the evidence.[4] It lacks the type of charge to the jury that is found in England for the reason that in most courts of the United States the

---

[1] Karlen (1963)., pp. 111–13, 150.

[2] Ibid., pp. 149–50. In England, the term 'brief' generally refers to the instructions given by the solicitor to the barrister.

[3] Ibid., p. 149.

[4] Ibid., pp. 16–17, 150. Several of the Circuit Courts of Appeal have eliminated the requirement that the entire record be printed, and substituted a rule that the parties should print as appendices to their briefs only those portions of the record which they desire the Court to read. Appellate Delay, *Report*, p. 8.

judge is discouraged from summarizing the evidence, or commenting upon it. The charge tends to consist of little more than abstract propositions of law, which are of little help to the appellate court in understanding what transpired below. The absence of the type of charge known to English practice may be one of the reasons that it is traditional in the United States to provide the appellate court with a transcript of much of the evidence in the ordinary case. The record on appeal may take the form of appendices to the briefs, or it may take the form of a separate document.

Another contrast between English and American practice is that the record on appeal in England is always mimeographed, whereas in the United States it sometimes has to be printed at great expense. On this point, however, the practice varies from one court to another, with a strong trend today towards permitting mimeographing and other relatively cheap forms of duplication.[1]

ORAL ARGUMENTS

Since there are no written briefs in England, oral arguments assume primary importance in that nation. They are not arbitrarily limited in duration, although they tend to be shorter in the Court of Criminal Appeal, averaging only twenty or thirty minutes per case for both sides, than in other appellate courts in England, where arguments sometimes go on for days or weeks. That is because the judges of the Court of Criminal Appeal customarily study the records before the oral arguments commence, sometimes in connexion with the applications for leave to appeal, sometimes independently of them. The same papers that are used on an application for leave to appeal are used on the appeal itself, supplemented, if the judges so desire, by all or part of the transcript of evidence. Having read these papers, the judges are spared having to listen to counsel read at length the record of trial, as is done in the Court of Appeal in hearing civil appeals. The only reading likely to take place is from the legal authorities cited by counsel. There are seldom more than two or three such cases, frequently none, because unnecessary citations are discouraged by the judges. Counsel ordinarily take it for granted that the judges are familiar with the governing legal principles—an assumption justified not only because of the specialization of the

---

[1] Karlen (1963), p. 150. See Willcox, Karlen & Roemer, 'Justice Lost—By What Appellate Papers Cost', 33 *N.Y.U. L. Rev.* 934 (1958).

court, but also because of the small bulk of reported criminal cases. When cases are cited, it becomes necessary to read them in open court since there are no briefs, and since the decision of the court is ordinarily rendered immediately upon the close of oral argument.[1]

It is not uncommon for the court to dispense with oral argument by the respondent. If the judges, after hearing counsel for the appellant, are satisfied that the judgment should be affirmed, they refuse to waste time in listening to the other side.[2]

In the United States oral arguments are secondary in importance to written briefs, and in some cases are dispensed with entirely, the judges preferring to have cases submitted on the briefs alone. Most appellate courts, however, want both. The time for oral argument is generally limited, each side being allowed fifteen minutes, a half hour, or an hour. The reading aloud by counsel of any material is frowned upon. The judges do not wish to hear what they can read for themselves, expecting to get all the information they need about the proceedings below and the authorities relied upon from studying the briefs and the record on appeal. They discourage counsel from discussing in detail the precedents claimed to govern the decision on the assumption that they can better do that job themselves in the privacy of their chambers, with the assistance of their law clerks. Since the practice of American appellate courts is not to render decision immediately upon the conclusion of oral argument, there is no pressure upon them to learn all about the case from the oral argument.[3]

THE DECISION

In the United States substantially all decisions are reserved and rendered in written form. This is as true in criminal cases as in civil cases. The practice is also the same in both types of cases as to dissenting and concurring opinions. The ideal is to have a single opinion for the court as a whole, but, if the judges cannot agree, concurring opinions are considered quite proper, as are also dissenting opinions.[4]

One of the consequences of this method of proceeding is that cases are heard in groups. The court may sit for a week hearing a dozen or

---

[1] Karlen (1963), pp. 113–14. [2] Ibid., pp. 114; 151–2.
[3] Ibid., pp. 150–2.
[4] Chief Justice Charles Evans Hughes said: 'While it may be regrettable that [the justices] cannot always agree, it is better that their independence should be maintained and recognized than that unanimity should be secured through its sacrifice . . .'. Hughes, *The Supreme Court of the United States*, (1936) p. 67.

more cases and then adjourn for three or four weeks, while the judges prepare their opinions and try to reach agreement upon them. Conferences, both formal and informal, are necessary to secure agreement (or as much agreement as possible) among the judges, as are also exchanges of memoranda and draft opinions. Most of the time of the American judge is spent working in chambers, doing solitary reading and writing, interspersed with conferences with colleagues.[1]

In England judges follow a vastly different pattern. They hear and decide cases one at a time, with judgment being rendered immediately upon the conclusion of oral argument. The practice is for only a single opinion to be rendered.[2] That is usually given orally and extemporaneously. The Lord Chief Justice sits on a great number of appeals, and usually but not invariably delivers the judgment of the Court. English judges spend most of their working time together on the bench, listening and talking rather than reading and writing. They hold brief whispered discussions to agree upon the disposition of each case, but these are very brief, seldom taking more than a minute or two. Ordinarily there are no full-scale conferences or exchanges of memoranda or draft opinions.

Apart from differences in internal operating procedures caused by differences in the way that English and American decisions are rendered, there are also differences in the work-product of the judges under the two systems. English opinions tend to be short statements of general principle with a minimum of supporting authority, rather than carefully drafted, lengthy and documented opinions such as are often found in the United States. On the other hand, because so many appeals can be taken in the United States as of right, and because so many of them turn out to be frivolous, American courts are sometimes given to affirming cases *per curiam*, giving no reasons, or very brief reasons, for rejecting appeals which should never have been brought.[3]

There is also a difference in the manner in which opinions in criminal cases in the two nations are published. In the United States it is the practice to publish virtually every opinion, civil or criminal,

---

[1] Karlen (1963), pp. 152–4.

[2] By statute, the Court of Criminal Appeal is required to deliver only one judgment unless the Court directs otherwise when the question is one of law and the Court states that separate judgments are desirable. This rarely happens. In the House of Lords, however, dissenting and concurring opinions in criminal as well as civil cases are possible and not uncommon. See ibid., pp. 115, 127–8.

[3] Ibid., pp. 28, 39, 51, 53–54.

written by an appellate court. The result is a constantly increasing bulk of case law, growing to proportions which are becoming less and less within the competency of individual judges and lawyers to master, even if they are specialists.[1] In England only about 10 per cent. of the opinions of the Court of Criminal Appeal are published in the law reports.[2] The English philosophy is that only cases which enunciate new principles should be published; those which merely apply well settled principles to unique sets of facts should not be. The selection is made by barrister-reporters, who are also in charge of editing the opinions for publication. In addition to the quasi-official law reports, published under the aegis of the Incorporated Council of Law Reporting for England and Wales, there are special reports, including a series of opinions of the Court of Criminal Appeal. Even taking into account those which appear in this series, there is nothing in England to approach the complete publication of opinions that takes place in the United States.

The net result of the limited publication of opinions in criminal appeals in England is that the law of England stays relatively simple and easy to comprehend. This may be one reason why it attracts and holds widespread support in the profession and the general public, and why the number of trials and appeals is relatively small.

FINALITY AND DELAY

For reasons suggested in earlier parts of this chapter, English criminal proceedings are concluded more quickly and with greater finality than American criminal proceedings. There is likely to be no appeal at all in England, since few appeals are allowed as a matter of right, and comparatively few even in the exercise of judicial discretion. If there is an appeal, it is a once only affair with almost no likelihood of further review at a higher level. The appeal comes on quickly, for there is no need to wait for the preparation of briefs or an elaborate record on appeal. There is a need to wait for the transcript of the judge's charge and the related material described above, but this takes on the average only about six or seven weeks. When the case is reached for hearing, the judgment is pronounced promptly, ordinarily immediately upon the close of oral arguments. Finally, there are

---

[1] Karlen (1964), pp. 94–95.
[2] Karlen (1963), p. 116; and for a description of the way opinions are reported and published, see ibid., pp. 98–104.

no rehearings and no further proceedings by way of collateral attack.

In every respect American procedure provides a sharp contrast. There are many appeals as of right, and many layers of appellate courts. Cases are long delayed while records on appeal and briefs are being prepared, and further delayed while judges are reaching their decisions and writing their opinions. Finally, still further delays are occasioned by applications for rehearings and collateral attacks through writs of habeas corpus, *coram nobis*, and the like.

Even apart from situations where convictions are subjected to collateral attack, the time that elapses in the United States between sentence and final disposition is much greater than in England. According to findings of a recent American Bar Association committee to study appellate delay in criminal cases, the average time between the imposition of sentence and the final disposition of an appeal (non-collateral attack) varies from about ten to eighteen months in the various states in the United States.[1] In England the interval between sentence and final disposition in the Court of Criminal Appeal is on the average ten to twelve weeks.

[1] *Appellate Delay Report*, p. 5. In the federal courts, the interval between the filing of notice of appeal in the district court and final disposition by the Court of Appeals varies from about six months (in the First Circuit) to about twelve months (in the Eighth Circuit). Ibid.

GENERAL INDEX

INDEX TO CASES